CW01301361

The War of Spartacus

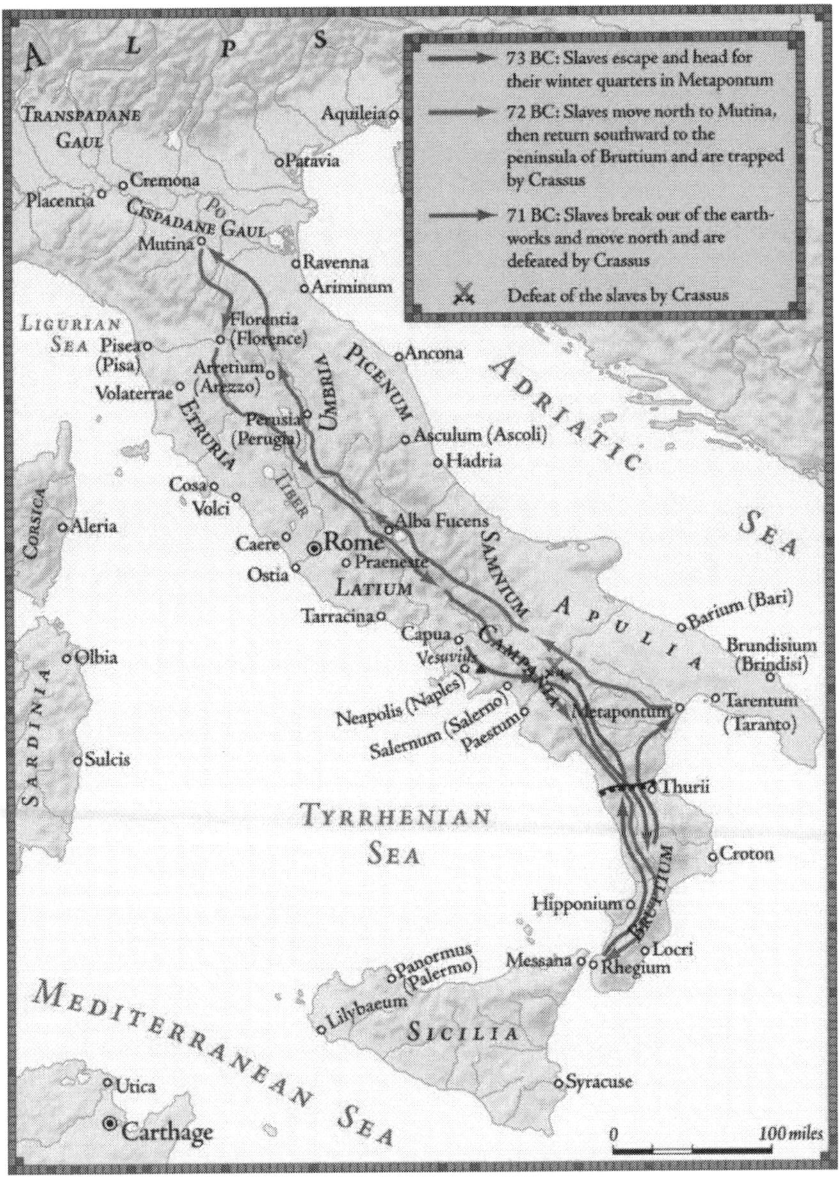

73 BC: Slaves escape and head for their winter quarters in Metapontum
72 BC: Slaves move north to Mutina, then return southward to the peninsula of Bruttium and are trapped by Crassus
71 BC: Slaves break out of the earthworks and move north and are defeated by Crassus
Defeat of the slaves by Crassus
ALPS
TRANSPADANE GAUL
CISPADANE GAUL
Po
Aquileia
Patavia
Cremona
Placentia
Mutina
Ravenna
Ariminum
LIGURIAN SEA
Pisea (Pisa)
Florentia (Florence)
Arretium (Arezzo)
Volaterrae
ETRURIA
UMBRIA
PICENUM
Ancona
Perusia (Perugia)
Asculum (Ascoli)
Hadria
ADRIATIC SEA
Cosa
Volci
TIBER
CORSICA
Aleria
Alba Fucens
SAMNIUM
Caere
Rome
Praeneste
Ostia
LATIUM
Tarracina
APULIA
Barium (Bari)
Brundisium (Brindisi)
Capua
Vesuvius
CAMPANIA
Olbia
SARDINIA
Neapolis (Naples)
Salernum (Salerno)
Paestum
Metapontum
Tarentum (Taranto)
Sulcis
Thurii
TYRRHENIAN SEA
Croton
BRUTTIUM
Hipponium
Locri
Messana
Rhegium
Panormus (Palermo)
Lilybaeum
SICILIA
MEDITERRANEAN SEA
Syracuse
Utica
Carthage
0
100 miles

"TO A ROMAN, A BEND IN A THRACIAN BLADE IS AN IMPERFECTION, BUT LITTLE DO THEY KNOW THAT IT'S THE IMPERFECTIONS THAT MAKE IT WORK SO WELL."

- SPARTACUS

I

On a windy dirt path through the hills of Capua, there was a wagon bustling back and forth with the unhappy cargo of several Roman army deserters. The men had been captured trying to flee to the war in the Mediterranean. In 73 BCE Rome was fighting for control of the sea on two fronts, to the west in Iberia, and to the east in Armenia. These deserters had been unwilling soldiers for the Roman Empire in the first place, finding themselves more in common with the so-called enemy, the King of Pontus, Mithridates. Amongst these dissident soldiers was a Thracian cavalryman named Spartacus. About the age of thirty he'd been fighting one way or another for most of his life, and had the scars to prove it. But in his wagon, it wasn't the scars that were gaining attention from his armored Roman captors, it was the sighting of a familiar tattoo on the inside of his left forearm. The Romans had seen it before, a pattern of seven dots in a circle, the one in the center just ever so bigger than the other six. When asking Spartacus what the tattoo meant the Roman captors were met with the same lack of cordial response as the other bearer of this mark, and they snickered with each other as they pulled up to their destination tucked away in the countryside, hot, and entirely unassuming.

Spartacus leaned out the wagon to see where he had been brought. He knew he had been bought as a gladiator, meant to fight, and die for the Romans amusement. Fighting was the only thing he was good at, though it brought him no fulfillment. There was a long rock wall with wooden gates that they were slow to open for the wagon to pass inside. A small sign beside the dirt path said that they had arrived at the House of Batiatus, hardly a stately manor of Rome. The clashing of wooden weapons inside could be heard, along with tufts of brown dust rising above the walls. The wooden doors creaked terribly when they opened, as if in near disrepair. There was no sense of confidence being pulled inside. Lanista Lentulus Batiatus was waiting just in the courtyard for the presentation of his new gladiators. The men were rustled out of the wagon with no ceremony, and lined up in the dirt like some sort of criminals. Batiatus wasn't a large man, sometimes an entire head shorter than the deserters who had been brought to him. As he walked up and down the line, observing his new men, he seemed dissatisfied with most, but pleased with Spartacus. The Thracian was the biggest of the lot, and seemed to wear a permanently angry expression, readable even through his gnarled beard. The tattoo on his forearm was acknowledged by the Romans, and this brought a smile to Batiatus' face. Spartacus snarled in response, but the lanista simply snapped his fingers and the Romans took their empty wagon and left the grounds. The deserters were then given a brief tour of their new home including the barracks, prison, training facilities, and kitchen. Outside one of the small shelters in the training arena, there was a hulking man with arms the size of most men's legs. His name was Oenomaus, a prisoner from the Marcomanni tribe in the Germania wars. As a gladiator, his position was known as a *cestus*, meaning he was a boxer who fought without weapons or armor. Spartacus saw a branding iron in the man's large hands, and made the quick assumption as what was about to happen. Slowly, the biggest men from the arena encircled these new gladiators, to decrease the likelihood of anything unpleasant happening. One by one the branding process began, searing the sigil of a B on the right inner forearms of the men. Spartacus was at the back of this line. Just before him was his uneasy acquaintance, Crixus, a Gaul from Parisii who'd provided like minded conversation on the ride over.

Crixus presented a challenge. He was a man in his late thirties, with a family and a life to get back to. His time in the Roman army had an expiration. He had served his duty, and had been lied to upon release. He'd been wrongly picked up as a deserter, and ever since then he'd been fighting every step of the way to make sure the Romans knew they'd made a mistake. Spartacus watched as Crixus tried to fight with this Oenomaus. It was over before it began. Like Spartacus, Crixus was considered a *murmillo* gladiator, or a heavyweight. Due to their large size, they would be burdened to fight with up to forty pounds of armor and weaponry. Crixus thought he had a chance to get around this branding, but Oenomaus had seen such resistance before, and was able to quickly overcome any trick the Gaul might have had to his name. In the end, the struggle lasted less than a minute, and Crixus was branded just like the rest of the men, cursing in tongues every step of the way, but branded none the less. Spartacus took in his surroundings, the little lanista man behind him whose name was all over this place. He thought highly of himself. Spartacus didn't want a confrontation, he put out his arm and willingly and took the mark. Oenomaus had many marks of his own, mostly tattoos. Being from Germania he had the emblems of deer on his chest and shoulders, with swirls all along his shaved head. Surely the pain endured while taking in that made something as fast as a brand easy to stomach. Spartacus nodded to the man, as they stood eye to eye in the shade.

"You'll get used to it fast enough. Of all the places I've been made to fight, this one isn't so bad. Batiatus is a little fool. He barely knows what he's doing. Such a little fish in the ocean of Rome. You win your first couple of matches; you'll see what I mean. My name is Oenomaus, what's yours?"

"Spartacus."

"What did they pick you up on?"

"Desertion."

"Ah! Been bringing in a lot of those the past few weeks."

"Anything I should be worried about?"

"You? No. You seem smart enough to handle yourself. Just stay away from the gladiatrices, and you shouldn't have a problem."

"The what?"

"*Female* gladiators."

"I thought they were just prostitutes? Roman whores."

"Some of them are. Batiatus aims to please all sorts. The ones he's collected are serious fighters. Catch yourself in the dark with one of them, and you might walk away missing something *very* important, if you know what I mean."

"Thanks for the warning, Oenomaus. I think I should go find myself a bed now."

"The Thracians sleep in the eastern barracks."

"How did you know I was Thracian?"

"I've seen your tattoo before. The dots. Only ever seen that on one other Thracian, just assumed."

Spartacus nodded, and walked to the western barracks before settling on an abandoned bed in the eastern ones. He didn't know anyone there, but a few of the Thracians speaking of home did comfort him. They were polite enough to see him, encouraged they wouldn't have to fight him because they were so much smaller. Spartacus wouldn't have to begin training until tomorrow as it was already dinner time. A smaller man with curly hair named Castus was collecting all of the broken training weapons in the arena as dusk approached. Spartacus watched him through the open window in the stone wall. He was a *beastiarus* gladiator, one trained to fight animals. His quick feet and agility were key aspects to his survival, coordination wasn't his strong suit though. Spartacus watched the man drop several armfuls of wood fragments before going out to help him. Due to the nature of preservation and needing an audience for death, the gladiators never trained with actual weapons, but wooden replicas instead. It was also much cheaper, and Batiatus was a man of low funds but expensive taste. At the end of every day more broken replicas would be brought to the lanista's door for repair and inventory. Castus had volunteered for the job as it allowed him access to where the gladiatrices were quartered. There was only a small fraction of them here, but Spartacus recognized that Castus must have been fond of one of them, hence his volunteering. With Oenamaus' warning to keep away from the women, Spartacus was all the more interested as to what the lanista was hiding behind his stone walls.

    Like the gladiators, the gladiatrices had been training all day, and were now beginning to line up beside their door to the kitchen for their dinner rations. It was the only place in all of the House of Batiatus that the two could have any kind of mingling opportunity, and even then, it was limited at best. Not really conducive to anything private or intimate. Spartacus kept his head on a swivel, trying to memorize the layout of his new surroundings while following Castus through the halls and dumping the wooden scraps. Batiatus seemed bothered this evening, and waved the two men off with little attention being paid to them at all. Castus seemed used to this treatment, half bowed out of submissiveness, and saw himself out to the wall of the gladiatrices' barracks, hoping for a chance encounter. There was a lot of giggling inside. Spartacus was able to pick up pieces of conversations as he passed by the open windows, something about a very important, very rich Senator coming to visit tonight. There was the consensus that a marriage to a Senator would free the women of a life of fighting and prostitution, and while this visit was only for one of them in particular, they would all try their hand at getting noticed. This one woman was being quite fussed over for her special selection. There were wash bins to clean her from the dirt of the past few days, and someone was doing her long black hair up in knots and twists of the latest Roman fashion. It didn't sound like this one woman was all that pleased, and it was this one woman that all the gladiatrices knew Castus was after. He posed no threat to them, and was taken in as a friend at the last door to the barracks.

Spartacus however was wary of entry. The women welcoming Castus inside did not look at the curly haired man the way they looked at Spartacus. They could tell he was new, with the bleeding brand on his forearm and confused to the rules of the House. He was attractive, and worth getting in trouble for, but his tattoo made him untouchable. The little seven dots. They knew the tattoo, because the woman seeing the Senator tonight had the same one on her forearm. The women parted as Castus snuck in to hug his friend, and Spartacus was able to see her, and her familiar glowing green eyes. She was miserable about this meeting, but hugging Castus made her smile for a brief second. She was wrapped in an off-white piece of fabric that made her dark tan skin all the more apparent that she did not belong here. She was Thracian, and belonged in the east. The wavy lines tattooed up and down her arms and legs were proof she was an outsider, foreign, and exotic. Spartacus couldn't believe his eyes when he saw her, and she gasped when she realized who he was. It didn't make sense to either of them. She gently pushed her friend Castus off to the side, and walked up to the new gladiator. Each woman was seething with jealousy.

"Well, if it isn't the infamous Two Dagger Téadora?"

"Could it *really* be you? Slick footed Spartacus?!"

"No one's called me that since I was…not in years."

"Hmm. Maybe that's because you've decided to quit tripping over your feet, and just started tripping over your words instead?"

"I've only ever misspoke around you."

"What's so special about me?"

"Everything."

"Look at you, all battle worn. I bet you tell all the women you cross that you think they're special. Make them weak in the knees."

"There's never been any other woman for me but you, Téa."

"Really?"

"Really. You look…*different* tonight."

"I look a fool. That damned little lanista out there thinks he can whore me out to a Senator of his choosing to secure funds to expand this dump he calls a training facility."

"And this is not what you want?"

"Has it been so long since we have last seen each other that you have to ask me such a thing?"

"What will you do?"

"Something that will probably get me locked in the prison for a few nights. But, it's not like I haven't been there before."

"How long have you been here?"

"A few years. It'll be five this winter. If I'm still here by then."

"So, this is home now?"

"No, Spartacus. Only home is home for me. Samothraki. I will see it again one day, but today is not that day. It's good to see you, though you should know if anyone catches you here, they'll have that man beat you who branded you."

"Oenomaus? No. I don't think so."

"Oh, are you two friends now?"

"All my friends are dead, but he could be an ally."

"Am *I* not a friend?"

"You are…Téa."

"Yes, I am. And I am also late to see this infernal Senator. You should go back to the men's side with Castus. He knows his way around."

"Will I see you again?"

"Don't we always manage to bump into each other?"

"Last time I saw you we were running through the fields of Thrace. Teenagers. I don't want to have to wait that long to see you again."

"Then don't wait that long."

When Téadora turned to run out of the gladiatrices' barracks she gave a flicker of a smile that she had always given Spartacus when they were about to do something that would get them into trouble. The two had known each other practically all of their lives. They were both Thracians, part of the Strength of the Seven, and their families were trading partners for generations. Spartacus was from a mountain tribe, called the Maedi. They lived on the mainland, whereas Téadora was from the island of Samothraki in the Aegean Sea. Multiple times a year the tribes would congregate for the celebration of the changing of the seasons and marriage rites. Téadora was a prize amongst her people as the lone child of a chief, but Spartacus had never seen her as anything more than his best friend. They had once, in their youth, brilliant plans to run away together, but fate intervened. Spartacus was to go to war, and Téadora was not allowed to go with him. They gave each other their dotted tattoos in the forests, in the hopes it might remind them of their promises. Romans never seemed to cease fighting, and so, Spartacus spent all of his years from sixteen up until now as a cavalryman. He was dutiful, and obedient to a fault, but it was killing him inside. He'd been wanting to go home for years, start a family, build a house, tend a farm. Seeing Téadora only strengthened that urge in him. At eighteen, she had been promised to a man from a wealthy Roman household. They were politically ambitious, and the Thracians were desperate to avoid the ire of the Romans. But on the eve of her wedding, Téadora slipped away in the middle of the night, and ran off with a bunch of Cilician pirates of questionable morals willing to take her on. It was there during her time at sea that she learned to fight. In the gladiator arenas she was called a *dimachaerus*, because she fought with two blades and no shield. Sica blades were her weapon of choice, because they were bent towards the end, a Thracian trade secret. She kept at least one on her person at all times, even tonight, against the advices of her fellow gladiatrices. It was concealed not so discreetly in the folds of her off white wrappings, as Spartacus was keen on watching her skip away into a place he could not follow. But before she was entirely out of view, Téadora turned around and stared at Spartacus one more time while she hung in the doorway of the lanista's private residence where she was to meet with the Senator. Spartacus reached up, and squeezed the little silver ring hanging around his neck. His sole personal possession, all that was left of his mother. He'd worn it since he was a child. He'd fought to the death to keep this necklace over the years, and Téadora remembered it. Seeing him grip onto the little piece, made her absent mindedly clutch at her own neck before she disappeared. A few of the women were eyeing Spartacus like a piece of meat in their barracks before Castus cleared his throat, and noted to a path they could take to return to the men's side of things. Spartacus was heavy footed to follow, but made his way into the kitchen without issue. His slop of watery gruel was less than appetizing, but he had eaten all day, and was pleased to get something down his throat. Spartacus sat at a table with a spurned Crixus and the other handful of new gladiators still nursing their fresh brands while Oenomaus guarded the door to keep them all inside the kitchen. Outside the windows it could be seen that the Senator had arrived.

  Senator Felix Furius was a picturesque Roman man. He was tall, frail in stature, not at all built for manual labor or fighting. His hair was as light blonde as his eyes were light blue, and from the tint of his white skin, it was easily assumed he spent most of his time inside a building. From the limited knowledge Spartacus had been piecing together since his arrival, he was gathering that Batiatus wanted to be a much more influential man than he currently was, and since he was still building up his reputation as a lanista, he was not yet in the good graces of the Roman Empire as a whole. If he was making deals with politicians, they would not be the most influential men either. This Senator Furius was too young to have been a politician long, and most likely had inherited a title from an ailing father who knew better than to frequent a facility like the House of Batiatus. But from what Téadora said, and the unsavory reputation that gladiatrices had in general, it was clear this Senator had come with ulterior motives in mind tonight. Spartacus found himself peering anxiously through multiple windows to try and see what was going on, but the Batiatus private residence was housed behind stone walls, and therefore, the gladiator was out of luck. Oenomaus saw this and chuckled to himself. Spartacus was hardly the first man to get disappointed at not being able to get his hands on the likes of Two Dagger Téadora, but she was hardly about to settle down and become some fresh-faced Senator's pretty little wife either. It was unfortunate to be rude to him, because Furius, despite his name, was quite a gentle soul. He was polite upon first laying eyes on Téadora, all cleaned up for once. He had been following her through the countryside for months now, catching every single one of her matches. He was the House of Batiatus' greatest sponsor. No expense spared. He'd made a lot of money betting on her, though she had no idea. Batiatus took all profits for himself and to keeping his wife happy, which was somewhat of an impossible endeavor. She was gone tonight, though the lanista remained. He was not at all needed for the meeting. This was a private rendezvous with the Senator and his gladiatrix. Téadora was increasingly uncomfortable as they circled the rooms in Batiatus' residence. She didn't want to be alone with the white man that seemed to exude light like the sun. He kept smiling at her with kind eyes, and it gave her the chills though she was sweating. Eventually, he figured she was more interested in studying him from a distance than speaking to him, so he'd have to be the man and force the conversation upon her. He cornered her in a windowless spot of the residence. She could have easily fought her way out of this, but that seemed like inappropriate behavior to exhibit on a man as soft as a Senator. Téadora settled on the arm of a chair, and Furius matched her pose beside her on the same chair. She wasn't fond of having to look at him, and leaned away when he leaned towards her.

"I won't bite, you know?"

"I won't die because a Senator dared to touch me when he should not have. My life is worth more to me than yours."

"Fair enough. But I mean you no harm, Téadora."

"Our definition of *harm* is no doubt different."

"No doubt. You seem to have more scars on you than I have homes."

"That was terribly arrogant of you to say."

"It was, wasn't it? I'm sorry. I didn't mean it to sound like that."

"Then why did you say it like that?"

"I'm nervous."

"You're a Senator. Why the nerves? You hold all the power here. If you were to say jump, everyone in the House of Batiatus would be off their feet in a heartbeat."

"That's not what I would want."

"Then what do you want? Why are you here? Why ask for me?"

"Have you not seen me before at your matches? I never miss them."

"You have a lust for blood sport. Forgive me. I do not dare make memories of the faces jeering at me from the crowds."

"I've never once *jeered*."

"Do you want praise for that? You still paid to see me. You still paid for blood. You support violence."

"I paid to see *you*. I support *you*. I am your biggest support."

"You are the man keeping this place open, aren't you?"

"Batiatus is a fledgling lanista. He needs all the help he can get, and I do as well. If one of us succeeds, we both rise in the eyes of Rome, and isn't that what every man truly desires?"

"A true man desires to rise in the eyes of one good woman, not all of Rome, and not with blood on his hands. You are no man of interest to me, Senator."

"Now, that is a shame. You asked me why I was here. I…I had hoped you'd consider marrying me."

"Are you mad?! I'd ruin your reputation. Society would scorn you. I am Thracian. I am low."

"You are strong, and brave, and honorable as you are beautiful. You are a fearsome thing to behold and I am very fond of you. I have heard you are Batiatus' favorite champion."

"It is always good to be someone's favorite something. They try not to kill the favorites, unless enough money is involved. I've had a good run so far. That's all any of us can hope for, a good run."

"So, what do you say? Would you consider becoming a humble Senator's wife, Téadora? There's nothing I couldn't give you. Anything you ask for would be yours."

"I fear what I want most is something you could not give. Excuse me, Senator. I must be going now."

"Where are you going?"

"A prison cell, more than likely."

"Why would you say that?"

"For what I'm about to do next."

II

Téadora pulled her sica blade from the folds in her off white coverings and slashed at the bared thigh of the Senator beside her on the arm of the chair. While the man screamed, she ran for the nearest door she could reach. She'd already circled the rooms enough times to know her closest exit. It led to the courtyard, from there she could scale the stone wall and drop down into the men's side of the facility. If she could make it that far, getting back to her own barracks wouldn't be much of a challenge, but she knew she wouldn't get that far. Lentulus was watching everything too closely, hoping she didn't foul up this deal. He needed the Senator's money so bad he could taste it, and at the first sign of a struggle, he sent his guards in after Téadora. She had been manhandled by the pair several times before for some altercation or another. She wasn't fond of authority, or being used for blood sport. The guards cut off Téadora's first exit choice, truly the only ideal one that could lead her back to her barracks. The next closest door was the front door, which was currently being blocked by Lentulus' pretty little teenaged daughter. Téadora shook her head no, pleaing to the girl with her eyes to move out of the way. Téadora had saved the daughter once from a sticky situation a year ago, and the gladiatrix was hoping a favor might be repaid to her now in her time of need. Unfortunately, she was her father's daughter, and as Lentulus began barking orders at her to stay at the front door, Téadora had no choice but the shove the girl aside with her bloody curved blade still firmly in hand. Lentulus wanted to know how she had gotten her hands on a metal weapon when all the training facility was allowed to use was wood. The metal used in matches was locked under guard, but some of the men here could be very easily swayed by their favorite gladiatrix. One of Téadora's friends allowed her to slip into the weapon stores unnoticed a few months ago and she'd been stowing her blade for safe keeping ever since. Now she was at risk at losing it for the umpteenth time and she bolted for the courtyard. Her wrappings failed her, tripped her up as she darted for the wall and lunged herself up for the top row of stones. Heavy hands seized her by her waist, dropped her to the ground and she didn't have a fighting chance. The two men overpowered her, wrenched the blade from her hands by bending her wrists backwards and causing her to cry out in pain. Téadora was then picked up off her feet, and forcibly carried into her usual corner cell in the facilities' own prison. Oenomaus was keeping guard on the kitchen when this was all going down. At the sound of Téadora's scream he chuckled and shook his head, knowing she had gotten herself in trouble yet again. Spartacus was not immune to the woman's cries though, and instantly bolted up from his bench and sorry little bowl of gruel. Other men in the kitchen had heard the woman's cries, but knew they could do nothing about it, and were quickly involved back in their own conversations and idle chatter about training and the upcoming matches. Spartacus walked to the door and wanted Oenomaus to step aside. The Germanian shook his head no.

"She does this all the time, Spartacus. It's best not to get involved."

"If you want to keep me in this kitchen right now, you're going to have to try a lot harder."

"Don't make me hit you, Spartacus."

"That's *exactly* what I want you to do."

With two strong hands Spartacus lunged for Oenomaus' throat. It was nothing personal. The Thracian wanted to get into trouble. The brawl spilled out of the closed kitchen and into the dusty courtyard, drawing the attention of the Senator's guards still waiting outside the Batiatus private residence. As the Senator was being cleaned up from his gash on his leg, they were standing there bored and uneasy. Lentulus was already in a foul mood, yelling at Téadora while she was being carried across to the prison. When the guards finished with her, they were to come back for Spartacus, the obvious man at fault for this latest showing. Oenomaus had a good reputation with his lanista, and even though he was on top of Spartacus, pinning the large Thracian to the ground with bloody knuckles and a smile, he was innocent. Spartacus was smiling too though, unafraid of taking a couple of hits or two to get what he wanted. Oenomaus didn't know what to make of all of that. The two men kept staring at each other, trying to have a silent conversation so the Romans around them would be none the wiser. It was getting dark now, and the torches had to be lit. The Senator should have been making his way out, back to a more respectable lodging, but he was hobbling towards the prison. Oenomaus watched in confusion before being yelled at for not getting back to his duties watching the men in the kitchen. Lentulus had such a shrill tone when he yelled that Oenomaus merely left the courtyard for respite rather than obedience. He waved off the lanista and went inside with a smirk, still careful to keep an eye on the happenings in the prison across the way. It lit windows he was able to make up stories about the progressions of the shadows, and relay his thoughts back to Castus beside him, who was anxious for a happy resolution to this whole mess. As the curly haired man sat on the edge of his bench, his older ginger haired cousin beside him, Gannicus, took hold of his bowl of gruel and downed them both. Gannicus and Castus looked and acted nothing alike for being cousins. There was a fifteen-year age gap between the two, and Gannicus often acted more like a father to Castus than anything else. The men were both beastiarus' from the Trinovantes tribe in Britania. While Gannicus had been busy at the House of Batiatus making allies of fellow Celts, Castus had gone off and made a dangerous connection with Téadora. She was the young man's only friend in this facility, and Gannicus was worried that was going to break his cousin's heart when she finally got herself into a mess, she couldn't fight her way out of. Oenamaus was quite amused by the whole thing, as he usually was. He had blood on his knuckles from Spartacus' nose, and she had a Senator's blood dripped across her. While the Germanian was speculating what might be going down in the prison, and taking great joy in upsetting Castus, Gannicus was having none of it. The three men all hunched over their table together, and lowered their voices, careful of anyone hearing what they might have to say. Castus knew when meetings like this occurred, he was merely to be an observer, not a participant, so he held his tongue, and allowed his eyes to dart back and forth from the large man to his cousin. Meanwhile, at the next table over, Crixus was deeply involved in eavesdropping. He had been a fellow cavalryman with Spartacus for a few years, and not once seen the man bested in a fight, sans for their capture when they had been drunk and the fight unfair. Crixus knew something was up tonight, and that Spartacus had a plan, which now involved the men whispering beside him. He slowly sipped that cold gruel in front of him while never loosing eye contact with Oenamaus' swirled tattooed head.

"I'm telling you, Gannicus, this Spartacus could be *just* the man we have been waiting for."

"Don't give your hopes up, Oenamaus. You and Téadora have been plotting to break out of here for years, and nothing's ever come of it but promotions for you and scars for her. She's lucky she's as talented as she is or she would have died years ago. Can you imagine how many more matches she's going to have to win to get over this? A *Senator*?! Rome could *kill* her for drawing that man's blood."

"Lentulus would never let her die. She makes him more money than any three of us combined. And you know nothing is more important to that man than his money. That Senator is a lucky man. You know she could have killed him if she had wanted to."

"What was she thinking?!"

"I don't know. But now she's got an audience with Spartacus, and something is telling me those two know each other. Did you see the tattoo? The dots?"

"Castus told me. I don't think it's as significant as you think. Many tribes mark themselves. They could be strangers."

"They *weren't* strangers."

"Quiet Castus!"

"They *weren't* strangers, Oenamaus. Spartacus came with me to drop off the broken training weapons. When I went to see Téadora in her barracks, I could tell the two knew each other. I couldn't quite hear what they were saying, but she smiled at him like she's never smiled since she came here. And *I* would know."

"Yes, Castus, we all know you're in love with the woman, but how many times have I told you? She's not safe."

"Yes, cousin, I know. And you could tell me a million more times but it will not sway me."

"Gannicus, this could be a good thing for us."

"How so, Oenomaus?"

"Spartacus is tough. That one named Crixus who came in with him, the one who fought me at the branding table, he's just the sort we need too. I bet all the deserters brought in today would be willing to break out with us. They don't want to be here long, not like us. They won't grow discontent; they'll fight to the death for their freedom."

"And how many men have we already lost to your and Téadora's half brained ideas?"

"They were the wrong sort. Spartacus is the right sort. I know it. You'll see. Téadora's actions tonight will tell us everything."

Oenamaus clapped his hand on the table twice, very matter of factly, and nodded his head. Gannicus rolled his eyes and began stroking his ginger beard. He had no faith in Téadora. She was violent, and too unpredictable. Hoards of Celts had been lost in the last attempt at an uprising. Gannicus had lost many close friends. This had not been lost on Oenomaus. Over the years, he'd seen many of his friends die as well, but he had not forgotten about home, and how badly he wanted, needed to return. Castus craned his head back to see around Oenamaus and study the shadows in the prison windows. Everyone was inside now, so whatever happened was anyone's guess. Worry was painted all over the curly haired man's face. He was too obvious about it, and it annoyed his cousin so much that Gannicus excused himself for bed. Oenamaus insisted Castus should go too, and that he'd stay up to keep an eye on Téadora, tell him all about it in the morning. Castus was reluctantly obedient, but followed his cousin out who had waited for him at the door. Crixus was still drawing out his cold bowl of gruel at a table alone now, staring at Oenamaus. Crixus wanted in on any sort of uprising or attempt to break out. He'd keep a weathered ear out for anything useful, and remained in the kitchen until cleaning duty forced him to his barracks for the evening. He too, was keeping an eye on the shadows in the prison windows. No one could figure out what was taking so long. The Senator, despite his leg injury, wanted to pay for Téadora's release. She didn't want his kindness, but she was overruled because Lentulus wanted the money. Under armed guard, Téadora was removed from her cell without a single word being able to be exchanged with Spartacus. Lentulus had the woman carried all the way back to her barracks while the Senator was left alone in the prison with Spartacus. The Thracian's captivation by Téadora, and their matching tattoos, had the Senator more than a little uneasy. Furius took up a stool and drew it near Spartacus' barred cell so it would be easier for him to talk. Spartacus had no interest for the Senator, nor any idea why this conversation was about to take place.

"You know her, don't you, slave?"

"I'm not a slave. I'm Spartacus."

"Is that supposed to mean something to me?"

"Not *yet*, but maybe one day it will."

"Why were you looking at Téadora?"

"Is it a crime for me to look at her, Senator? She was the only woman in the room, of course I was going to look at her."

"You two have matching tattoos."

"So?"

"What do they mean?"

"You're new in Rome, aren't you?"

"Excuse me?"

"You have no idea what you're doing here or how to do any of this. Visiting a little gladiator school, speaking with prisoners, chasing a woman you haven't got the *slightest* chance of ever having."

"And why don't I have a chance with her? I just paid her bail. She owes me."

"Téa doesn't do debts. She does, well, look at your thigh. *That's* what she's good at."

"I'm well aware of the woman's talents. I've been following her matches across the countryside. That's why I mean to marry her."

"*Marry* her?!"

"That upsets you?"

"It surprises me. You mean to make her your wife for the purpose of bearing children or providing you with protection?"

"Ideally both."

"You truly have no idea what you're doing."

"And you, a man locked in prison, you know more than me?"

"You and I are two very different men, Senator. I don't pretend to know you, so don't pretend to know me. But I do know Téadora, and I also know that you will *never* know her like I do."

"I don't need to know what you know about her to make her my wife. I have all the money she could ever desire."

"She doesn't place any value in money or titles. She judges people on their character."

"I am of good stock."

"She took a blade to your thigh!"

"She will come around. She will realize I can give her freedom from the arena. I can give her a life."

"She won't want whatever you can give."

"You speak from a point of jealously."

"I speak the truth. You will never have her. She'd just assume kill herself before becoming your wife."

"Of this you are certain?"

"As certain as I am about the sun rising in the morning."

"Well, we'll just have to see about that, now, won't we?"

"I suppose we will."

"I am *not* your enemy, Spartacus."

"You are hardly my friend, Senator."

"We'll have to see about that too. Good night."

Furius struggled to stand without wincing in front of Spartacus, and appearing as small as he felt inside. The young Senator was well aware that he was as new to politics and the world of back door negotiations, but he was trying to learn as fast as possible. He was not in the business of making enemies. One always was more successful when surrounded by good connections, and so that was what the Senator tried to foster on his way out of the prison. He dropped more money on the front table for Lentulus, and paid Spartacus' bail too. Spartacus was still trying to make sense of his conversation with the Senator when the guards came to unlock his cell. Spartacus was allowed to go back to his barracks where the other Thracian gladiators slept. He was not tired, but full of questions. He kept thinking about Téadora, and how desperate he was to speak with her. But there would be no opportunities so long as they were inside these walls. Spartacus was not made to be anyone's prisoner. He'd given all of his adult life for Rome, and he would not be used for blood sport now. He'd served his time and then some for the empire. He wanted to go home. As Spartacus rolled back and forth on his small, itchy, bottom bunk on a rack of three, a familiar face came crawling through the darkness to see him. Crixus was bounding on hands and knees with his eyes bulging out of his head. He held a finger to his lips to be quiet, and then scurried back into the darkness, wanting Spartacus to follow. There seemed no harm in it, it'd been a hell of a day already, what more harm could possibly be done? Crixus was waiting in the empty section of barracks so the two men could more easily speak. They sat down cross legged on the dirt floor, a far cry from the Roman camps they had spent years together in. They had never been friends, but had passed each other enough to respect one another. There was trust there, more than anything, and if something was bothering Crixus, Spartacus owed it to him to hear the man out. The Gaul clearly had a lot to say, constantly taking in inventory of their surroundings.

"You're unusually nervous this evening, Crixus."

"There's word that an uprising is being planned here, and *you're* the man who's going to lead it!"

"This is the first I've heard of anything."

"That man who branded us, the one you fought with…"

"It wasn't a real fight. I was just trying to…"

"To get to that woman. I know. She's the mastermind of the whole thing, apparently. Didn't she speak to you in the prison?"

"No. We didn't get the chance."

"That's a shame. I'd have liked to heard her plan."

"You and me both. An uprising, you say?"

"I overheard that tattooed Germanian speaking of it with the ginger man and that curly haired welp."

"Castus is a kind kid."

"That woman is our way out of here, Spartacus. If she means to use you in this uprising, I want in. You and I have fought too long together for us to be separated now."

"I don't know anything about this uprising, Crixus. And I don't know how to go about finding out either. They keep the men and women separated here."

"But you know the way across. You got across tonight."

"We've been here less than a day. These walls around you have made you mad. You need to get some sleep and calm down. With a level head, we can start to make sense of all of this."

"I've never known you to back down from a fight, Spartacus."

"I'm not backing down from anything. But a good soldier knows to get the facts before he goes drawing his weapon. Be smart about this, Crixus. Come morning, we'll start asking questions."

"Come morning it will already be too late."

"Crixus! Wait! Where are you going?! Crixus!"

"*I'm* going to go get my facts. *You* can go to sleep."

Crixus crawled off into the darkness again. Spartacus would not follow a man who could not listen to reason. He was curious though if there was any truth to the matter. Before he went back to his bunk, Spartacus trekked though the halls to find where the Germanians slept in the barracks. Oenomaus was asleep on a middle bunk, but with a little shaking he was wide awake, and came to with fists flying out of instinct. Spartacus dodged the half-asleep attack, and Oenomaus was happy to engage in discussion once the uprising was mentioned. In fact, all of the Germanians were interested as they started to wake each other up one by one until the whole portion of the barrack was gathering around Spartacus. It was true that the gladiators had been biding their time for the right moment to strike. Téadora had tried half a dozen times to organize an uprising and each time it had failed because a lack of faith and morale. No one enjoyed staying at the House of Batiatus, but many had lost hope in ever going back home or having a life again. They had lost too much. For those dead inside, death was not a threat, but a goal. There were a few Germanians now who Spartacus could tell had this look about them. They listened to the words of an uprising, but had now glow to their eyes that it could actually be achieved. While Oenomaus was giving a laundry list as to how all the other attempts had failed, Spartacus was finding a commonality in all of them. The men did not stick together. There was not the unwavering belief they could succeed, and so before they ever got started, they had failed. Spartacus had seen it on the battlefields too, men retreating without orders, running for their lives. It never got them anywhere but a prison cell. Spartacus had just been released from one of those after spending a grand total of less than an hour in one. And thanks to a Senator. Spartacus still wasn't sure what that was all about, but would keep that fact to himself until it became useful. What he would share though was that Crixus apparently was conducting research of his own at this very moment to try and find a way out of the House of Batiatus. Come morning, they would see what he had found.

    It was dawn when Crixus made his move. Alone, but with the fervent hope of being supported en masse, the Gaul from Parisii armed with nothing more than a hot branding iron, began his attack. The uprising had begun. Two hundred men and women were woken in an instant by the familiar scream of a man's flesh being burned. Crixus had attacked the two guards at the front of Batiatus' private residence. Like a flood, the gladiators came pouring out of their barracks, grabbing anything they could get their hands on. Rocks, sticks, shields, furniture, all of it became a weapon. Crixus had run into the kitchen. The back doors were open. The gladiatrices, with Téadora at the lead, made it into the kitchen before the men. The jumped on benches and flipped over tables more as if wild animals had been let loose inside. They armed themselves with utensils, spoons, knives, and anything small enough to be handheld. Their screams led the men to the open doors. By now, Batiatus was awake, and was screaming for his protection. Roman guards pooled from their sleeping quarters, but they were slow to arm themselves and prepare against the onslaught of the gladiators. It was a ravenous fight before the sun could even crest the horizon and begin painting the dirt orange in the training arena. Men were falling. In the madness and chaos of the stampede of activity, many did not survive to see themselves outside those open kitchen doors. Spartacus reunited with Crixus first. Oenomaus was not far behind the gladiatrices. Gannicus had Castus by the elbow as they tumbled into the free countryside. Seventy-five out of two hundred made it out. With their bare hands or kitchen utensils the runaways were able to ambush a wagon full of weapons and armor bound for another gladiator school down the road. It wasn't much, but it was better than nothing. Téadora began running for high ground, and Spartacus led whoever was willing to follow him, right after her.

III

When Senator Felix Furius received word about what had happened at the House of Batiatus he turned his entourage away from Rome and started right back for Capua. It wasn't until he looked upon the carnage with his own eyes did he believe what had happened. The night before it had been so quiet. Now he was looking upon over a hundred dead bodies baking in the morning sun. Faces he had just seen hours earlier. The guards from the prison who had carried Téadora were lying face down in the center of the arena, but the Senator recognized them by their armor and size. Crixus had cut them down by their necks with a kitchen knife. Pools of blood had soaked the sand beneath them. Furius could barely keep himself from vomiting. He'd never seen a dead body before, and now he was saturated in death. He could not believe his colleagues in Rome had ever seen such a sight as this. Surely, they could not have, and yet, the decisions they made every day caused scenes like this. Some of them might have been heads of legions, but they were removed from the fighting as they were deemed too important to the empire to lose. As the Senator grappled with the sheer amount of devastation around him, Lentulus Batiatus was in a fit of rage. The short man was coming undone, pacing in circles, babbling about money.

"How am I supposed to show up to the match in Campania in three days' time with not a *single* gladiator to my name?! Senator?! Thoughts?!"

"We will find them, Batiatus."

"And how will we do that? All my money's just run off across the countryside to god only knows where!"

"We will find them. Your men were deserters before and Rome found them. They can do it again."

"They killed all my guards. I have no one to send out in search. Senator, how am I supposed to pay my taxes, feed my family?"

"No shortage of resources will be used to return your business to you, I promise."

"I need more than a promise, Senator."

"I will keep your business afloat until we can fill your walls with gladiators again. If not the ones you lost, then new ones. There's no shortage of slaves, deserters, or the poor. Don't worry, Batiatus, we are friends. I will look out for your best interests, trust me."

"It's not a lack of trust in *you* that I am having trouble coming to terms with right now. People pay me to see Two Dagger Téadora. If I don't have her, I have nothing. I can't replace her. I must have her back or I lose it all."

"I want to find her as much as you do."

"You'll never get your hands on her. She'll be the death of you."

"Why do you say that, Batiatus?"

"The men protect her. That one you freed last night, Spartacus, you'll have to kill him to get to her. And he *won't* be killed."

Senator Furius wouldn't be killing anyone. He was a man of words and wit, and would get what he wanted without more bloodshed. He was sure of this, and not at all dissuaded by the lanista's heavy warning. While Lentulus continued to pace over his wrecked business, and rifle sweaty fists through his hair, the Senator backed out of the gates and tried to come up with a plan. Tracking down runaways usually wasn't too difficult if one was quick about it. The Roman guards in Furius' employ were eager to say anything the Senator wanted to hear. Keeping him happy meant a prosperous, and rewarding career safe from the backbreaking work of a soldier. They were lying through their teeth, but the Senator believed them enough to send them scattered across the hills of Capua. Little did they know, the gladiators were nowhere near the school anymore. Téadora was running for high ground, and by nightfall she was seeking refuge on the slopes of Mons Vesuvius. While the volcano was steeped in legend of catastrophic eruptions, there had not been note of any such happenings in recent centuries. The ground here was fertile, and the farms plentiful for raiding. The gladiators would not go hungry while they figured out their next move. They also held the all-important scenic view. No one could sneak up on them here, and most vital was the lack of stone walls. Crixus' mind had been appeased. He was not wholly settled though. Heavy on the minds of the gladiators and gladiatrices alike was revenge. For the most part, it wasn't even specific in nature. This was no personal bounty hunting mission, but more an opportunity to send a message to Rome itself. Good people had been turned into criminals, and forced to fight to the death for far too long. Families had been severed. Spartacus had been elected as a de facto leader for the gladiators. It wasn't entirely intentional or formal. It just sort of came together while makeshift camps were made. The men stuck to their own. Oenomaus had his Germanians, Gannicus had Castus and the Celts. Crixus kept the Gauls at his side while the Thracians flocked to Spartacus in blind admiration. Téadora had the women in her ranks, and many of them were anxious to make known the faces attached to the men's names from the gladiator school they had heard so much about. Spartacus was a bit ill at ease over the whole revenge plot, more interested in going home than anything else. Téadora sat on the volcanic hillside beside him, tired from walking the twenty miles it took them to get here from Capua. It had been such a hot day and the dried sweat was sticky on her arms and back. Spartacus surprised himself with an audible chuckle when she leaned into his bare shoulder and they stuck together. It was still warm outside even in the dark of night. The two hadn't had the chance to sit together like this in over sixteen years, and suddenly, it was as if no time had passed between them. Téadora let out a sigh as she took in the view of farms all around the base of the volcano, all of the opportunities that awaited them. Spartacus was embarrassingly nervous. She clearly wanted to talk and he didn't know what to say, so before he started bumbling over his words again, he reached up and gripped the little silver rink necklace he wore, and wished somehow his long dead mother might give him some sort of courage to be the man Téadora was hoping he had become.

"Is it nice for you to be able to see the sea again, Téa?"

"You know how much I love the water, Spartacus. It might not be home, but it is better than those stone walls I have come to know. I am glad you ran with me today."

"What kind of man would I have been if I had not followed you?"

"I heard some of the men say you were unsure about breaking out."

"Crixus came to me like a madman and it all seemed too good to be true. I couldn't imagine seeing you again and gaining my freedom all in the same day."

"And now, how do you feel? The gladiators chose you as their leader. You must be pleased."

"I don't know what they expect of me. All I've ever known is how to get by. It's not some envious skill I possess, Téa. It's human instinct. There's nothing special about me."

"Which is *exactly* why they chose to follow you. You do not seek power. You are a good man, an honorable man."

"You think that highly of me?"

"I have *always* thought highly of you. If you only knew how much I looked forward to our tribes meeting when we were younger, you'd have never paid me any attention at all. Just another girl falling at your feet. Slick footed Spartacus."

"I tripped on the way here."

"You did?!"

"Kicked my ankles together running through Neopolis. Went right down on my face."

"And I missed it?!"

"Look, I scraped my forearms up trying to catch myself."

"Nothing a little saltwater won't fix."

"Yes, I remember. That was always your solution to everything. Got a cut? Go in the sea. Feeling sick? Go in the sea. Sad? Go in the sea. I could always find you in the water."

"Nothing bad has ever happened to me in the water."

"I hate to think anything bad has happened to you *ever*. But I know better than to believe our time away from each other has been free of issue. What was it that got you locked up in the House of Batiatus in the first place?"

"I trusted the wrong people."

"I'm sorry. We don't need to talk about it if it makes you feel uncomfortable. I know I'm not proud of how they caught me. Drunk as a fish in a taberna in Brindisi."

"But you don't drink?"

"I know. I was humoring Crixus."

"A friend of yours?"

"We've fought together for years. I don't know that we're friends, but we watch each other's backs. His death would bring me no more pleasure than mine would his."

"What brought you down to Brindisi?"

"We were planning on buying passage on a Cilician pirate ship to join King Mithridates' army."

"And what foolish soul told you trusting a Cilician was a good idea? They'd have robbed you blind."

"What do you know of Cilician pirates?"

"More than I care to admit."

"Téa?"

"Another story for another time, Spartacus. Perhaps once I can find the words to explain myself without hating my naivety."

"It has been a long day. Maybe you need to go down to the sea and heal yourself?"

"It's a mile out to the water. I've walked enough for one day. I should probably just go make a campsite for myself and get some rest."

"I'm sorry. Have I said something wrong?"

"You've done nothing wrong. You just reminded me of something I'd rather forget. Here you were being a noble soldier for all these years and I…I am not as proud of my youth as you. I've made one bad decision after another. I'm just hoping that for the first time in a long time, today, I've done something right. Good night, Spartacus."

Téadora leaned away from her friend, stood up and dusted herself off. Spartacus motioned to stand up too but she held a hand out for him to wait. She was right. He had traded in his clumsy feet for a clumsy tongue around her and now he was watching her walk away. There was nothing to make a camp out of for the runaways. Many gladiatrices had found themselves a man to keep the night's company with and Téadora had secured herself a little cliff to call home. Spartacus watched her from the hillside until she fell asleep. He was tired too, but he couldn't shut his head off. The mounting pressure of people counting on him kept his thoughts racing. Come morning, they would need food. There was shelter to secure, supplies. They needed more weapons, most of them had no armor. If this was to be a successful runaway, they couldn't be captured in a mere day's time. They had to keep up the resistance. Keep up the fight. While most of the men and women slept, Spartacus took to making the round of base of Mons Vesuvius. He was making a mental note of the farmland, which villages to exploit. There was one road up and down the volcano. It was easy to secure. No one would bother them up there, and anyone stupid enough to try wouldn't live long enough to tell anyone about it. This could actually be doable. It wasn't entirely as far fetched as he once feared. They were out. They had open sky above them, no walls around them, no Romans barking orders. Spartacus did feel pleased with himself by the time he laid down beneath the little cliff face Téadora was sleeping on top of. He was careful not to make a sound as he crawled onto the grass and curled himself up on his side. Just a couple of hours later when she woke with the sun, she grinned like a fool to see Spartacus had taken up beneath her. She bit her lip to keep from giggling out loud, and made her way down the dirt path to the sea to fix herself. A few gladiators came with her to bathe, Castus among them. He was never too fond of being dirty. By the time they had finished, the day was just barely getting started, and shop owners on the shoreline were opening for business. None of the gladiators had a bit of money to their name, but they had quick hands, and Téadora had a pretty face. She shamelessly flirted with a few older men to secure a basket full of grapes from one shop, and fish from another. Cheese from a fat man on the corner, and bread from a woman who didn't know any better to keep watch. Not wanting to press their luck the gladiators fled with Téadora back to their volcanic hideaway by sunrise, and Castus had his arms full of eggs from a farm. More raiding parties would be assembled as the day pressed on, but for one morning, the spoils were well enough to feed the seventy-five runaways. When Spartacus woke, it was to the sound of happy chatter, and the smell of scrambled eggs. Téadora and a handful of the other women had amassed a large campfire and flat stones for cooking. Eggs had been cracked, and cheese was melting. The men were huddled around in dire anticipation to get a handful of goodness. Spits were being constructed and sticks collected for cooking the fish. Spartacus couldn't contain his smiles any longer. This was all the proof he needed that they could really do this. He looked down at Téadora, doling out her eggs in true Thracian fashion, a recipe she'd learned from her mother. She flashed a grin up at Spartacus over her shoulder as if she could feel him staring, and he turned away, red in the face. Scraping off a portion of eggs and cheese onto a flat stone she ran the food up to Spartacus while he was talking to some of the other Thracians.

"It's not the best I can make, but it'll do for now. When I went down to the sea this morning, I found a whole bunch of farms ripe for the picking, Spartacus. Half of them are barely being tended to as it is. If we're careful, we can stay here for a while until we get things figured out."

"So, you've got all the answers, have you, Téa?"

"Not all the answers, but some. I want to make sure that when the men come to you with questions, you can answer them. A good leader always has the answers."

"You think I can be the leader these men want?"

"I do. Now eat up before the food gets cold. I have to go."

"Where are you going?"

"I have a lot of mouths to feed."

Téadora was always happiest when she was busy. Spartacus followed her orders to eat the eggs and cheese she had made him and it tasted better than anything he had had in years. He ate with a smile on his face the entire time, and when Crixus got his fill of breakfast, he went up to speak with his friend. It was the consensus among the gladiators and gladiatrices alike that Téadora was something of a mastermind for this breakout. She had worked for years talking to the fighters in the arena and gladiator schools to get a lay of the land. Her knowledge, combined with Oenomaus' years in the Roman army led them all to this point. If everyone chipped in and pulled their weight, they could not fail. Rome had abused everyone. The people in the countryside were more apt to take the runaways' side of things than their oppressors. Taxes had robbed these farms, made average families poverty stricken, and funding the wars in the Mediterranean were bleeding the people dry. The empire had pushed too far. Spartacus nodded as Crixus laid out potential plans for moving forward. Sooner rather than later the gladiators would be forced to fight the Romans. Someone would be looking for them. Lentulus wasn't just about to sit on his hands while his entire fortune walked away. When word got out about their escape, other gladiator schools might try to conduct uprisings of their own. Slaves from all over the place would flock to wherever they could find freedom and support. Crixus had delusions of grandeur, this mass overthrow of the Roman empire. Spartacus did not see such visions, but he did see possibilities. He wanted justice too. He wanted revenge. He wanted to right the wrongs done to him, and to others no longer alive to fight. But first, if there was to be any flocking, any army raised, there would need to be a base of operations. Vesuvius could be that place, but as it stood this morning, it was nothing more than patches of matted grass from where they had slept the night before. Spartacus gathered his would-be commanders, Crixus, Gannicus, and Oenomaus. Raiding parties were established. Schedules were made. The countryside would be systematically canvassed.

 Spartacus himself took some Thracians and went through the streets of Neopolis, eager to find something useful to bring back to the volcano. He found that in a veterans home, who was vainly displaying the souvenirs of his warring days above the hearth. Two sets of sica blades were crossed on the wall. After harassing the homeowners and scaring them down the street, Spartacus took kindly to removing the weapons of his homeland, and stashing them on his person before continuing to raid the kitchen and bedrooms. It took less than an hour before Spartacus and his men had loaded enough loot in their arms for a good day's raid. They met little in the way of any kind of serious resistance to their actions. No Romans guarded these farms. Most of the males were either too old or too young to put up much of a fight. A few women tried their damndest to keep hold of their food, but the Thracians were a rough bunch with their darker skin and tattoos. Spartacus felt a bit guilty seeing some of the children crying, holding onto their mother's, but this was all for a just cause. When they were older, they would understand that. One of Spartacus' men had to pull him away from a mother holding her baby and crying on her knees in the street. The gladiator was half tempted to return some of her items to her when Spartacus was reminded how little the runaways had to their name. He nodded, and ran for the volcano, laden down with goods to share with everyone. Oenomaus and the Germanians had fine luck raiding some nearby vineyards, and returned with barrels of wine for the camp. As a fair offering to his de facto leader, Oenomaus took the first cup of wine to Spartacus, who merely held it up to get a cheer from the runaways before lowering it, and holding it awkwardly in his hands. Oenomaus could see the man was distracted, and followed his gaze to a bundle of sheets tied up on a little cliffside perch. The Germanian leader knew that had been where Téadora had slept the night before, and elbowed Spartacus in the ribs.

"What did you bring back from the raid for her?"

"She can make a proper tent for herself out of those sheets. Inside there's a pan so she can make meals easier, and a pair of sica blades so she can defend herself. She is called Two Dagger Téadora after all. Can't have her reputation ruined on account of me."

"Why did you leave them on the rock there? Why not hand them to her yourself so she knows they came from you?"

"I don't need the praise. Just knowing she has them and is more comfortable here is all the reward I need."

"If she asks me, I'll tell her it was from you."

"Oenomaus, no!"

"You're like a little boy! What's the excitement about?"

"Téa's very important to me, that's all. With everything going on, I don't need to risk losing her. We need to stay focused."

"Well, no one could be more focused on Téadora than you. We've all seen it, that's why we followed you out here."

"It is?"

"Téadora's a good woman. One of the finest I met. We've been friends for years in that gladiator school. If ever a woman could hold her own, it's that one. She has my greatest respect. And it seems you have hers. If she trusts you, I do too, and that goes for a lot of the men and women here. You have nothing to worry about, Spartacus."

"It is the Roman way to take what a man loves most and destroy it in front of him. I watched it happen for years, and it nearly broke me. If we get overtaken, there will be consequences to pay. I know what the Romans will do. They will hurt her to get to me. I can't do that to her."

"Then we just need to make sure the Romans never catch us."

"Are you delusional, Oenomaus?"

"I was a soldier in their armies once, same as you. Many of us were deserters at one time or another. We know how the Romans fight. We know how they think. We know their strengths as well as we know their weaknesses. If we are smart and careful, we don't need to lose this fight. We can be the victors in this story."

Spartacus took a look around at the runaways as they returned with their spoils of the day. Some of these men hadn't smiled so deeply in years, it brought tears to their dirty faces. Men were dancing with each other, singing around campfires. They were free. They were probably being hunted, but for now, they were making their own decisions. Spartacus had to take pride in that, but he was modest in the congratulations he was receiving as he took in the foundations of the camp along the hillsides. All the while he was keeping an eye out for when Téadora might return. While he had been out in Neopolis, she'd returned to the sea. She took a different path this time, tested some new shoreline. Her raiding party was one of the last to return. They had hit a few snags and some resistance with a batch of young men, and therefore hid out in some alleys until darkness fell and they could make a clean run for the volcano. Spartacus was very anxious to see what she thought of the gifts he left for her. He tried to be nonchalant about it from higher up on the volcano, always peering down as she slowly made her way back to the cliffside. It seemed everyone wanted to talk to her. All the women had something to say. Lots of hugging, and laughing. When she finally saw the bundle, all tied up for her she clasped both hands over her mouth in joy. She hadn't even untied anything yet to see what was inside. Just the fact something had been left for her, anything, meant the world to her. When she did kneel down and took to revealing her gifts, she grinned at seeing the pan, then she paused at the pair of sica blades. Her fingers traced the curves in the daggers like she knew them by heart. To have something from home, she could have cried, but she didn't. At this point Spartacus came down to the little perch she called home and without a word being spoken between them she pulled him in for a full body hug.

"Thracian blades belong in Thracian hands. And there's no finer Thracian I could think of than you, Téa."

"I can think of one. Let me make this up to you. Name your price."

"Just stay with me. That's all I could ever ask of you."

"As if I'd want to be anywhere else?"

IV

After a week Senator Furius was no closer to finding the runaway gladiators than he had been on the morning they escaped. The news in Capua was more consuming to the public because when word got out that Lentulus Batiatus had pulled out of his matches across the countryside, it gave rise to other small schools to try and break out. None of them succeeded, but there were scores of men that either died trying, or were murdered for insubordination. The only reason Batiatus hadn't been entirely laughed out of business was because Senator Furius was paying his bills and searching for replacements. Had either of the men widened their circle of search, they would have realized that the runaways under Spartacus' watchful eye were thriving on the hillsides of Mons Vesuvius, and absolutely harassing the local townspeople of Neopolis. Routines were being set up now, each group had their day of the week to go raiding. Gannicus and Castus would take the Celts out first. There'd be a day off to keep things safe before Oenomaus took the Germanians out through another neighborhood. Another day off and Téadora would lead women to the sea to fish and flirt with shop owners who didn't know any better. Then after another day off Spartacus would take Thracians and raise hell on the farms while

Crixus kept Romans busy in the city running pickpocketing rings and having a mighty good time. In a week, the volcanic hillside was shaping up nicely into a proper looking camp. There were shelters and cooking stations, rows of men and women in neat fashion. There were sentry duties assigned, patrols made, resource gatherers. Dinner was held at sundown, fires maintained. The runaways were even building their ranks. The original seventy-five which had made their escape from Capua had swelled to nearly twice their size from the help of local poor, and thieving opportunists desperate to fit in somewhere. No one was turned away. The enemy of an enemy was a friend, and Rome was in no shirt supply of enemies. They'd hurt a lot of good people in their push to the top. Gannicus kept an eye on the new recruits though. It was the father figure in him, being one of the older men in the group nearing forty. He pulled Spartacus aside and stroked his ginger beard like he had wisdom to share.

"We must watch these new men coming in, Spartacus. Keep a close eye on their movements. They're not like us."

"And what binds us together, Gannicus? We are all criminals in our own right, aren't we? Who are we to judge those who come to us seeking help?"

"I just think we need to be careful. We ran from Batiatus with a common hate between us. These new men don't share that. How can we trust that they will watch our backs on a raid that goes wrong? Or a battle when the Romans finally catch on to us? I mean, we're not exactly being careful out here. Someone will report us sooner rather than later."

"We're not making camp because we intend on staying hidden. I am not afraid of what Rome has to throw at us. Any solider worth their salt is fighting in the Mediterranean, either to the west or to the east. All that's at home to keep the empire under control is old men or young boys. I fear neither."

"Rome *will* come for us, Spartacus. Not all men of fighting age are gone. We will have to defend what we have here."

"I knew what was at stake when we ran from Batiatus. I was not made to be anybody's prisoner. I will fight and die for my freedom if I must. Anyone willing to share that sentiment is more than welcome to stand by me as long as I remain standing. Anyone wanting to go home is also free to do so anytime they wish. If you are uncomfortable, Gannicus, you can take Castus and head north. I would not think any less of you. You're a long way from home."

"There's nothing left for me up there. When the Romans came up and fought with my tribe, they massacred us. They wouldn't leave us alone. Every couple of years they just kept coming with more and more men. Castus lost everything when my family took him in. When I should have been going off finding myself a wife to settle down with, I had this little boy running at my side. Castus is a sweet man. I couldn't leave him any easier today than I could back then. There will be no taking him away from Téadora. She gives him strength like no other. No. I'm staying, Spartacus. I just want to know that *you* know what we've all gotten ourselves into."

"I'm well aware."

"Tell me, what do you know of the past slave wars?"

"I know they didn't end well. I heard a few stories from soldiers while I served in Rome's armies. But back home in Thracian tribes, the failed exploits of our people did not get circulated with pride."

"Then let me enlighten you. About sixty years ago the first slave war broke out. They had their wins and losses, but ultimately twenty thousand men ended up on a cross for Roman amusement. About thirty years ago the slaves tried to free themselves again. This time a thousand of them were caught in the end, and forced to fight each other in the arena. Together they decided that mass suicide was a more dignified way to go. So, you see, now it's our turn to change history. I have no plans on ending up on a cross, Spartacus."

"I don't think any man here wants to be crucified, Gannicus. But we are not fighting the Romans of sixty or thirty years ago either."

"Are we smarter than the men who died before us?"

"I think so."

"Why do you think that?"

"I believe in us. I can't say why, but I do. It's just a feeling."

"I heard the rumors of your hesitation back at the House of Batiatus. It wasn't *you* who started the escape, it was Crixus. *You* wanted to wait and gather facts."

"I have fought with Crixus. It is his way to charge into battle and prepare for what might happen later. I've just never thought that way. And yet, somehow, we've both managed to make it this far."

"What changed your mind?"

"About what?"

"You didn't believe in us a week ago. Why do you believe now?"

"You know. Are you really going to make me say it?"

"You mock my cousin for his weakness for Téadora, when you share the same weakness. I know Téadora. That woman is as fierce as they come. She has spoken of freedom to me ever since I met her at that gladiator school. She has fought in matches for time served. She has fought for Batiatus' wealth and marriage. She has fought for everything and everyone. I fear her life means nothing to her. She wants to go home so bad she can taste it, but I don't know that she'll ever get there. She would die to know others got it though. She believes in this cause so much."

"And I believe in her. I want what she wants. I want to go home. I want to take her home. I want us both to get out of whatever comes at us alive. I won't let the Romans break her. I won't. She is the beating heart of this whole camp. I know that."

"Then you need to be more careful around her."

"What do you mean?"

"A woman like that can't be smothered or controlled any easier than a man can tame a fire."

"I don't want to smother her or control her. I just want to take care of her."

"She doesn't need you. She's been taking care of herself for years."

"Then it's about time I give her a break. I owe her for being away so long. It was never my intention."

"You *owe* her? Just what are you two to each other? Were you betrothed from years ago?"

"No. We were never betrothed, not officially, but I think we were both hopeful of such a promise. We had talked of running away together more than once. When I was taken for the Roman army, it was supposed to be a set term of service. I was to come back to her. And to this day I've still never gone back home. It's just fate that brought us together again. Or the gods. I don't know. I don't want to go asking questions. Seeing her every day, I feel like I'm in some sort of dream I don't deserve, and I'm terrified of waking up for fear of losing her."

"This is no dream, Spartacus. But you *can* lose her. Romans don't treat us with any sort of mercy in these slave wars. And we may not be slaves anymore, but they will always see us that way. Just be careful, alright? Enjoy what you have while you have it and leave it at that."

"Thank you, Gannicus."

"You're welcome. You looked like you needed someone to talk to."

"Can I ask you something?"

"Of course."

"You speak like a man who's lived and lost."

"That's because I have."

"You're not so much older than me. I wonder, if it might be alright for me to ask you why you have the wisdom that you have?"

"You mean, you want to know what the Romans have taken from me, don't you?"

"You don't have to tell me if you don't want to."

"I had a girl to call my own once. We too had talked of a life together. I was going to build us a house on the river she liked. She wanted three little girls, so they could grow up like her and her sisters."

"They killed her, didn't they?"

"A legion was passing through my tribe's lands. They weren't near my home, but they were near hers. We had been watching them and their camps get closer and closer for days. You know how the Romans camp, they're not exactly subtle. Her family had a decent sized farm, lots of livestock. I wanted her to stay with me until the legion passed, but her parents would not stand for it because we were not yet husband and wife. I woke up one night to the sound of women screaming. The Romans were taking everything, killing anyone who resisted, burning homes, raping women. To this day it's still one of the most brutal things I've ever seen. Castus lost everything. The only reason he survived was because he had hidden in the water trough for the horses. His mother, my uncle, his two brothers, and younger sister were all slaughtered. I found them burning in their home. And I found my beautiful Muire, with her sisters and mother, all bloody and beaten, raped to death with their bright blue eyes staring up at a ceiling full of flames."

"I'm so sorry, Gannicus."

"That's what keeps me going. Hate. It is a powerful motivator. It is much different than love. Much less forgiving. I know firsthand the pain of seeing the woman you love dead at a Roman's hands, and I do not wish that on my worst enemy, not alone a friend. It changes a man, and not for the better. I am not proud of what I have done because of my pain. But I will do it again to make sure no one else feels what I have felt. So, just be careful, Spartacus. Please?"

"I will be. You be careful too, Gannicus."

"I don't need to be careful. The Romans can try all they want, but they can't kill a dead man."

"You're far from dead to me."

"I'm deader than you think. Don't let this smile fool you. Ah, I should let you go. It sounds like the women are coming back home. I hear their war cries!"

Spartacus admired Gannicus' strength as the man walked away stroking his ginger beard as carefree as he usually did. No one could have known the things he had seen. Spartacus wondered how many of the other men carried such heavy burdens on their shoulders. How many of the women too? The women especially. When Spartacus had mentioned the Cilician pirates, it had rubbed Téadora the wrong way. He had brought up something painful for her without realizing it. She wore a smile often as well. She seemed to be enjoying her time here on the sides of the volcano this past week. She cooked for the men in the morning and evenings with the pan Spartacus had stolen for her. Téadora had always been fond of taking care of people though, the more the better. What secret horrors could she have been hiding? Spartacus hoped she didn't have anything too painful in her memories, or if she did, she would find a way to tell him about them in her own way. Maybe not today, or tomorrow, but one day. As the women came running up the hill howling like a pack of rabid wolves it was clear they had been victorious in their raiding, but had run into trouble just like the last time they had been out. Some of them were bloody as they set their spoils down for the men to admire. One woman was being carried back on the shoulder of another. Spartacus hadn't seen Téadora yet. As usual, she was the last to come up the path, as a good leader should be. She was carrying an unfamiliar face on her back. Spartacus went down to relieve of her of the new recruit. A healer then took the girl from Spartacus and began tending to her wounds. Now he had blood on him too, but he hadn't noticed because he was too busy scanning Téadora up and down for injury. She laughed off his concern as she crossed two clean sica blades behind her back.

"Calm down, Spartacus. None of its mine."

"That's a relief. You look good in Roman blood."

"You too."

"What?"

"Look at yourself. You didn't even notice. Come here. Let me wipe it off of you. You can be such a mess sometimes, Spartacus. I swear to the gods it's amazing you lived as long as you have without someone looking after you all the time. You're always paying attention to something else."

"I was paying attention to you."

"I'm fine. Nothing to pay attention to."

"You were out a long time today. I was starting to get worried."

"Gladiatrices can handle ourselves."

"I know, but still, I was worried."

"No. There's something more going on. There is pain on you face. Why? Tell me what's wrong."

"It's nothing. I was just speaking to Gannicus."

"Was he telling you about Muire?"

"You know about her?"

"He usually only talked about her with me or Castus. I guess he trusts you enough to tell you too now. He gets really serious when he talks about her. I try to just let him feel comfortable telling me whatever he wants without poking in with too many questions. I want to respect the man. It usually bothers him more in the warmer months. It must have been an important time for them. She sounds like she was a lovely girl, doesn't she?"

"The Romans took her from him."

"You were a soldier in their ranks for years. Surely that shouldn't have surprised you to hear such a thing."

"I want you to know I never did that to women while I served."

"I know."

"You do?"

"You're a good man, Spartacus."

"I don't feel like everything I have done has been good though. When I went raiding here the first day, the home where I got your blades, there was a woman I left screaming out in the road with her little boy. I stole from her when she barely had anything to her name. What kind of good man does that?"

"Did you lay a hand on that woman?"

"No."

"Did you lay a hand on her boy?"

"No."

"Did you spill any blood at all on that raid?"

"No."

"You are a good man."

"If you say so. You wouldn't lie to me, Téa."

"No, Spartacus. I *have* never and *would* never lie to you."

"But there's more to that."

"What you don't know can't hurt you. Besides, don't men like their women with a little bit of mystery?"

"Gannicus has horrors in his head, and a smile on his face. I just want to know if you are the same?"

"I do not hide horrors from you, only foolish mistakes."

"You promise?"

"I promise."

"Then I think you are as good a woman as I am a man."

"Now that I must correct you on."

"Why?"

"Look at me, Spartacus."

"All I can do when I am around you is look at you."

"I am covered in Roman blood."

"Yes."

"I am not a good woman like you are a good man."

"You killed on your raid today?"

"Yes."

"Who did you kill?"

"That girl that I carried up here, I killed her father. She was screaming at me from her window. He had put bars on there to keep her in. She wanted to run away. She had a man waiting for her that her father did not approve of. So I went to their door, and I killed him before he could speak his case."

"But why is *she* the one bleeding?"

"He had hurt her for trying to leave him."

"Sounds like you were right to save her."

"But was I right to kill the father?"

"Perhaps."

"Perhaps not? I do not feel good about it. But in the moment, I did not think. All I saw was myself when I was younger."

"I remember your father did not approve of our closeness."

"He wanted me to marry that *arrogant* son of his friend. If I had a coin for every time I cried myself to sleep at night after you left…"

"You what?"

"Like I said, Spartacus, I have no horrors to hide from you, only shameful acts of my youth. I was not strong then like I am now."

"You cried for me?"

"You said you were coming back for me. You never came back."

"I tried. The army kept me away. I was halfway across the empire from you. But never a *day* went by when I didn't think of you."

"I didn't know that. My father kept telling me you had died, and that I needed to marry before I got too old. I couldn't take it anymore so I ran. I ran to the water, like I always did. It just so happened that when I did this, the Cilician pirates were docking on our shores. It wasn't violent or anything, no raids. Everything was peaceful and quiet. I was going to stow myself away and get off at the next shore, but they found me before we ever took off. I was able to buy my way and work my keep for a while. I asked about you, but no one wanted to talk to me about what the Romans were doing. They thought anyone in the army was worthy of a traitor's death, and that only made me more upset. Eventually, I had to deal with the fact that I was never going to see you again, and it hardened me. I started to kill with the pirates, and I was good at it. I was *really* good at it, actually. I liked being good at something, receiving praise. The captain became like a father to me, and when he died, his son took over. Nothing was the same after that. I started to be used more and more. It became a business rather than a family. I tried to run away multiple times but he just kept finding me. That man *always* found me. Then he sold me to Batiatus, and I was used once again. I made him money, and all my attempts to run away were thwarted. But I made it out this time. I finally ran far enough away, and I won't be used by *any* man *ever* again. And if I can save just *one* more girl like me, *all* of my struggles will be worth it. I *had* to save that girl today, Spartacus, and I *had* to kill her father. I *had* to. That does not make me a good woman, but it feels good in my heart."

"If it feels good then it can't be wrong."

"You don't think any less of me for telling you all of that?"

"No. It makes me love you even more than I already did."

V

After three weeks of raiding the camp on the hillsides of Mons Vesuvius had grown from seventy-five people, to a couple thousand. Among the new recruits were the poor with nothing left to lose, disaffected farmers, young widows, old veterans, runaway slaves, and local rebels. They trickled in nearly daily up the lone path from the surrounding countrysides. No one was turned away. The original force was heavily outnumbered, and new groups were forming. Spartacus still held his commanders in high regard. Gannicus looked out for the Celts, Crixus, the Gauls, Oenomaus the Germanians, Téadora the women. Local people filled in where they were accepted. The Thracians were in short supply under Spartacus, and tended to make their shelters a little way off from everyone else. Growing their numbers was a good thing. It really was. It meant they stood more of a chance. Rumors were starting to circulate around campfires that the Romans were on to them. Any day now an army was expected to come marching up to the volcano for a slaughter. The general feeling was eager anticipation. Weapons were a major commodity, not so much armor. Death wasn't a threat for many involved. The idea of home had been ruined for them long ago. Téadora could not share in that sentiment. Crixus' way of thinking, to take down as many Romans as possible or die trying, it was not what she wanted. Revenge sure, but not at the cost of her life. She was realistic. She wasn't the luckiest of souls. It was more than likely she would die in this fight for freedom, but it wasn't what she hoped for. She wanted to know Spartacus' opinion on the matter as tensions grew but he was embroiled in an endless back and forth with Crixus tonight, on plans moving forward. The man from Parisii was no plans and all action. He wanted to go find the Romans on a trail somewhere, ambush their camp, catch them unaware. Spartacus didn't want to approve the separating of their forces for that suicide mission. From across the way Téadora could see him fiddling with his mother's silver ring necklace, pinching it between his fingers during the rise and fall of the argument. She wanted to go intervene, save him, but she didn't know what to say or if it'd be appropriate. Crixus was a difficult man she tried to steer clear from as much as possible. He was very confrontational, very one sided. There was no persuading that man to do anything he hadn't already convinced himself of. She sighed, and turned back to her campfire to tend to the fish she was roasting. She wasn't even hungry, but she knew she had to eat. Her mind was racing with these rumors of the Romans coming. She'd been living in a removed fantasy the past couple of weeks. It wasn't that she thought she could live this way forever, but she had been enjoying herself more than she should have. There was this guilt pressing down on her shoulders as she sat down and let the fire warm her. It wasn't cold out, just the opposite, but she had unsettling chills all the same. Oenomaus invited himself to sit beside her with his typically jolly smile and lighthearted wisdom. For such an intimidating looking man with all his tattoos and busted teeth, he was always a sight for sore eyes for Téadora.

"What's bothering you tonight, Téadora?"

"Everyone seems to have their own opinion about the Romans coming for us. I just don't see us coming out of this too well."

"You had to have known they'd come for us."

"No, I knew. I think I just wanted more time here."

"You enjoy being with Spartacus again, don't you?"

"It took me years to try and accept that he was dead. You can imagine the state of shock I was in when I saw him before me in the House of Batiatus. Every day since then has felt unreal. We are happy together like we used to be, like no time has passed. The Romans showing up will ruin all of that. It's just selfish. I wanted more time before death came between us again. And I can't tell him that. He's got enough to deal with. Every time I look at him, he's arguing with another man about some suicide mission."

"Some of the men have good ideas."

"Oh yeah?"

"We're not leaving the volcano. You can count on that. A smart soldier never abandons their high ground without due cause."

"A group of us leave this volcano every day. We've been abusing our freedom doing these raids. We should have been more careful. We got greedy. Look around you. We've taken too much."

"You're just scared. You're speaking from a point of fear. I've seen it from you before. But you worry for nothing, Téadora. You've never come out of a fight on the wrong side."

"We've all ended up on the wrong side of life before, that's why we're here now."

"Some of us are luckier than others. You forget your good fortune."

"What have I forgotten, Oenomaus?"

"You have the admiration of a Senator on your side."

"A lowly Senator with next to no influence."

"Having the good favor of a Senator is nothing to overlook."

"I don't want his favor. I want *nothing* from him."

"His admiration for you might just be enough to save your neck one day, or give you political asylum, leverage if nothing else. You're a smart woman. You can use him to help us."

"Easy for you to say, you're a man."

"What does that have to do with anything?"

"I will not sell my body for politics."

"What a woman chooses to do with her body is her own business. I know if the gods had made me a woman, I'd be the biggest whore the world had ever seen! Senators would bow at my feet!"

"Perhaps that is why the gods made you a man then, to keep you *humble*, Oenomaus!"

"You mock me?!"

"Only a little."

"You remind me to be humble, Téadora. Just one look at you and I am reminded of home, and everything I have to fight for. You remind me so much of my wife. You two would be the best of friends if you ever met. She is headstrong like you. Fierce."

"And would you advise your wife to befriend a Senator, entertain a proposal of marriage for the good of freedom?"

"I know where her heart lies. It lies with me, regardless of whatever happens elsewhere. She would do whatever it took to have me back in her arms, as would I."

"I wouldn't even know how to get the Senator's attention if I *did* want it, Oenomaus."

"What have you heard of the rumors in camp?"

"That the Romans are coming. No one knows how many or from what direction."

"Would you like to know?"

"Do *you* know something?"

"I know where a Roman guard is. Beat him up pretty good on my raid today. Left him to die in the shade of this crumbling stone house out in the middle of a vineyard to the east."

"I don't know my way around the vineyards. That's not my territory. I prefer to stick to…"

"To the water, yes, I know. But where do you think all the injured Romans are taken when they do not die?"

"I do not know."

"To the water! Téadora, they take them on ships and sail back up to Rome. They don't risk travelling by land. They're too afraid of us. If you go down to the sea tonight, you can surely ask about your friendly Senator. Send word to him. He will be more than happy to hear from you."

"I am not comfortable with this."

"As if a woman as pretty as you has never used a man before."

"This is different. This is dangerous. Thousands of lives could be on the line if I am not careful. I am no practiced politician. I don't know what to do!"

"A woman needs no practice in politics to manipulate a man. You have all the tools you need. Trust me. I see the looks that follow you just around this camp. You can do this."

"What do I tell Spartacus of this?"

"Tell him nothing until you have something to tell."

"He will notice I am gone."

"I will cover for you."

"Why are you doing this, Oenomaus?"

"We need intelligence on the Romans. You are our best chance at getting the information we need. I can't live with just rumors."

"I will go and see what I can do. Tell me about this vineyard you were in today?"

Spartacus looked over at Téadora's campfire and was eager to run away and talk to her while Crixus droned on and on about being allowed to go out on a scouting mission at the very least to try and cover the hillsides weak points. She looked busy though, watching Oenamaus detailed hand gestures on the landscape. He was telling her how to get somewhere, and her eyes were wide to take in every detail. Spartacus looked back at Crixus to excuse himself, and wave off his old fighting companion, but when he began walking down to Téadora's campfire she was gone. Oenomaus was helping himself to the fish she had nearly burnt to a crisp and was bad at playing clueless as to where the woman had walked off to. He made it sound like it was nothing serious, a harmless follow up to a question of hers. She'd be back soon enough and Spartacus could talk to her then, or he was more than welcome to talk to the Germanian. Spartacus was done talking to everyone right now. He clapped a heavy hand on Oenomaus' bare shoulder and winced at the sound of the fish being crunched between the tattooed man's battered teeth. Crixus was ecstatic at rounding up volunteers for a scouting mission and there was no shortage of new recruits who wanted to get themselves dirty with some Roman blood. Spartacus went back to his tent and tried to sleep. With campfires raging all around him however it was no use, and he propped his stolen sheet up on a foundation of apple piles in order to see Téadora's cliffside perch. His mind would not allow him to rest until he saw her return. So, he lied there in wait, as the hours passed by.

Téadora was able to track down Oenamaus' raiding victim with relative ease. The vineyards were some of the closest farms to the volcano. She didn't have to work too hard to climb over the fences and sneak across the terrain overnight. What presented a challenge was hauling this dying Roman on her back to the shore. She was playing the part of distressed homeowner this evening. Her guard had been injured on her property. She was asking any man willing enough to look her way to sell her story, and ask for directions to where the Roman's were landing their ship. No one wanted any trouble, and they believe her fake tears well enough. She could muster a good cry in a matter of seconds. It was a trick she learned at a very young age, and had never been more thankful for perfecting it than she was now. This Roman on her back was a stout man, dense and ridiculous to maneuver. She thought about dropping him in the street and just dragging him like a dead animal more than once, but she had to fake compassion here for her charade to get results. Once she was near enough to the sea, there was more activity in the streets, and a pair of brothers coming in from fishing helped carry the Roman guard to the docks for loading. They could tell Téadora was clearly upset, and felt bad about leaving her unattended at such a late hour. One brother had to tend to the catch of the day, but the older man, who was probably much younger than he looked but the days out on the sea had aged him far beyond his years, took pity on the young woman. She sniffled, and tried to come up with details as to what to say to steer this impending conversation where she needed it to go. All the while, in the back of her head, Oenomaus' toothy grin was reminding her how badly the camp needed this information she was searching for. Thousands of lives weighed on her conscience. She sniffled, and as a tear trickled down her face it about broke the fisherman's heart.

"Is there anything else I can do for you?"

"Oh, no. Don't mind me. You've helped enough. Truly. It's just…"

"Go on now. It's alright. You can talk to me. You're safe."

"This is the only guard I have left at the vineyard. With my husband off with the army, I have no one left to protect my land. I'm all alone out there and I'm afraid with all these raids happening…"

"Have you had trouble out there?"

"I fear for my life some days. This man, he was like a member of my family. I mean, look at what those… *heathens* did to him!"

"Those slaves have no decency. But it'll be alright soon enough. I've heard that the Senate is supposed to be sending a legion down here to Neopolis to help us."

"A legion? But I thought all the armies were at sea?"

"Not all of them apparently. Rome has not abandoned us. You'll see soon enough. Help is coming. You'll be alright."

"Any word on when this legion might arrive? How long will I have to protect my land on my own?"

"A few weeks as best I can figure. If you want, I'm usually busy fishing with my brother during the day, but I can stop by your vineyard until the Romans arrive. Give it a walkaround for you, just so the slaves know you're not alone?"

"Oh no! I could never ask that of you. You are too kind. You've already done more than enough to help me. Just knowing a legion is coming, it has brought me peace. Really. Thank you so much!"

"Are you… would you like me to walk you home? Just in case any of those slaves are out on the streets tonight?"

"I'll be fine, I think."

"It's really no trouble."

Téadora reached up on her tiptoes and placed the lightest of kisses on the fisherman's cheek before bursting into a flood of fake tears that made her words incomprehensible as she spoke gibberish and fluttered off into the darkness. This news of a legion coming her way was unsettling. It had been comforting up until now to think no organized army was left in Rome to come for the runaways. Now, the danger had just become all the more real. She needed to get back to camp as soon as possible and warn Spartacus without causing too much of a panic. She needed to find her words. Téadora was careful to keep up her charade by running up the streets towards the vineyards until she was sure she was out of the fisherman's sight. From up on higher ground, she could look down across the shoreline and see the bodies of other Romans being brought down in the darkness and abandoned like trash heaps at the water's edge. A ship was coming in off the coast. It was only a tiny dot of firelight now, but she could see it, rolling in. That was the way the legion was going to come in too. Come in on a ship and be at the volcano in a matter of no time. Téadora picked up the pace as she ran for her familiar hillsides now, leaving the charade firmly behind her. She wiped her cheeks dry on the back of her hands that wreaked of Roman blood. That man had died on her back, but he had served his purpose. To the men loading the dead and dying on the ship, it was little more important than moving any other kind of cargo. But when this ship pulled into the Roman harbor, it was a much different story. Women were crying on their knees, and the Senate was bombarded by the public to do something. Furious was attempting to spearhead more of a response to the attacks around Vesuvius but no one wanted to lead a slave hunt. It was about as inglorious a task as you could ask of a man in politics. There was nothing in it for him but appeasing a few widows. Young men new to the world, like Furius, were the only ones interested for a slight step up in status and influence. Eight, highly expendable men had been selected for the cause, all of them inherited praetors who didn't know any better to refuse. Among these eight doomed souls, Furius found the one displaying the most nerves. His name was Gaius Glaber, and he had more freckles on his face than there were waves in the ocean. In comparison, Furius was a fine-looking man, and rich beyond words. When he came up to Glaber, the praetor was shaking in his sandals.

"Senator Furius! It is an honor to be assigned to the slave retrieval. I just want to take the time to show my appreciation. My mother has been begging for me to get an assignment for months now. This will truly please her! Such a savior, Senator!"

"Alright, alright. I'm no hero, Glaber. I just wanted to pull you aside and talk to you. You seem to be the only one here who really cares for this assignment. I want to let you know that means a lot to me. You see, there's a slave in particular I am very concerned about."

"You…concerned for a slave? I don't think I understand."

"Do you know anything about these slaves, Glaber?"

"Only that they must be stopped as soon as possible."

"Yes, the raiding and killing must stop, but these slaves are not our enemies, at least not all of them. There are women among them."

"Women slaves?"

"You have seen them, no doubt. These aren't domestic house servants, the kind that tend to your mother. No, these women…these women are much more than all of that."

"You're the Senator that attends all of the gladiatrix matches in the countryside, aren't you?"

"Yes. And it seems by no fault of my own, I have become quite fond of one of the women from those matches. She ran away, and I believe her to be in that camp in Vesuvius we have been told about. Can I trust you with something, Glaber?"

"Anything! Of course!"

"If I were to task you with a special request, do you think you could return this particular woman to me?"

"I will do everything in my power."

"*Alive*, Glaber, you do understand that my conditions are for this woman to be brought back to me in the best of conditions, yes?"

"I will try my hardest. Who is this woman?"

"Her name is Téadora. Two Dagger Téadora to be specific. She has long black hair, dark tanned skin, and bright green eyes. Do you think that you can remember that?"

"Black hair, dark skin, bright eyes."

"Bright *green* eyes. *Green*. They glow you see in the most…well, you understand then?"

"I understand."

"I will reward you handsomely for this should you succeed, Glaber."

"Yes. Yes, I understand, Senator. I will find this woman for you and bring her back. It will be my greatest honor to reunite the two of you. She will probably be ecstatic at my rescue."

"Glaber, have you ever spoken with a slave before?"

"Aside from giving orders, no, not really. Is that a problem?"

"No. Its perfect, actually. One more question, have you ever been in a fight before?"

"No. But my mother made sure I received the best combat training. My father was in the army for years. I'm sure I'll be a natural."

"I'm not sure that's how it works, but I have the utmost faith in you. Oh, and, this isn't really important, but…could you keep this little task I've given you just between us? You wouldn't want one of the other praetors to come in and steal this bounty for themselves."

Glaber took a look around the hall at his colleagues and eyed them with disdain. In a matter of minutes Senator Furius had managed to take the weakest link in the bunch and give him enough confidence to think he was nearly invincible. Any smarter a man would have refused the Senator's task and promise of money, but Glaber did not have that luxury or wisdom. He was friends with none of the other praetors assigned to the slave mission, though they all seemed to be friends enough amongst themselves. Glaber was the odd one out, and was now determined to remain that way in the hopes of pleasing his mother and all those who had ever made fun of him, of which there were many. Senator Furius felt a bit guilty for using the freckle faced boy in such a manner, but if it got him Téadora, then it didn't really matter. Even if Glaber fell, he was sure one of the other praetors would come to him for the reward. They eyed him now in the hall, curious, and eager to please. Furius passed them with measured steps and a fake smile, but deep down, he was terrified this was all going to backfire on him in humiliating fashion. Getting Téadora back to Rome was no small feat. She would not go peacefully. Furius rubbed the still healing gash on his thigh he kept under protective cover to avoid awkward questions. Why should he be interested in a lowly gladiatrix when all the women were known for was doubling as a fighter and a prostitute? How could he possibly explain his interest to his fellow politicians in a way they would understand? It was better to just act without their knowledge, and face their stares later, once he had the woman he wanted in his arms. She could come to love him, and realize the perks of being with a Senator. If it was home she so desired, they could visit as often as she wanted. He had that power. Furius tried to talk himself into a successful future all the way back to his chambers. By the time he came to his door he was sure that this task would not end in failure. Téadora would be beside him one day, holding him, and smiling. He was so fond of her smile. He could close his eyes and see it as clear as if she were standing right in front of him. But she wasn't, and that was because she was on the hills of Mons Vesuvius, sharpening her sica blades for a war. In fact, all of the slave army was preparing for war. This wasn't going to be the fight of the men sixty years ago, or thirty years ago. This was going to be different, because they had what no one else had. They had Spartacus.

VI

It took the praetor legion several weeks to drum up support for their slave mission. Families had already given enough for the empire, and to be asked to give even more, it was like trying to get blood from a stone. Many women were already asking about where their husbands were at sea, many mothers worried for sons, and sisters about brothers. Women were tending the farms and livestock. Women were out fishing and butchering animals. Women were in the shops making deals. They had children with them, all running about. The praetors divided into neighborhoods when they reached a village. It was always picking up a man here or there. Maybe picking up a group of friends, never more than five would come back to the ship at a time. It was slow going. All the while Glaber kept his secret to Senator Furius close to his heart. This struggle and sacrifice was all going to lead up to something one day. No one knew where Two Dagger Téadora was when Glaber went asking questions in the countryside. Many of them had known of her from her matches as a gladiatrix, and her reputation for being undefeated. She had made a lot of people a lot of money. The closer the Romans got to Neopolis, the better their leads became. Slaves had been terrorizing and harassing wider and wider ranges from Mons Vesuvius as their numbers grew. Mothers had complained they had no sons to give to the empire because Spartacus had already taken them. They knew Spartacus by name. He was the face of the enemy. His commanders all came back to him. Spoils were levied out by him. Decisions were made by him. Townspeople were fed up, but they sought very little relief in Glaber or his fellow praetors. It was clear the group of eight were highly inexperienced in the field. Even after amassing three thousand soldiers to their name, Spartacus had at least twice that many on the volcanic hillsides. With so many mouths to feed, the raids had increased in size and frequency. Commanders teamed up now on their searches. Spartacus usually went with Gannicus to collect supplies in the fields to the north, but today Gannicus was sick with a fever, and Crixus volunteered his Gauls to step in. There really wasn't telling the man no, so Spartacus led the Thracians out first, leaving his characteristic seven dotted tattoo mark on the grassy hills as they were deemed clear and safe. He'd take his fist to clear a dirted symbol. Crixus scoffed as the men continued walking.

"What's wrong now, Crixus?"

"I just think it unwise of you to go marking the landscape, Spartacus. If the Romans come tracking us from this direction, they'll have a clear path right back to camp, and you."

"They'll already have a clear path back to camp. What man in his right mind can't see thousands of us up on the hills? We're not trying to hide. If we didn't want a fight, we'd have run as soon as Téa came back that night and told us the Romans were coming. It's been weeks now. They're close enough."

"So why the dots?"

"Téa comes through this way sometimes. If she sees our dots…"

"*Our* dots?"

"The *Thracian* dots. If she sees a mark from home, she'll know the path is safe."

"That woman is going to be the death of you if you're not careful."

"I can't think of a more fitting way for a man to go than for the woman he loves."

"You're hopeless. She is a weakness. You have thousands of people depending on you and you can't afford to have weaknesses."

"Every man has a weakness, and every woman too. So, what if she is mine and I am hers? We fight stronger together. Everyone can see it. It's not like I am the only man in camp to take up a gladiatrix in his arms. Almost every one of those women is spoken for."

"That's because the lot of them are whores. They're not good and loyal women. They'd bed any man. And as soon as the Romans start cutting us down, they'll find another man to bed, and another and another, until sooner or later they've gotten into a Roman bed, and they're taken care of. You should be careful. I heard a Senator's already got his eyes on your woman."

"Téa has no interest in Senator Furius. Besides, she's no whore, and most of her women aren't either. You speak unkindly and unfairly about our allies."

"It is the truth. If women could be trusted, they'd be in every army around the world. They're not, and for good reason. They make men weak in battle. They pull attention away from where it ought to be."

"What are you getting at, Crixus?"

"I've fought with you for years. I know you, Spartacus. You are different now with Téadora. You hesitate. You doubt. How many men did we watch die who were crying over missing their wife the night before?"

"I do not hesitate anymore than I ever have. But you are right, I *am* different. I am more cautious. I have something to lose now, whereas before, I thought I'd already lost her."

"Like I said, she's a weakness."

"It is useless trying to talk to you. You don't care for anything or anyone. You don't care about going home, or having a family. You are consumed with revenge. But you'll never be satisfied because the men that hurt you when you were younger are long gone now, and killing these new Romans will have nothing to do with the healing you so desperately need."

"I don't need to heal anything. I am *not* a broken man."

"Well, you certainly aren't a solid man. You question everyone in camp. You trust no one. You think everyone is out to get you all the time. It is a lonely path you lead, Crixus. So angry all the time. It's not right. It must be exhausting."

"At least I am aware of the seriousness of the situation."

"I am just as aware as you, if not more so."

"Humor me."

"No. The last time I did that we ended up drunk and bound in the back of a Roman wagon headed for the House of Batiatus. I've never been so humiliated in my life to be bought and sold like an animal."

"And you blame *me* for all of that? I didn't put the wine in your mouth that night."

"You might as well have. You were as unreasonable then as you are right now and I will not make the same mistake twice. Call me weak, doubt my decisions all you want, but you leave the women out of this. You will not speak ill of Téa to me again, or any of the other gladiatrices or you will find yourself fighting the Romans alone, and you will lose, Crixus."

"You would kick me out of the camp? I thought you took in all the rejects of the world?"

"I will not keep a man who doesn't want to fight with the others."

"I want to fight."

"But you don't want to listen. You don't want to compromise. An army is a *team*, Crixus. You have to depend on each other. You have to trust each other."

"Every man I've ever trusted is dead, except for you, Spartacus."

"You've never told me that."

"I didn't want to have to. I don't need you thinking you're important to me."

"There's no shame in having a friend, Crixus."

"I would get myself killed to avenge your death."

"And I would you."

"No, you wouldn't. You have someone to live for. I don't have anyone. That's the difference between you and me. I want Roman blood. And I want *all* of it. You're right, about me. I will never get my fill of death. Rome has taken my happiness. When I was a boy, I used to laugh all the time. I had a family and friends. I had girls chasing me. I had everything I could have wanted and took it all for granted. I walked away from them. I wanted to be a hero. I had heard what the Romans did in tribes all over the lands far away. I wanted part of that. I wanted the scars and the stories. I was the biggest fool. Now I have all the scars and stories a man could ever dream of, and I am so unhappy. I have no one, and I have made it that way. There is no future for me. No hope. There is only death. And I am not afraid. I am excited, Spartacus. I am eager. But I still want it to mean something when I go out in my hail of glory."

"It will bring me no joy the day I see you fall, Crixus."

"Then I shall make sure you never see it. But the day is fast approaching. I can feel it in my bones. It feels…like coming home."

"When was the last time you were home?"

"I was thirteen. I was so tall for my age, when I lied to get into the army, no one questioned it."

"Why did you volunteer so young? Didn't anyone warn you?"

"People could have told me anything, but I wouldn't have listened. I want what I want and I go after it. It's the way I've always been. And it's kept me alive this long, so who's to say I'm wrong?"

"You smile, but I don't believe it. Gannicus has told me everyone's smiles hide pain. I thought he was being dramatic, but now…"

"You smile in pain too, Spartacus."

"Do I?"

"All anyone has to do is mention Téadora's name, and if she isn't close enough for you to reach out and touch, she's too far for your liking. That's all I was trying to say earlier. It's almost as if you care too much for the woman. She will die no different than we will, and the men can't have you as a leader halfway through this war, and then watch you fall apart. If we lose you, we lose everything."

"This isn't my war."

"Are you sure about that?"

"*You* led the escape from the House of Batiatus. Not me. *You* started all of this, Crixus."

"I just gave you the push you needed."

"Was this really what *I* needed?"

"You're a soldier, Spartacus. If we had stayed in that gladiator school, Rome would have made a fool of you. We are men, we demand respect. We are not mere animals who fight for blood sport while some little lanista can get rich off of us. Haven't you talked to Téadora about how much that destroyed her?"

"I don't like talking about things that upset her."

"Well over the past few weeks I have heard enough stories to know that the life of a gladiator is no life at all. A man needs his freedom. It's unnatural to keep us in cages."

"I still feel caged. I hate waiting for the Romans to come and find us. I am so used to being on the other side of things."

"Don't worry, you'll be getting your blades wet soon enough. I can smell it in the air. The legion is close."

"I have had Oenamaus manning the Germanians on patrols in all directions around the volcano. He's told me nothing of their camps."

"That's because they're not stupid enough to come by land. They'll come in from the sea. Your woman was right about that much. As much as I hate to admit it, she knows her stuff. A sea attack would be safer, and we're not dealing with the best of the best here. These little boys that'll be coming for us, they'll be so green. We're going to slaughter them! It'll almost be too easy for me to enjoy. *Almost.*"

"Don't get too confident. There might be some boys worth their salt. Once we get a first battle under our belt, I'll feel much better about what we're up against."

"You should go back to camp, Spartacus. Talk to Téadora."

"What about the raid? We have a lot of land to cover still."

"I'll keep an eye on the Gauls and your Thracians. You're just not in it today. You need your woman. Go. I insist."

Spartacus gripped the reins on his horse and wasted no time getting back to camp. Crixus could tell from the smile on his face that Spartacus needed this time away from incessant duty to get his head on straight. A distracted man was a dead man on the battlefield. Crixus knew a fight was on the horizon. More than a smell in the air or a feeling in his bones, he just knew. He'd been on raids with Téadora all last week down by the water. Shop owners were talking. The Romans were coming down the coast, and the praetors were desperate for soldiers. They were damn near taking anybody they could, old veterans, and young boys. They'd land overnight and filter through towns, be gone by the next morning. Crixus was going to try and talk to Oenomaus about giving the Germanians a reprieve from their sentry duties, but that negotiation was unlikely to go smoothly. Crixus still scorned that B burned into his flesh by the large tattooed brute he had to call an ally now. There was no love loss between those two men, but they just so happened to call Spartacus a friend and Rome an enemy, so they remained in camp together. Oenamaus thought something was wrong when Spartacus ran back early today, and alone, but before any man could run up to the man with an idea or request, he had scooped up Téadora in his arms as she was sharpening her sica blades on her cliffside perch.

"Spartacus?! I thought you were raiding? Is something wrong?!"

"Nothing's wrong. I just missed you."

"Well, I'm right here. Nothing to miss. Can you help me finishing sharpening my blades? You always were better at this than me."

"I'd rather do something else right now."

"Like what?"

"Want to go down and spend the day on the beach?"

"You sure that's wise? I raid the beaches."

"Come spend the day with me, Téa, please?"

She was searching the big Thracians eyes for some hint at to what was wrong. There was a shake in his voice when he spoke to her, and his arms clung to her waist like he had a goodbye choked off in his throat. She would tend to her blades another time, and set them down in her sheeted tent. Spartacus took her up on his horse with him so they could run down to the shore and waste no more time in the day. It was already well into the afternoon by the time the pair were able to swim out into the salty water. Téadora was the best swimmer, it was the island upbringing in her shining through. Spartacus stayed only waist deep to watch her. He needed her smile, her true smile. Not the kind that he was surrounded with now on the hillsides of the volcano. Everyone lied to him, but she could not. She laughed in the water. She didn't laugh anywhere else. It was her home away from home, as close as he could get her right now. If Crixus was right, and the Romans really were closing in on them, he wanted this moment of unspoiled happiness with her. He needed it like food or water. He needed her. She was indeed a weakness, and a crippling one at that, but he was just fine with that. Téadora kept swimming back for him, trying to pull him out farther from the sand. The Thracian wouldn't budge. He was like a rock on the shore, and she the water just continuously pouring in around him, surrounding him until they were one. The Romans could not take this moment from him, no matter how hard they tried. They could kill him, but this moment, this memory would remain. Spartacus kept Téadora close through the rest of the day, and she did not pester him once as to disclose what was nagging at his mind. She just tried to be a positive force, and enjoy the closeness she had dreamed of for so long. This wasn't their beach, but it was good enough. This wasn't their shoreline or their people, but for the moment, it would do. And that wasn't their sunset that they watched, but it was sweet all the same as she leaned back into his chest and he wrapped his arms around her shoulders. When the stars came out, Spartacus helped Téadora back up on his horse and they rode for the camp. Oenomaus and his Germanians had been replaced by Crixus and his Gauls on sentry duty. There had been no argument about it because Crixus had lied and said it was Spartacus' idea. Spartacus hoped there would be no fault in this, and played along. Téadora went back to sharpening her sica blades, and it was quiet for the evening.

A couple of hours before sunrise, a ship landed in the harbor of Neopolis. The praetor legion had arrived, and they were armed for a fight. They lined up and marched up into the villages that had been so used to raids that they didn't even bother heading to their windows to see what the commotion was. Crixus was alerted by his southern facing men that they had company. Crixus then went to Spartacus, Téadora, Oenomaus, and Gannicus to rally the commanders together and figure out what needed to be done. While they spoke in frustrated whispers in Spartacus' tent, the Romans marched closer and closer. Crixus' Gauls kept coming up to the tent every five minutes with updates, counts on the soldiers, and what they were carrying, where they were coming from, where they were going. It was so much that no one could think. Oenomaus finally cut the meeting short to just go out on the hillsides and watch the enemy coming for him with his own two eyes. They were indeed a bunch of new recruits. A handful of older veterans were sprinkled in at regular intervals. The eight praetors rode in the back on matching white horses. It had to have been an intentional decision. Oenomaus scoffed, spit, and was joined by the other commanders. Some people were starting to wake up in camp, and tend to their morning campfires. Seeing all the leaders converging on the front hillside meant something was wrong. Small huddles began to form, whispers turned to anxious chatter. The tension grew heavy. Téadora was right. The Romans came from the sea, a single legion, some three thousand men. They used the word men loosely. Some of Téadora's women were more men than the boys down in the streets. But this was no preparation for battle, at least not yet. There was no urgency in their steps. The soldiers stopped at the base of the volcano, surrounding the outer edges in all directions until Spartacus and his camp were isolated on Vesuvius. The lone path up and down from camp was overtaken by the praetors, all paraded in formation on their white horses. That was the Roman's grand master plan. They didn't have what it took to engage in combat, so they would wait things out, forcibly starve their enemy into a surrender. A man from Crixus' sentry duty ran up breathless to the gathering of commanders. After disclosing his information to Crixus, he left to return to his post on the north facing side of the volcano. Téadora stepped forward, wanting transparency amongst allies.

"What did your man have to say, Crixus?"

"It seems the Romans left us an escape path."

"What do you mean? They lined up to surround us. Did they not *fully* surround the volcano?"

"On the north side they seem to have left a gap in their formation. It might just be temporary, or an oversight, but for now, it is our only way out."

"Why would they do that intentionally if not for baiting us into a trap? I don't like this."

"Come now, Téadora, do you really think those boys wise enough to lay a trap?"

"Then why leave a gap, Crixus?"

"The north face is extremely steep, and the soils shifty. We've been avoiding it for weeks."

"Shifty soil?"

"Yes. As in difficult to…"

"I know what *shifty* means, Crixus! I'm a woman, not stupid. But I grew up on an island. I raid the sand all the time. Me and my women are excellent in shifty soils. With a little determination, it's nothing we can't deal with."

"And the steepness of the northern slope? How do you suggest we handle that?"

"I don't know. But I'm not the only one thinking up here. Spartacus? Gannicus? Oenomaus? Any bright ideas?"

"We need rope."

"I don't know if you've noticed, Spartacus, but the camp is a little short on the amount of rope it would take to get some six thousand men off the side of a volcano."

"Thank you, Crixus, for the wonderful observation. But like Téa said, she was born on an island, she knows sea and sand. I wad born in the mountains. I know hilly terrain. I've been making rope since before I could walk. It's not hard. And we are not entirely without supplies. I mean, look at all of the grapes we have harvested. The vines have just been kindling for fires, but we can use them. They are gnarled and hearty. I need all of you to go back to your people. Tell them to spare the grapevines. Do not burn them in the morning fires. I need everyone with any sort of weaving experience to pull together. I will teach them how to make a rope worth using. I've never had one break on me yet."

"Are you sure about this, Spartacus?"

"Don't worry, Gannicus. I know what I'm doing. I will get us off of this volcano. We are not trapped. But let the Romans think they've gotten the victory of the day. Crixus, keep your men on that north face. You let me know the second someone moves in on that gap."

"I will watch the north personally, Spartacus."

"Téa, can you collect your women. I feel like if any weavers are in this camp, they might be our best bet."

"I'll go see who I can find."

"Oenomaus?"

"Yes, Spartacus?"

"Gather your most intimidating looking men. I want you to scare those boys down there. Keep them on their toes while we're busy."

"It would be my pleasure!"

VII

Up on the hillsides the entire day was spent packing up camp and preparing for war. Those who could weave wracked their fingers to the bones twisting and twining grapevine fibers together into long expanses of rope. There were five in total, all bound to massive volcanic stones and coiled out of view from the Roman troops down below. Blades were sharpened, and campfires burned in the middle of the day. Women took charcoal to paint their eyes black, and some of the men smeared lines across their face as well. Oenomaus and the Germanians demonstrated the might of the slave army for hours, just screaming and clanging weapons together from a safe distance, out of range of any archers. In some cases, the slaves were twice the age of the Roman boys at the base of the volcano. Only the veterans seemed to stay outside and watch the show. The praetors stayed in one tent or another all day. Oenomaus saw Glaber the most. His fiery orange hair was doing him no favors in this environment. The dirt was black and the grasses green. And this young man kept popping out, staring at the hills for minutes at a time. Oenomaus wanted to kill him first, fearing he might know more than the others in his company. While walking around the volcano, terrorizing, and harassing each part of the legion, Oenomaus crossed Crixus' position, and the two men nodded to one another. Up until now, the only time the two men had exchanged words was when Oenomaus branded Crixus at the House of Batiatus and they fought. Crixus was in no mood to pretend the men were friends now, but Oenomaus came up to his spot on the hill anyways, and swallowed his pride for the purpose of information.

"If Spartacus sent you over here, I have nothing new to tell him from the last runner I sent back around the volcano."

"Spartacus didn't send me, Crixus. I'm here for myself."

"What do you want?"

"I'd like to know before this gets ugly that I don't have to worry about you driving a dagger into the back of my neck down there."

"I'll be too busy stabbing Romans to worry about what's going on with you, Oenomaus."

"I guess that's good enough. I also wanted to ask you a favor."

"Why?"

"It's not for me, it's for Spartacus, because I know he won't ask himself. I already told my men to keep an eye on the women when this opens up. You know as well as I do the life of a prisoner looks far different for a man than a woman."

"I've been told more than once how well the women can handle themselves."

"Yes, I know you have. I've been told the same thing. But see, I was also raised by a man who told me to protect women, and I don't see why that should change now."

"My father told me the same thing. Don't worry. The Gauls will keep an eye on the women too."

"Thank you, Crixus."

"Is that all, Oenomaus? Shouldn't you be down there screaming at the little boys or something?"

"My throat needs a rest."

"Then don't stand here talking to me. Rest in silence."

"Do you really hate me so much you can't even handle being civil right now?"

"We don't need to be friends just because we are allies."

"No, but it does make fighting a war easier when you can trust the man beside you."

"I trust you to be a good fighter, Oenomaus. What more do you want from me?"

"Nothing, I guess. Forgive me for thinking you were capable of more. I'll move my men around to another position soon enough. Then I'll see you later tonight when we make our move."

"Is that still the plan?"

"As far as I know. Gannicus wants us to wait a few hours after sunset, so the Romans are good and settled. If we're to catch them unaware, we'll need to move off these hillsides fast."

"Nothing faster than falling."

"You have no faith in Spartacus' rope idea?"

"I have faith in nothing. But one way or another our army will be face to face with the Romans. However we get down there, it will be a blood bath all the same. That's what's important. I want that ship to be empty when it goes back to Rome."

Oenomaus took a step back. He hated the Romans, the entire slave army did too, but no one hated like Crixus. That man was excited to get his hands dirty tonight, and a glimmer of a smile upturned his lips. It was unsettling to look at, so the tattooed Germanian excused himself and went back to screaming with his men, banging swords on shields, and yelling curses. The Romans were setting up their tents, legitimate tents, not the makeshift pieces the slaves had been used to working with. The boys down there had food too, nice packs, rations, cooking equipment. They were clean, clean armor, clean hands, clean faces. Their pale skin glowed as the sun began to set. By the time Oenomaus had rounded the volcano after a whole day of demonstrating, he and his men were allowed a break to eat and sleep. They would be woken when it was time to descend on the ropes, but that was still a couple of hours off. Spartacus and Gannicus had drawn up battle plans in the dirt hillsides, scraping free the grass for a clean view. Téadora and Castus put in their opinions here and there. All the commanders were assigned their area of the legion to attack. Oenomaus' request to kill the ginger headed praetor was factored into these assignments. Spartacus wanted the praetor's fleet of eight white horses. The animals were healthy and strong, good for a long trek. Thinking of a victory tonight, that was the next hurdle to jump, where to take the war next. They had made quite a home for themselves here on Vesuvius, and been content raiding the farms. Six thousand men went through a lot of food and water in a day. They needed some sort of shelter. Some sort of safety, and promise of direction. Spartacus suggested heading north, back in the direction of Capua. Gannicus thought it unwise to go tempting familiar areas so soon, and since Rome was north of Capua, it was suggested and urged that the army press south. To the south they could winter over. Summer was on it's way out right now, and the further south would make it easier to keep an army happy. Morale was important to maintain unity. Spartacus nodded a lot, and spent more time listening to what Gannicus had to say. The man knew an awful lot for spending most of his days quietly following orders. But the time to be content on the volcano was over. Spartacus was somewhat sad to be leaving these hillsides. Gannicus could see his leader's reluctance, and clapped a fatherly hand on the Thracian's shoulder.

"South is the right way to go, Spartacus. Trust me."

"I *do* trust you, Gannicus. I just wonder how many of us will be heading south."

"We outnumber the Romans two to one right now, and if you factor in experience, there's no way we can lose."

"If I had a coin for every time I heard an officer say that there was no way we could lose, and we lost, I'd be a very rich man."

"Are you afraid of suffering defeat tonight?"

"No. I'm just afraid of who we are going to lose."

"Is it Téadora?"

"No. Crixus."

"That man is an unhappy as they come. Should he fall tonight, it would not have a single negative effect on the rest of us."

"That's what bothers me. The man has no friends. He fights for blood and blood alone. There is no going home for him. He's different than you, and the men you say are dead inside. You're not looking forward to dying, but Crixus is. He's got hundreds of Gauls following him."

"If he falls, another Gaul can take his place."

"I just wish he had a better attitude about all of this. We're on the same side. I think once we get down there, and go our separate ways to push through the legion, he might do something I can't stop him from doing."

"His actions are his own, Spartacus. You're not responsible for him."

"I'm the leader. I'm responsible for everyone."

"That is a very heavy burden to place on your shoulders."

"I will bear it so no one else has to."

"That is admirable, but unnecessary."

"I need to go check and see how the weavers are doing with the ropes. Will you excuse me?"

"Téadora's not with the weavers."

"What?"

"Téadora's not with the weavers. I know you said you were going to go check on the weavers but you're going to go check on her. While you were speaking with the Thracians, she went down the path to try and set up a meeting with one of the legion's praetors."

"She did what?!"

"She asked me to come talk with you to cover her because she knew the second you found out what she was doing you'd try to stop her."

"She could get herself killed!"

"She can handle herself, Spartacus."

"I don't care if she can handle herself! I don't *want* her to have to handle anything. Gannicus, you…you…"

"I was just helping a friend."

"You go check on the weavers."

"Spartacus if you go running down there after her it could alert the legion. You need to trust her to do this on her own!"

"I *do* trust her."

"Then prove it. Don't go down there."

"If anything happens to her, it's her blood on your hands."

"Nothing is going to happen. This is a civil negotiation. Leaders in war do this all the time."

"This isn't like other wars, and she's a woman."

"Don't go down there, Spartacus."

"What am I supposed to do then?"

"There is plenty of other things to keep you busy right now. Your men and women are watching your every move. If you get upset, what are they supposed to think? A good leader is a calm leader. Pace yourself. You have plenty of time to go screaming your head off tonight. But wait for the right moment. Now is *not* it."

"Maybe I *should* go check on the weavers?"

"Why don't we both go? I need to pull my cousin aside anyways."

"Is he nervous?"

"Castus is no soldier. I'm sure you already knew that."

"But he was a gladiator for years. A beastiarus is no laughing matter. The man can wield a blade and protect himself."

"Just because he's good at killing animals, doesn't mean he's good at killing people. He's never taken a human life before."

"Oh."

"I promised to protect him as long as I could. I need to know that he remembers that. If there was a way I could keep him safe, and out of this, I would. But, there's no clean way out of this. Not this time."

"If worse comes to worse, I'll keep an eye on him too, Gannicus."

"Thank you."

"I'm serious."

"No, I know you think you're serious, Spartacus. But I've fought in battles before too. I know what happens in the heat of the moment, and how fast it can all come undone. No matter how careful you try to be, and no matter how many precautions you take, sometimes it's just not your day."

"Or night. But you told me earlier you were sure of a victory?"

"Every victory comes at a cost. I'm just trying to figure out what this one will be. I'm no good at seeing the future. We should go check on those weavers now. We're starting to lose daylight."

Gannicus walked ahead. He would no longer hold eye contact with Spartacus, and kept his hands from trembling by stroking his long ginger beard. It was unsettling to see a calm man shake. Spartacus tried to keep it all in perspective. Some of the men in this camp hadn't fought in a battle in years, or ever. Some of them only knew the rigged games in arenas and gladiator matches. This battle they were in for, it didn't follow any sort of rules, and there was no almighty Roman ready to pass judgement at the end of this. This was real. And this was going to get messy. Spartacus was pleased with the weaver's progress. The ropes were all longer than they needed to be, and attached to progress from hours earlier secured on the northern side of the volcano. Crixus was still watching the gap. It had remained open and untouched all day. That was promising. Spartacus began to move the camp to the northern hills as the Romans lit their campfires. It wasn't until the flames began to dim could they begin their descent to the base of the volcano. Spartacus waited and waited on the south side facing the sea for Téadora to come back. He was alone on her cliffside perch when she returned. She looked absolutely defeated as she came up the path. No one was willing to talk to her. She had spent hours trying to get through to someone. All she did was take mental notes on the men's readiness. The praetors had next to no training. There was something about a bounty on her head but only Glaber was allowed to take her. She was under the impression no one respected Glaber. Spartacus told her Oenomaus wanted that man's head, and it seemed to please her enough to take Spartacus' hand and walk to the north side. She hesitated though, when they began to round the volcano, and the sea started to fade from view. Spartacus put a gentle hand on the small of her back and urger her forwards.

"It is not the last time you will see the water, Téa. I promise."

"It's just, I went years without seeing it. I felt like part of me was dying. I don't want to ever feel like that again."

"You won't. Stick with me, and I'll make sure of it."

She nodded, and he placed a kiss on top of her head. Her hair was all tied in braids for the fight tonight, and her eyes blackened with streaks of charcoal. By the time Spartacus and Téadora arrived at the northern side of Vesuvius, most of the fires in the Roman camps were dwindling into embers. On five ropes the slave army descended, roughly a thousand per rope. Not one of them busted, frayed, or weakened. As they crept down the shifty soils and steep slope, they kept careful footing, and talking to a minimum. Down between the gap in the Roman lines, the slaves gathered in groups according to their commanders in the various pockets of greenery and overgrown shrubs. Gannicus, Castus, and Crixus were to go left, and wrap around until they met up with Spartacus, Oenomaus, and Téadora going right. Taking the praetors was high priority, as well as any man barking orders or who knew what they were doing. Spartacus wanted the horses alive. All weapons, armor, supplies, and food were to be looted as much as possible. Nothing useful was to be left behind. Everyone had to carry their own weight. The injured were to be tended to. Rome could not take prisoners from this fight. Crixus pulled away first. He was not quiet about it, which forced the other five commanders to act in kind. The Germanians were the loudest, and by the far the most brutal to watch. Even the allies had to take a minute to stop and stare at the brutal power they displayed. Téadora and the women were more clever in their attacks, sneaking up on men from behind so as to not be overpowered. But the Germanians had size on their side. They towered over the Roman boys, and sent them running with frantic tears into the darkness. The slave army had caught the Romans by complete surprise. By accident, Téadora had acted as a perfect distraction for the praetors. They were not ready for this, nor would any amount of time had made them ready. The soldiers were not good in hand-to-hand combat. Any lucky veteran that did manage to get a jab in or two, was quickly overtaken by a slave and his friends. At the rendezvous, it was Oenomaus and Crixus who had rounded the base of the volcano first, with everyone else straggling along and cleaning up their messes. The man exchanged bloody grins in the moonlight before setting after the praetors. The leaders had gaggled in one tent, no one could say why except for fear. One of the eight had already been killed, and left outside. Crixus charged in first, hacking away while Oenomaus followed inside and seized the redheaded Glaber by the neck of his armor and threw him outside. Oenomaus wanted an honorable fight, but Glaber was scurrying on the ground like a child. He was demanding mercy, a pardon. Oenomaus followed him menacingly as Glaber tried to throw camp items in the Germanians' way to slow him down. Oenomaus could not, and would not be stopped.

"You have a bounty on my friend's head. Now, I must take *your* head, and bring it to her."

"The bounty's off! I swear. I want no one. The bounty's off!"

"No. You don't get to make decisions anymore, little praetor. *You* came to *my* camp. And that will be your *last* mistake. Come here and face me like a man! Stop running!"

"I should have never come here! No one wanted to come. The senate said you slaves were a *filthy* lot. You're not a good man!"

"Good enough to kill you."

Oenomaus pounced on the praetor, pinning him between his body and the earth. With such ease he took his right fist and knocked the freckled man unconscious. After his body went limp, Oenomaus wrenched him around the neck until he heard the bones snap, and proceeded to haul to body up to the volcano's edge where Crixus was lining up the other six. By the time Gannicus and Castus arrived from the west, seven praetors had been killed, and Crixus was torturing the last one by tying him two horses, and seeing what information the Roman had to spew. He was not cooperating. A few minutes later Spartacus and Téadora arrived from the east. They were coated in blood, and had a far tougher go at plowing through the Germanians' aftermath. But it had been a successful night, that was what was most important. The six commanders convened in a happy huddle, pressing their foreheads together and sighing the biggest sighs of relief. Castus was already beginning to tend to the wounded and trying to speak to the praetor in a Celtic language. Turns out he wasn't really Roman at all, or speaking Celt out of fear. Gannicus wanted to keep him alive, send him back to Rome alone as a message to the senate. Crixus wanted to kill him. Oenomaus didn't care either way. He'd got his man, and displayed the redheaded bounty hunter to Téadora. She was pleased, and sided with Gannicus to send this lone praetor back as an omen of what was to come. Spartacus took the majority vote, and Crixus was sore about it, but punched the praetor in the gut one more time for good measure to feel better about the night. Spoils were being collected amongst the slaves. There were great cheers in the darkness. Spartacus and Gannicus hoisted the bound praetor up on a stolen black horse the slaves had been using, tied him to the reins, and slapped the horse as it ran back to the town of Neopolis. All eight of the praetors white horses remained with Spartacus. Every commander was to take their favorite. While Téadora was making the rounds, trying to choose her new companion, Castus came over to her, and noticed she was limping. She didn't want to draw attention to herself for fear of worrying Spartacus, but she had twisted her ankle, and Castus wanted to see if it was anything more serious. For her curly haired friend, she would obey his guidance to sit and take a rest. She untied her shoes and revealed a swollen ankle, as well as fresh cuts to her feet. Castus scolded her mildly while

Oenomaus came up and placed Glaber's severed head beside the pair. Castus nearly vomited in his own lap while Téadora giggled at his expense. Oenomaus was the jolliest of souls while he squatted down to check on Téadora's injury.

"It's nothing, Oenomaus, really. Just a twisted ankle. I'll be plenty fine. I look worse than I feel."

"Well, I think you look great. Our little praetor friend on the other hand…you know he called us filthy slaves?"

"Us? Filthy? And he's the one with mud all over his face."

"Should I wash it off for him?"

"You're not going to carry that head around with you like some kind of trophy, are you, Oenomaus?"

"I don't know. I might. Ward off evil spirits."

"Ha! The smell alone in this heat would be well enough to ward off even the gods themselves."

"What shall you have me do with it then?"

"Why are you asking me? It's *your* kill."

"I only killed him because he was coming after *you*. That bounty would have put money in his pocket in exchange for your life. *You* get to decide what becomes of his remains. It's the least I can do."

"Put it in a bag for me. Come morning I will put him in the sea. I want to get my feet wet one more time before the army moves."

"I'll find a good bag for you, Téadora. You take care of our girl now, won't you, Castus? I want her as good as new!"

"Don't worry, Oenomaus. Castus always takes good care of me."

VIII

Spartacus had the army on the move by dawn. Téadora had gotten up before the sun even began to crest the horizon, and dumped Glaber's head in the sea. She watched it tumble about in the waves for a couple of minutes before washing her hands of the whole thing. Leaving Vesuvius was more like leaving home than the House of Batiatus. She had been there for several years, and here only several months. The quality of time she had spent here though was better than any one single day at the gladiator school. All the commanders in the army now rode the Roman praetor's team of white horses. Behind them the army crawled on in makeshift legions of their own. Everyone found a place somewhere. The few dead had been buried at the base of the volcano, and the Romans left out to rot for the locals to handle. The plan was to move south, keep with the nicer weather until they could figure out just how the Senate was going to retaliate against them for the previous night's one-sided slaughter. Their reaction would be very telling of how this war was going to go. Crixus wanted to make a march on Rome itself, to instigate further violence, but he was quickly and unanimously overruled in favor of not looking for a fight if they didn't have to. To compensate for his sour attitude, Crixus took a rear-guard position as the army marched south, trying hard to find like minded men interested in taking on the might of all mights in the Senate. A lot of the army wanted revenge, and rightly so, but they were not so eager as Crixus to die doing it. They wanted to enjoy their spoils for a little while, and take a tour terrorizing the countryside as they went. It took a lot of food to keep an army marching and in fighting condition. Raiding parties kept their daily schedules from the Vesuvius camp, and rotated duties to maintain the army as a whole.

It was an uneventful couple of weeks moving south before the Senate could send a response to Spartacus. Rather than a team of ill-equipped praetors, green and underinformed with a makeshift legion of volunteers, one praetor was sent, with a little trick up his sleeve. Publius Varinius was a young man, wise beyond his years and shrewd to the core. His cropped blonde hair made him easy to spot on the field, or on horseback. Constantly at his side was an eastern woman, a seer named Dacia. Her pale skin was illuminated by her long, dark hair, and crudely applied ashen tattoos all up and down her body. They were a mixture of dots, lines, swirls, and tribal symbols. She'd given most of them to herself in her youth. She was not yet that old now, but time in the harsh sun and woods had aged her. The woman did herself no favors, living a life as an outcast, bought and sold more times than she could count. Her talents were renown, but when a man heard something, he didn't like, he'd give her a good beating and send her on her war. She had the scars to prove it. A gash from an Egyptian across her abdomen, a chunk of her lip missing from a Gaul, a patch of hair that wouldn't grow on the back of her head from a firefight in Greece when she was a teenager. But she smiled at the life she had lived regardless. Now her talents were in the hands of a Roman praetor. He had been different than her past owners, treating her more like a wife than an employee. He made sure she was tended to, had food, water, adequate shelter. Where he travelled, she followed. He woke to her prognostications every morning, and fell asleep to them every night. An outsider might assume the two were some kind of lovers, but it was hard to tell. A seer could only ever be trusted so much, and a praetor not at all. Spartacus and Téadora were out on scouting maneuvers this morning when the Roman legion could be spotted parked in the valley the slave army had been intending to cross that night. Téadora sunk down against the rocks the two were using for shelter and sighed, hiding her face in her hands. Some small part of her had convinced herself they'd gotten past this, and that there would be no war. Spartacus tried to stifle his excitement at a possible engagement in the near future. He gripped the little silver ring that hung around his neck and thanked his mother silently for this change of pace. He felt the travels had grown stale and the army restless over the past couple of weeks. This was just the sort of news the men needed to keep their spirits up. When Téadora looked over to him at her side she could see him smiling, biting his lip as he peered over the rocks. Perhaps she was just taking this all too personally. She tried taking up the view that Spartacus was so focused on, and furrowed her brow. There was someone down in the Roman camp she recognized. Spartacus could feel the tension seething out of Téadora just by looking at her.

"It's alright, Téa."

"What about Dacia the Seer being with the Romans makes you think that anything could be alright, Spartacus?"

"Dacia isn't always clear about what she sees."

"She's clear enough to lead the Romans right to us. You know that's no accident. That woman has *always* been able to find people."

"You mean she's always been able to find *you*."

"I've been running from that woman for most of my adult life. When I was with the Cilician pirates, she kept popping up at *every* port we made, no matter where we were. My father paid her so well. My only peace from her was when Batiatus had me."

"You know, it wasn't *always* your father who paid her."

"It wasn't?"

"Like you said, she's always been able to find you."

"Are you saying *you* entertained the talents of Dacia the Seer?"

"A couple of years ago I fell off of my horse in a skirmish, and I was out healing from the army for a couple of months. I thought about you more in that few months than I had in years. If I was busy, I could put the thought of you out of my mind most days, and only be haunted by the sound of your laugh in my dreams. When I was hurt, I couldn't help but feel this crushing guilt for never having gotten back to you like I promised. I wanted to find you, see you again if at all possible. I paid a bounty hunter to find Dacia, and bring her to me. She said she could find you, because you and I were so close. I paid every coin I had to my name. She was with me when I was captured as a deserter. Dacia insisted the best way to find you was to get on a ship. I tried to spare her when the Romans took us. I said she was my wife, to earn her mercy. They separated us, and I didn't see her again. Then I was at the House of Batiatus, and all of this has happened. It was money well spent. I'm here with you now."

"You said Dacia was your wife?"

"I told you; it was only an attempt to gain her mercy."

"Who would be stupid enough to think Dacia the Seer would ever take a husband?"

"The Romans."

"That explains so much. I had no idea you missed me so badly."

"I've always missed you, Téa. I miss you even now when we are separated on raids. Why do you think I asked all the other commanders to pretend to be busy this morning so I could go scouting with you?"

"You're the leader of this army. You don't need to beg for permission to see me. You can just see me. Assign us to be together."

"I don't want our only time together to be *assigned*."

"Then what *do* you want, Spartacus?"

"I'd like for you to want to spend as much time with me as I do you."

"Rest assured I do. I just don't want to bother you when you are busy talking with your men. I'm well aware women aren't appreciated in armies unless we are in subservient or sexual roles. But me and my women hold our own. I hope in time, the army can see that."

"They will see it, if we choose to lead by example. Back home, men and women are equals."

"But it is not that way in many cultures. I don't want to cause any division in the ranks. And we are very far from home. Very far, and yet Dacia the Seer is right down there in the valley before me."

"I won't let her take you for the Romans."

"It's not the Romans she's working for, it's only one or two in particular, that blond man, and that other blond in the Senate."

"Senator Furius? You think he's behind this?"

"A man doesn't beg you to be his wife without exerting a little effort, and the man has no shortage of money at his disposal to send an entire legion out looking for me. They have to know I'm with you. Dacia would know that much."

"She knows much more than just our location."

"So, what do we do, Spartacus? Do we run back and tell the others that we're trapped on high ground because the Romans have come again? Or do we try some elaborate baiting situation?"

"I'd like to wait it out if at all possible. I don't know how dangerous this blond praetor is. He looks more serious than what they sent after us on Vesuvius. I expected that much. The Senate would not make the same mistake twice."

"I don't want to sit here and wait too long. Dacia tracked me all across the Mediterranean, from one coast to another. She's within eyesight now. I'm very uncomfortable with that."

"Dacia does not owe allegiance to Rome. She's from the east, like we are. She would not sell us out."

"Everyone has a price. As honorable and loyal as you may find Dacia to be, she does not share that sentiment for me."

"But think of it this way, she may have tracked you from coast to coast as you say, but did she ever *once* take you back to your father?"

"The pirates protected me."

"Well, I'm no pirate, but you have my entire army at your disposal. We will protect you now."

"That's the first time you've claimed ownership over the army."

"It is? It can't be."

"You've sidestepped the issue for months, but now you've finally said it, and rightfully so. It *is* your army. The men and women, we all follow you. You have every right to claim it as yours."

"It is not necessarily the claim I was trying to make."

"Then what were you trying to say, slick tongued Spartacus?"

"Is that your new nickname for me?"

"I can't very well call you slick footed anymore. You've become quite the runner. I doubt my ability to keep up with you."

"You can more than keep up with me, Téa. Don't you ever worry about that. Besides, the view from behind is quite pleasing to my eye. I've never been bothered by coming in second to you."

"You mean to make me blush in the middle of the day?"

"I mean to make you blush all day every day if I was so capable. You do not need to keep your distance from me. Join me in my meetings with the men. Be my partner in this war, as you are in every other aspect of my life."

"This is what you want?"

"This is what I have *always* wanted."

"What kind of soldier would I be to deny such a request?"

"I'm not asking you soldier to soldier. I'm asking you man to woman, best friend to best friend. Stay with me, Téa, please?"

"I will stand by you, Spartacus, until neither of us can stand anymore. Please don't tell me about my laugh haunting your dreams again. Let me smile for you while we are awake, and enjoy what time together we do have before Rome rips it away."

"Rome will not come between us. I won't allow it."

"Oh, *you* won't allow it. And who are you, Spartacus, to be so mighty as to stop all of Rome?"

"I don't want to stop it; I just want to keep you. I'll do anything to keep you looking at me like you are right now."

"And how am I looking at you?"

"Like a woman in love."

"It is the way I have always looked at you."

"I know. I know that now. Forgive me for the years I was a boy and did not recognize it. Forgive me for my years away. Forgive me for anything and everything. From this point forward, we're together."

Spartacus reached his hand out for Téadora to take. When she placed her hand in his he pulled her palm to rest it over his heart. She giggled because it was beating so fast. He had never been this serious about anything in his entire life, and she knew it. She knew him. When he said the army was at her disposal, he meant it. Looking down at the valley now, Téadora was not as worried. Dacia might not have been the monster she'd been made out to be. Perhaps, it was Dacia's constant tracking that kept Téadora from being turned back over to father, rather than the opposite. If Spartacus had tried to save her, she couldn't be that bad. Téadora crept over the ledge of the rocks, lying flat on her stomach to survey the valley one more time. Dacia was on the back of a white horse by a large, blood red, Roman tent, the tent she would be sharing with the praetor. Even though there was hardly any reason for Dacia to take in the rocks on the hills above her, her eyes seemed to beam in right on Téadora's position. Neither woman faltered in their stance. Dacia knew she was being watched and smiled. Téadora couldn't see the seer's facial expressions, but she didn't need to. Somehow, she could feel that an accord had been struck between them, as it had in the past. Dacia would be near, but would not take her freedom from her. If anything, she the protector of it. Téadora slid down from the rocky perch and gripped Spartacus' hand. His body was in jitters beneath the skin, smiling like an absolute fool. She leaned against his chest to steady herself as she bounced up on her tiptoes to place a kiss on his cheek. Everything was going to be the way that it should. She didn't know how or why, but she trusted that it was so. Spartacus was ecstatic, and happily helped Téadora up onto the back of her white horse even though he didn't need to. She let him help her, which was a sign of things to come in and of itself. Téadora was not fond of asking or accepting help. For Spartacus she would make an exception. She would make all of the exceptions, and follow his lead as their horses ran back for the slave army's camp nestled in the hills. There would be no trip into the valley tonight, so they needed to get comfortable. As comfortable as runaways could be with a Roman legion in striking distance. But the masses didn't need to know that. Not yet. Spartacus told his commanders. Crixus volunteered for sentry duty but was denied in favor of Oenomaus' calmer mind. Gannicus warned caution, and Spartacus agreed.

Dacia advised Varinius against staying in the valley that night. Instead, she urged the legion to take up residence in the outskirts of Herculaneum, a nearby resort town. It would be good for morale boosting, and seeing as how the soldiers didn't want to be out catching slaves anyways, it was a wise move. All the men could talk about was what the mistakes must have been on Vesuvius to leave only one praetor alive, running back to Rome with nothing but absolute disgrace to his name. Varinius didn't think much of his fellow praetors. He talked politics with Dacia often but she tuned him out in favor of studying her surroundings. She was fond of people watching, and eavesdropping on conversations. It gave her mental clarity to make something out of nothing. Varinius walked around with her on his arm like they were something of an item, but in private, the seer sought her solitude. She was something of an eyesore to the legion. No one understood why Varinius kept her so close aside from the sexual pleasures she must have provided. It was common practice to have foreign whores in an army for companionship, and often bastard children running through camp only to be left behind when the call came to return to Rome. Families were decimated from one end of the Mediterranean to the other. But Dacia was not one of these women. She hated men, but tolerated them enough, played on their egos and manipulated them from the shadows. Dacia kept Varinius on his toes, and he viewed it as a keen maneuver. He thought he was so smart, so highly educated in the world. He'd never make the mistake of his colleagues. The Senate would soon recognize his prowess, and give him his own seat at the table. His family name would be honored, he'd have his choice of life. This slave catching business was just his step to the future he'd always dreamed for himself. He'd marry a rich woman, have sturdy sons, gorgeous daughters, and Dacia would be right there at his side. He'd take her along of course. She never outright refused the man his requests, but she slipped around them multiple times a day. She'd speak in tongues, shift her glances. Varinius was fascinated by her, but could not ever jeopardize his superior role. While the praetor was carelessly enjoying himself in the luxuries of the baths at Herculaneum, Dacia was busy in dark alleys, leading Varinius' nosy aide astray. Cossinius was nothing but a munifex, a foot soldier, but he asked too many questions for his own good.

Cossinius came from a wealthy mother who had tarnished her good name by marrying a lowly soldier. While the young man's father was away in the east with Rome's war in Iberia, the cocky Cossinius was eager to make a name for himself. Never struggling with the girls in his home town, it didn't take much effort for Dacia to lead the munifex to the most irreputable street in the entire resort town of Herculaneum. It was known to be a place where men cheated on their wives, and vice versa. There was no shortage of secrecy needing to be held here. All Dacia had to do was show Cossinius the way, and then let his own degenerate behaviors do the rest. The seer already knew how this was going to play out. Varinius would be so upset at the loss of his aide that he would no longer trust the position to be carried out by a young man. Dacia would fill the role herself, and thus, carry so much more stirring capability in how the army moved. A simple bat of her eyes could pick the camp up or set the camp down. It all depended on how lonely Varinius might be feeling on any given day. Usually, she didn't have to work too hard. It was always pleasing to her to get her way. The blind spots in manipulating too many people at once always cleared up when the main person involved was an easy read, and Cossinius was not a complicated young man. He'd been talking about sleeping with as many women as possible since Dacia had brought up the idea of Herculaneum. Now, he was going to have his chance. But Dacia knew something the young man did not. He would have his fun, and he would pay the woman for her time. Then by fate, or the will of the gods, or a well-placed seer in a shop down the road, a husband would be alerted that his wife was in danger. A robbery! As an honorable, albeit misinformed husband, the man would run back home, to where his wife ran a taberna. What the husband thought was a taberna for weary travelers was actually a lupanaria, for those weary in spirit and self-esteem but profitable nonetheless. Now while young Cossinius would be in a panic, rushing to tie himself back into his clothes and sandals, the man would be running upstairs, and the munifex would be caught red handed, as well as red faced. The wife would cry assault to protect her dignity, and the arrogant Cossinius would be killed, with a knife plunged into his heart and his body thrown from a second story window, left to be found by no one who cared. Dacia nearly giggled while she listened to all of this play out from her hiding place. She had seen it in her head that morning, and it worked so perfectly she could hardly contain her excitement for the entire day. Sure enough, after the husband and wife had settled their argument and parted ways, Dacia went to see Cossinius' body with her own two eyes. The fall alone could have killed him, but he was dead before the drop. Blood pooled into the stones beneath him. Passersby were beginning to point. Dacia put on the act of a disturbed woman and shrieked to draw attention. Other soldiers in town came to her aid, and carried the munifex's body back to camp on the outskirts of Herculaneum. Cossinius was wrapped in cloth before Varinius finally strolled back to his tent, exhausted from the day at the baths. The praetor cared little for the dead man, and quite pleased at the prospect of having an aid vacancy as far as the Senate was concerned. Dacia aided him more anyway than any young boy ever could. While Cossinius was burned by some of his acquaintances, Varinius nodded for Dacia to follow him back to their tent. The seer had rearranged their sleeping arrangements so they were as far as the blood red tent would allow. He did not seem pleased, and she did not care as she sat on the ground and tended to unknotting her long hair.

"Have I done something to upset you, Dacia?"

"No."

"Have I overlooked something you said to me?"

"Not that I know of."

"Have you seen something troubling?"

"The future seems quite obliging to your aims, Varinius."

"Then why leave me all day?"

"Do we not spend most days and nights together?"

"Yes. But I wanted to have you on my arm today."

"I'd have only gotten in the way. Besides, judging by the grin on your lips when you returned from the baths, I'd say your day was quite filled with pleasure."

"You saw that?"

"I see everything, Varinius."

"Everything? So, you saw what I did today without you?"

"If I had chosen to see it, I would have."

"But you chose not to?"

"Something else occupied my mind today."

"And what was that?"

"Your military prowess."

"Might I ask about these victories I am to endure?"

"When the time comes, I will tell you all you need to know."

"You keep things from me, Dacia?"

"It is better that way."

"Better for who?"

"You do not need to know the burdens I bear, Varinius."

"So, you keep secrets to protect me? Is it safe for me to assume that is because you…you care for me?"

"You keep me alive, Varinius. Why would I want to do anything to get in the way of that?"

IX

Rome was having no luck with the slave army. Weeks turned into months without any altercations. Despite Dacia's excellent tracking ability to keep Téadora within a day's reach, Varinius could never could the jump on his enemy. The slaves kept moving, and growing their numbers at exponential rates. Every countryside they raided; they came back with more soldiers. Every port town they harassed; they came back with more soldiers. Slaves from farms were liberated. Sons from abusive families were saved. Women in trapped households were rescued. As autumn stretched on and lands were harvested, the army was also able to add shepherds to their ranks. The men were durable, angry, and hearty fighters. They were a bit of a rough bunch who tended to follow Crixus' more violent way of thinking. Either way, the army had swelled to some seventy thousand strong by the time it came to decide what to do for winter quarters. Spartacus had all the commanders grouped up in his tent to try and make a unanimous decision that would please everyone. Rome was holding back for better weather, but they had far from given up the fight. Varinius lurked a day away at all times. Crixus wanted bloody revenge. Oenomaus admitted his Germanians were out for vengeance as well. Gannicus and Castus had calmer men more anxious to find a way home up in the north and reunite with families. The vote came down to Téadora and Spartacus. Speaking for the women, Téadora explained there was a lot of unsettled business to tend to. Spartacus wasn't happy to hear that. His Thracians as well were a little fed up. Seemed the tipping point was more in favor of staying until the weather improved and engaging in a war. The commanders split up to share the news in their various camps dotted all over the south in neighboring towns. The Gauls were in Nola with Crixus. The Celts were in Nuceria with Gannicus and Castus. Oenomaus took the Germanians to Thurii. Spartacus and Téadora planned to winter over in Metapontum. The gladiatrices and female soldiers were to ride ahead by one day to scout. Spartacus was a little put out by the temporary separation. Crixus clamped a heavy hand down on his leader's shoulder to try and get his head straight before the camp dismantled for a little while.

"I don't want to hear it, Crixus."

"You don't even know what I was going to say, Spartacus."

"You want to gloat about the decision. I don't want to hear about how many more men sided with you than me."

"The will of the army is what should be most important to the leader. It doesn't matter whose idea it was so long as the masses follow. I want no glory from this."

"Liar."

"Alright, maybe I want a little. But can you blame me? Téadora's made you soft, Spartacus. In all our time together, you were never so eager so go home and settle down as you are now."

"I have a woman counting on me to survive, and give her a life. If you had the same you would not be so willing to fight Rome."

"I am not fighting *all* of Rome. Just one little praetor is enough for me. One legion. I have overcome steeper odds before."

"There are so many lives depending on us to do this right. Our soldiers have heard the stories from their fathers and grandfathers of the past slave wars. We have to give them a better ending than what history has taught us. We can't make the same mistakes."

"And you feel that staying in the south is a *mistake*?"

"I want to go home. I want all the men to be able to go home, wherever that may be. For most of us, that means going north."

"Home is a long way off. It is hard on an army to maintain morale when all they do is march and raid."

"But with the promise of home, it can make the tiresome days worth it. I think."

"Spartacus, you will take Téadora home one day. I know this to be true. But until then, your head needs to be with the army, and what the army wants. They want to fight. They want justice."

"We can give that to them as we travel north just as much as we can being in the south. Only, there is the promise of a life worth living if we go north."

"I don't know if you've looked at a map lately, but the Alps are in the north."

"I know they are."

"Those aren't rolling hills, Spartacus. Those are huge mountains."

"I know. But they've been crossed before by armies, and they can be crossed again. Hannibal did it over a hundred and fifty years ago. Why can't we?"

"The man had elephants! We have shepherds, convicts, slaves, farmers, gladiators, rebels, boys, and women. We are *not* Hannibal. We need to forge our own path."

"I don't like the path we're forging."

"Then don't like it, but don't sabotage us either."

"I would never."

"You're doing it right now. The army looks to their leader, Spartacus, for everything. If you don't believe in us and what we're doing, then how do you expect any kind of unity?"

"I just want to know when I lay my head down at night that I am still a good man. I want to make my friends and loved ones proud. I can't do that if I'm cutting throats every day. I *can* do that, but I wouldn't be happy with myself. If I did nothing but terrorize for the sake of blood lust, that'd make me no better than the damn Romans we're fighting. I was forced to be in their army for years, but I will *NOT* be a Roman. I am better than that. I was raised better than that. I know better."

"You *are* better. But sometimes to get your point across you have to sink down to your enemy's level and play dirty."

"I don't believe that. Two wrongs don't make a right."

"They do if you try hard enough. Come now, Spartacus. Cheer up. Take the winter off. Spend it with your woman. Let her talk some sense into you. *She* wants to fight."

"She speaks for the women. The *women* want to fight. Not *her*. I saw her face. She wants to go home with me. We've been away for far too long."

"You need the winter off, Spartacus. Go to Metapontum. Regroup. When the weather warms, I know you'll come around to see my side of things. You just need time."

"And what if I don't come around? What if you and I can never see eye to eye on this war?"

Crixus just sighed and rolled his eyes. The men were just talking in circles. He excused himself and let Spartacus sulk in one questioning scenario after another on top his white horse. The men were all packed up and ready to go. The Thracians were the last to leave for their winter quarters. Spartacus wanted to make sure all of the other commanders knew their schedules for checking in with one another, and the need to send runners to him on a regular basis. The goal for the next few months was to lie low, build support, and make sure Rome got no further in tracking their whereabouts than they already knew. Spartacus was aware there was only so much preparation that could be done to try and protect his army. With Dacia the Seer leading Varinius and his legion about the countryside it was only a matter of time before a strike was made. And it'd be a heavy one too. No retaliation had yet come for the slaughter on Vesuvius' hillsides. It had been months, and the time spent waiting was killing Spartacus' nerves. He'd never been known as a terribly patient man, and lying low wasn't necessarily a specialty of his. The Thracians were a loud, wild bunch that needed to be satiated on the daily or else they grew restless. There was the small opportunity in Metapontum to start talking about the possibility of buying ships to go home, take a sea route to the east rather than the much longer land routes on foot or horseback. But Téadora had that hangup about the pirates which ruled the local shores. Spartacus didn't want to do anything that might upset her, but perhaps if he was careful, she would see that what he was doing was right in the long run. The leader battled back and forth in his head all day and night about what to do. The march to the winter quarters wasn't eventful enough to distract him from his racing thoughts. By the time he reached Metapontum, he was eager for relief in the form of Téadora's sweet smile, but she wasn't there. She was in town, but not in a secure location. The women in her ranks, specifically the gladiatrices, had found themselves in trouble. Téadora was right in the middle of it. She'd lost her horse somewhere along the way. While Spartacus ran for her, he found it in the hands of some local man. He'd taken it from her by force. He had the bloody face and missing teeth to prove it. His friend was also bleeding. Spartacus threw a bag of stolen coin at them in exchange for the horse, and continued on to try and help the women. Most of them were bloody. Téadora's sica blades had been taken from her. She was yelling in Latin, but when she cursed it was in Thracian. He had to chuckle at the foul language pouring out of her. The women had no respect in this town. They were just trying to secure lodging and the taberna wouldn't take them in. They'd all been called prostitutes and whores. They were not welcome. Spartacus reached back into his bags, and pulled out more sacks of stolen coin to distribute to the taberna owner, in possession of Téadora's sica blades. She gripped Spartacus by his forearm to try and stop him from interfering.

"I have this under control, Spartacus."

"Yes. It sure does look like it. He has your blades and all your women are bleeding."

"We can handle this."

"Why won't you just let me pay the man?"

"It's about principle."

"It's about shelter and peace."

"I don't want to secure my safety with stolen coin. I'll never be able to trust the man. He'll just keep asking for more."

"I would steal coin every day if it meant keeping you safe."

"I don't want that kind of debt on my shoulders."

"Then don't take it on. This is *my* stolen coin. Let me do this for you. Let me help you."

"I don't want to have to need your help."

"I *want* to do this."

"But *I* don't want you to do this."

"I bought your horse back with stolen coin. Should I return it too?"

"I was going to get my horse back. You came early. You said you were going to give me a day's head start."

"I did. Téa it's been almost *two* days."

"Oh. Well, I've been busy. I must have lost track of time."

"You never lose track of time. You've been struggling and are too proud to admit it, even to me. Why?"

"The last time I depended on a man to protect me…he *sold* me."

"But I'm not that man. I'm Spartacus. *Your* Spartacus."

"*My* Spartacus?"

"Yes."

"Then put your coin away and let me handle this the way I do."

"Horse and all?"

"Horse and all."

"Fine. When you're ready, I'll be camping with the Thracians just outside town. I've found a little valley we can tuck ourselves into."

"A valley? I can't see the water from a valley."

"It's a river valley that flows out into the sea. You can see all the water you like and then some. I'll set our tent up right on the water's edge if you want?"

"*Our* tent?"

"I'll take your smile as a yes. Try not to kill everyone."

Spartacus left a lingering kiss on Téadora's forehead before putting the coin away and stepping back. The owner in charge of the taberna had been so close to thinking the money was already his that he was in some sort of shock. Spartacus had not come to save the day. He'd been asked to leave, and so he was. The man of the taberna attempted to run back into his establishment, but the gladiatrices attacked him on all sides and tackled him into the stoney ground while his wife and daughters watched from the inside windows. The man was beaten to a bloody pulp, and when he was dying, choking on his last breath, Téadora walked up and took her sica blades back from him. Toying with his dignity, she traced the blade around his neck while he asked for mercy. She would not give it to him, and let him bleed out in pain. Once it was clear the man was dead the wife came to the door and said the gladiatrices were welcome anytime they wanted, so long as she and her daughters could be spared. There was no need for further negotiations. The gladiatrices cleaned up and ate. Passersby and nosy busybodies got back to their daily chores, and it was business as usual. As for Téadora and her horse situation, she had a score to settle. With her blades back in hand she tracked her horse down to the street where the men had taken it, again. They were still snickering to themselves about the turn of events, buying it, beating her, getting coin from Spartacus, losing the horse, then securing it again. It'd been quite an afternoon, but it wasn't over yet. Téadora went to confront the men alone, and she was not proud about it, but her arena skills were put to full use. With two blades she was unstoppable, and did not show the restraint she had earlier in the day in the hopes of promoting peace and a quiet entrance to town. She stabbed her curved blade into the belly of the first man, and upon pressing his lifeless body up against a white wall, and watching the blood pool at his feet, the second man ran away and got lost in the huddle of houses. Téadora's white horse was hers again, and her dignity in herself restored. She climbed up and rode for this valley Spartacus spoke of. She ran for the coast and then followed the river back into the green and gold hills. The Thracians were taking their sweet time setting up camp, but were ecstatic to see her riding towards them, blood splattered and victorious. They cheered for her as Spartacus came out of their tent, looking a bit disappointed. He nodded his head to the river and brought a cloth out for her to wash herself up. Her smile faded as she tied up her horse next to his. He'd made a makeshift post for them until a proper stable could be set up in the coming days. Téadora wanted to enjoy her success with Spartacus but he was quiet as he bucketed the river water up for her and wrang out her bloody cloth. This was new for him, to be the one cleaning and not the one being cleaned up. Téadora tried to take the cloth from his hands, but his grip was too strong for her to overcome.

"Let me help you, Téa."

"Why are you so adamant about this, Spartacus?"

"Why do you fight my kindness so much?"

"I am not fighting you."

"You are not making it easy on me."

"I'm sorry. It's instinct."

"You don't need instincts with me. You're safe."

"I just…I guess I don't trust kindness, that's all. People only do you favors to hold a debt over your head."

"I am holding nothing over your head, Téa. I'm just trying to help you and support you. But you won't let me."

"When men do nice things for a woman, it's because they want something from them. There's always a price. I don't want it to be like that between you and me."

"Then it won't be."

"That's it? It just won't be like every other man in my past?"

"Just how many men is every other man?"

"You want a body count?"

"No. Come to think of it, I don't. I just don't want to pay for what other men have done to you. Judge me for me, Téa."

"I don't judge you, Spartacus. You are above my criticism."

"I'm not above you in any regard. We are equals, you and I. It is the way we have always been. It is the way we will always be. Side by side if at all possible. Now hold still and let me get the blood out of your hair. I don't want to be smelling that all night."

"I'll unbraid it. Your fingers are clumsy."

"Being close to you makes me tremble sometimes."

"You surprised me when you said you'd be pitching up *our* tent."

"I thought I would. If you knew how nervous I was to tell you that, and how many hours I had thought of a way to say that in my head, you'd laugh at me."

"It couldn't have been that bad. What were you so afraid of?"

"You telling me no."

"Why would I do that?"

"You rejected my help in town."

"That was different."

"Why? All I want to do is be there for you but you are more comfortable pushing me away. Who hurt you so bad that you can't separate that pain from the man standing right in front of you? What is it? You told me you'd tell me one day, and I haven't pushed you for an answer, but I feel the more we spend time together, I'd like to know what you keep to yourself. *I* tell *you* everything."

"And I appreciate your candor, but I am not there yet. I don't want you to look at me with a shred of pity in your eyes, Spartacus."

"Why would that be a bad thing? I want to know everything there is to know about you. I need to make up for lost time."

"It's not your responsibility to fix what has gone wrong in my life. I don't need you to make me right. I just need you to accept me as I am, and trust that I will tell you what I can, when I can. Can you do that for me?"

"I can, but it is difficult to see you struggle when I know I can take some of that pain for you."

"I didn't want you to see me like that today."

"But if I hadn't come when I did, you would have never told me you had any trouble at all. You'd have lied to me."

"It would not have been a malicious lie. I just want to protect you like you want to protect me."

"Don't protect me from you. I want you, Téa. I want *all* of you."

"I worry I would overwhelm you. You have enough to think about with this army and the Romans chasing us. I will not add to that chaos in your mind."

"Add to it. Consume me."

"Are you sure?"

"Yes."

"There will be no going back if we do this."

"Good. I don't want to go back to a time when I couldn't have you in my arms. Come here."

Spartacus had not even finished washing all of the blood off Téadora when he pulled her up into his lap. She gasped and he had his lips clasped tight against hers before she could even take a breath. Kissing her was like coming home. Spartacus couldn't get enough, he couldn't hold her close enough, trace enough of her curves. He needed to have her memorized. She had her bloody, wet hands racing across his skin. They knocked the bucket into the river. Another Thracian had to pick it up as it drifted to avoid it washing out to sea. The camp cheered, whistled, and hollered in approval as the leaders went at it. Spartacus picked Téadora up in his arms, lips never parting, and dropped her inside their tent which was still being made. The center post was up, it was good enough. The grass was cool underneath her back as Spartacus hovered above. Téadora pulled him down on top of her by gripping his silver ring necklace she'd admired from afar for so many years. They clanked teeth as hands and hearts raced. As fleeting a moment as this was, it promised to be just the first of many. They laid together breathless and laughing in their half-pitched tent. All their worldly possession stuffed into a handful of bags. They didn't need much to be happy when they had each other. Téadora nestled into Spartacus, side, and was fascinated with running his fingers through her long black hair. She traced his collar bone with her fingertip and kept reaching up to plant kisses on his jawline.

"You can't stop smiling, Spartacus."

"You are amazing, Téa, better than my wildest dreams."

"You've dreamt of this moment between us?"

"I've begged the gods for it for years."

"You've begged? A mighty warrior does not beg."

"I begged hard, pleaded on my hands and knees."

"No man of mine need beg for such things when I will honor him willingly and happily. Lay back, and let me take the lead this time."

X

    Winter was over too soon, and with Spring fast approaching the Romans were dying to get their hands dirty. No more waiting. No more holding off. Dacia had run out of excuses to keep her praetor at bay. Varinius struck at Lucania. Spartacus and his army had been preparing all day. Scouting missions had led on that the enemy was on the move, but as daylight fell, it was clear this move was going to be underhanded to try and give them an advantage. The Romans didn't have the right numbers on their side. The slave army had only grown in the colder months. There were estimates Spartacus had a hundred thousand in his command. One legion didn't stand a chance, but their arrogance told them otherwise. Dacia ran from the camp in a fury of frustration. Varinius would not listen to a word she said about retreating. He would not heed her warnings. She was not a free woman, she did not run far, but just far enough to be able to see it all fall down. It was well coordinated from the slave's perspective. The Gauls from the north, Thracians from the south, Celts from the east, and Germanians from the west. They converged in perfect unison, screaming like wild animals in the middle of the night. The women were sprinkled into every little break in the men's lines. They were everywhere, and nowhere. The

Romans could not get their hands on them, though they tried fiercely. Like Téadora, the women had their eyes painted black with charcoal so their eye glowed like monsters in the flashes of campfires let loose. Romans scrambled. It was like Vesuvius all over again, almost a slaughter too unfair to take any enjoyment from. The horses were stolen, spoils for the slaves. Varinius had taken up shelter in a collapsed blood red tent. A passing soldier might have thought nothing of it, but Oenomaus' men had been tracking the praetor for their commander, and pointed the tattooed man right to where the blond man was cowering in his own waste. He'd soiled himself out of fear, not a drop of blood on him. Oenomaus bared his teeth like a wolf and gripped his fists tight for the beating of a lifetime, but the battle had moved on. It was on the other side of the valley, moving quick into the hills. From her high vantage point Dacia could see the flickering shadows of Oenomaus poised to deliver the death blows to the man who owned her, and she just couldn't watch anymore. Oenomaus himself was hesitating as he stood above the crying blond man.

"I should kill you."

"You're…you're not?"

"You've been chasing us for months. I *should* kill you. It wouldn't even be hard. I could do it with my bare hands."

"But…you're…you're *sparing* me?"

"The battle has moved on. I may only be a slave to *you* little praetor, but I will still fight with honor when I can. There's no glory in killing a man like you alone in the dark. *You* deserve the audience of your army when you fall."

"Aren't you the man who massacred the praetors at Vesuvius?"

"Yes. But when I killed them, they had no woman crying over their bodies. Go to your seer. Enjoy her while you can. I will come for you another day. Téadora sends her regards, Dacia."

Oenomaus stepped back and bowed his head as the seer came into the light of the flames. Varinius scampered up from the fetal position he'd been holding on the ground, and up into her arms. She was ashamed to be found crying. It wasn't intentional. As quickly as it fell upon her, it vanished, and she was able to sniffle herself into composure. So, Téadora was aware she was being followed, and had chosen to tell the men around her not to go after the seer. Dacia gulped hard, and wondered what strategy Téadora might be playing at. The women weren't friends or allies, but they were women deeply entrenched in a man's war. There could be an accord perhaps, an understanding. Dacia gripped at Varinius' clothes and tried to get him to stand up on his own two feet to run away, but he was shaking so bad he could hardly stand. They disappeared haggardly into the night with the rest of the survivors, straggling about the countryside with little left to their name but an abundance of shame while they watched the enemy dance upon the remains of their friends and fellow soldiers. All their weapons and armor were stolen, their food and supplies commandeered. Crixus took the rods and axes, the symbol of the legion's power and prestige, held them up in the air as he pranced in laps on the back of his stolen white horse, and screamed in his local Gaulish dialect at the top of his lungs. It made the Romans shudder as they hid in the night. Crixus then broke the symbols of the legion over his bended knee and discarded them into a campfire like they meant little more to him than a piece of trash. The flag bearer for the legion, a young man of barely sixteen who had been hiding since the battle first broke, now revealed his location to Crixus, calling the commander out personally. Crixus smiled wickedly at the prospect of a challenge, but Spartacus held his arm out for Crixus to refuse.

"Crixus, *please*!"

"Let a man have his fun, Spartacus."

"He's a *boy*! He does not know what he's doing by taunting you. Rise above this. You've had your fill of blood for one night."

"No. You've had yours. I'm still thirsty!"

Spartacus was going to try and chase Crixus down on horseback as he pursued the lone flag bearer, but Gannicus intervened on his own stolen white horse, and shook his head no. Spartacus screamed after his commander, cursing in Thracian. Téadora's ears perked up at her leader's discontent and ran for his side as quickly as she could. There was a lot of ground in-between the two though, and reaching Spartacus was easier said than done. The camp had been laid to waste, and now what was left of it had to be searched thoroughly for anyone hiding or anything useful. The women were trying their best to carve paths through the carnage with the Celts, but it was slow going. The Romans didn't really travel light under Varinius. They'd become quite sedentary in their approach. Then again, these weren't real soldiers, but merely stand-ins. As Dacia lugged Varinius into safety on her high hideaway, she watched as Téadora methodically moved through the camp. She had a very particular, streamlined approach to surveying the damage. Dacia didn't think the slave army was in the practice of taking prisoners, but the seer was aware that Téadora would have a tough decision to make in the upcoming minutes. Cowering nearby in a collapsed blood red tent were two men who had no business being here. Varinius was still shaking by Dacia's side, trying to understand how he'd survived and been given mercy by the brute of a man that was Oenomaus. The praetor was very caught up on the smell of his enemy, the peculiar wreak, while Dacia began tuning him out behind her. She laid flat on her stomach and peered for a better view as Téadora uncovered the hiding pair of Senator Felix Furius and Lanista Lentulus Batiatus. It hadn't been paranoia after all. The men had come for her, and Dacia had led them right to her. When Téadora reached around behind her for her sica blades, the Senator stood up and dusted himself off, running a sweaty hand through his pretty blonde hair. The lanista on the other hand was inflated with an overwhelming and entirely inappropriate surge of confidence. His former prize fighter, his gladiatrix, his money maker, was now no longer in his control. And worse than that, she was thriving. He popped up to his feet, and despite the Senator's quiet urgings to be respectful, for the sake of their own lives, the lanista just puffed his chest out and tried to save face any desperate way he possibly could. Téadora rested her blades behind her. Neither man was a threat.

"Of all the sorry souls that have ever made me money, *you*, Téadora, by far, are the one I hate the most. I mean that."

"I know. But considering the profit you made off of my blood for five years, I figure, I earned my escape."

Batiatus reached up and slapped her in the face. Senator Furius gasped, and reflexively tried to shield himself for the attack to follow, but instead he found himself dropped to his knees for no apparent reason. Téadora smirked, but made no reach for her sica blades. She held up her hands for the women around her to leave the lanista untouched as he made his way into the darkness, thinking he'd won this small victory. Téadora clicked her tongue, and half laughed to herself with white knuckled fists. With any luck, that interaction would be the last one she'd have with her former owner. As Senator Furius stood back up, he reached out to Téadora's face but she stepped back and pulled one blade on the blonde man. She held the tip to the soft part underneath his chin, and he was floored by how pretty she looked in the firelight. Her restraint was as amazing as it was admirable. He knew he had made the right decision to track her all this way, and be persistent in his search of her. Téadora did not hold her blade out long, but tucked it back behind her and waved her hand in the direction Batiatus had taken to better allow her soldiers to revel in their spoils of the night. Senator Furius was steadfast in his position though, and the young woman rolled her eyes.

"I've come all this way. You must know, my offer to be your husband still stands, Téadora."

"You can't be serious. Senator, I must refuse you again. I am sorry if I gave you any indication prior to this that there was hope for happiness between the two of us. I cut you, and ran from you. Let me be as clear as possible, I do not want you, or anything you claim to be able to give me. Now please, make your escape before I come to my senses."

"So, that's it then? All this trouble, and you wish to be rid of me?"

"Yes! Now go before one of my fellow commanders comes in here and strikes you down where you stand. *I* may be capable of mercy, but many of them are not. Senator, *please*…go."

"I don't know where to go."

"Anywhere but here would be a fine start."

"Thoughts of you have been giving my life direction for months. If I am not following you, I simply have nowhere to go."

"Rome is north. Follow the river."

"I'd rather follow you."

"I am not yours to follow."

"To protect then?"

"You can't protect me anymore than you can protect yourself. Money and pretty words do no good in battle and you carry no weapon. You are a dead man walking if I have ever seen one. Now please go, I don't want to have to ask you again."

"I will make Batiatus pay for laying his hand on you."

"I'm sure the gods are already in striking distance of that man. Do not worry about that little slap. I've endured far worse from him."

"Still. Let me do this for you."

"I don't need or want you to do anything for me."

"All the same. I owe you for your mercy."

"Remove yourself, Senator, before you become another body for Spartacus' army to burn."

Senator Furius would not budge, so Téadora mounted her horse and left. It wasn't necessarily bravery or courage that kept the man there in the wreckage of the Roman tent, but fear and apprehension. Women with blood splattered faces and charcoal streaks across their eyes mowed through the Roman camp like it was nothing. They left him standing in place, and worked around him out of respect for their commander. When the Senator finally did move, the flames around him had dwindled to embers, and his eyes had adjusted to travel by starlight. It was fairly easy for him to find the survivors, as they whimpered and whispered in the darkness of the foliage. Senator Furius knew none of the men by name. All of them were looking for their officers. Anyone of rank had been killed aside from Varinius, but as far as the legion knew he'd been lost in battle. Only Dacia knew he was alive because she had dragged him away to safety. His composure was slowly but surely coming back as the slave army disappeared into the outskirts of Lucania. Dacia was waiting patiently for the praetor to fall asleep so she could trek down into the valley and see what was left of the legion. However, when she finally did go to make her move, she was surprised to be seized from behind by Varinius, who looked heartbroken at her decision. She had a sharpened chunk of rock in her hand, and he couldn't quite figure out why.

"You're going to kill someone with that, aren't you, Dacia?"

"It's none of your concern, Varinius. Go back to sleep. Please. I'll be back as soon as I can."

"I'm coming with you."

"No."

"You don't get to tell me what to do. You saved me from that slave back there. You got me out. You care for me, whether you want to say it out loud or not. Now, who is this rock for?"

"If I tell you, I need you to promise me that you will not try and stop me, or else, we stay here."

"Tell me."

"Lentulus Batiatus."

"The lanista who visited us? What would his death bring you?"

"This isn't about me."

"Then who is this about?"

"Does it matter? I want this man dead. I will kill him tonight. I don't need your permission. You might own me, but you do not get to make this decision."

"Give me the rock."

"No!"

"I am stronger than you. I will kill this lanista."

"You will?"

"I need to leave this battle behind me with blood on my hands. I can't be another embarrassed praetor running back to Rome without a damned thing to show for it. Give me the rock."

"Don't you have a sword?"

"It was…lost."

"It was *taken*, wasn't it?"

"Give me the rock. Let me feel like a man *once* tonight."

"You don't need to kill to feel like a man."

"I saw the way you watched that battle. You were not proud of me. I don't *ever* want to disappoint you like that again."

Dacia placed the rock in Varinius' hands. They were not shaking anymore. She was intentionally avoiding eye contact, but when the praetor went to say his goodbyes, he demanded her to look at him. Her eyes were glassy. He thought that might have been an invitation to kiss her, and cupped her face but she recoiled from his touch like he was poisonous, and it made him feel like a fool. Angrily, he took the sharp rock and stomped off for the remnants of his camp. He was positive the lanista would not have gone far, and he was right. Batiatus was mumbling and grumbling about, kicking up tent fragments in the hopes of finding something useful. No food had been left behind. No horses to run off on. The wagons had been stolen, ridden off by the slave army with jeers and cheers. Batiatus never saw the rock coming. Varinius threw it from some distance away, aiming for the man's head. It was a direct hit from behind. The lanista fell down face forward into a pile of embers and ash. Judging by the lack of removing himself from the smokey ground, Varinius assumed he'd killed the man. The sweet and sickening smell of burning flesh confirmed that assumption without needing to go over for visual confirmation. Varinius was sure he didn't have the stomach for that on a good day, not alone tonight. The deed was done. Maybe that would please his seer, make her able to look him in the eye again. Regardless of her approval, Varinius sat down in the ruins of what remained and tried to figure out how to move forward. After Vesuvius, the lone praetor left alive after the slave attack had run back to Rome in shame. The Senate laughed in his face, and he was removed from office. Varinius heard the man had killed himself in the weeks that followed. He did not want the same fate for himself. With a severely diminished fighting force, he did need help, but he'd have to go about getting it a different way than pleading with the Senate. While Varinius hit one mental obstacle after another, he was truly astonished when Dacia came to sit beside him in the carnage. There were dead bodies, and burning tents, and she didn't seem to care. She held herself close and leaned on the praetor's shoulder. An hour ago, he'd be bold enough to wrap an arm around the woman, but now, he kept to himself and avoided eye contact to try and keep what little pride he still had to his name. In front of them, Batiatus was slowly smoking. Dacia had seen this vision hours earlier and was content to get this closure.

"Tell me what's on your mind, Varinius."

"I wouldn't want to trouble you."

"You don't trouble me."

"But I don't *please* you either."

"It has been a difficult night. Excuse me if I chose to handle myself differently than you would have liked."

"I acknowledge our differences, Dacia. It's the act of pulling from me like I disgusted you that hurts."

"You took me by surprise, that was all."

"I have tried before to get close to you and you have pulled away during all of those attempts as well."

"You do not want to be close to me, Varinius."

"Don't I?"

"No, you don't. I am useful to you during this slave hunt, war, whatever it is you want to call it. Once I serve my purpose, you will not need me and I will be cast aside. You will live your life, marry, have children, get promotions, and I will not be part of any of that."

"I would keep you as long as you would let me."

"I have no desire to be owned until I die."

"Then don't think of me as owning you."

"I am not free, Varinius. I can't choose what I want to do, where I want to be. I am not living. I am merely staying alive to serve. It has been my burden my whole life. My talents curse me, and I am miserable every single day."

"I didn't know that."

"I have not told anyone that before. To be honest, no one has ever cared to listen."

"I am not like the other people who have bought your services, Dacia. I promise you I am not."

"But you are ambitious, and I will only get in your way."

"No! Not at all! How could you think that? I killed a man for you tonight without any reason at all. Is that not proof enough for what I feel for you? This is not just some employment opportunity. I am not just using you. I care for you, deeply."

"I wish you wouldn't have said that."

"Why?"

"I am a dangerous woman."

"I'm not afraid of you."

"You should be."

"You would never do anything to hurt me."

"You'd like to believe that."

"I have to believe that. You've given me no other choice. If not for your tears, I'd have been killed tonight."

"That is not why Oenomaus spared you. He was acting on orders."

"You know his name?"

"He is one of Spartacus' commanders. I know all of their names. He is good friends with the gladiatrix commander, Téadora."

"The woman that the lanista and Senator were after."

"One in the same."

"What's so special about her?"

"I don't know. Perhaps it is the fact she sees nothing special in herself that makes her so sought after. She is Spartacus' woman. She has been since they were children. Life could not do anything about that. It might as well be written in the stars. The gods themselves could not part those two."

"How do you know so much about her? Is it all visions?"

"I was in the employ of her father for over ten years. He was a very powerful Thracian chief before he died. I hated him. I watched her to make sure he could not get to her. Eventually, he figured out I was more interested in keeping her alive than following orders, and he sold me. Little did he know, Spartacus bought my services for a healthy bit of coin."

"You worked with Spartacus?!"

"He is a good man. Slave, deserter, or not. He is good on the inside, where it counts. He knows right from wrong. That's why it pains me so to work for you."

"You'd rather work for him again?"

"I'd rather work for no one. But I believe you when you say you care for me. No one has ever told me that before. I would take no pleasure in learning of Spartacus' death. But word of losing you..."

"You don't need to say it. I understand. There are no winners in war."

"I have had the most terrible dreams. So many faces dying. The road ahead of us is paved with blood, and there is no way any of us are getting out of it clean. Our names will haunt the ages."

XI

Despite two victorious nights against the Romans, the slave army was starting to divide. For some of the men, they had had their opportunities for vengeance, and they were satisfied. A life for a life, a kill for a kill, and that was all they wanted to accomplish. There was no desire to travel the countryside, no desire to leave their families behind. Upwards of half the army returned to their homes and villages. The shepherds had flocks to tend to, some of the men had babies ready to be born. Some women left too, for the chance at a new life. No one was shamed to leave, or pressured to stay. Spartacus was not about that. He knew all too well what it was like serving in an army his heart was not tied to. Never would he make someone go through what he had endured for nearly fifteen years. It was impossible however, not to lose a little morale amongst the men who hadn't finished what they set out to do. Seeing half the force leave camp, it was a quiet morning to say the least, but it also put things into focus for those who stayed. Spartacus was going to lead them north, to cross the Alps, and get them home. Crixus was not going with them. He wanted to stay in the south, and continue harassing Rome until there was nothing left for him to burn, or he was killed, whichever came first. Many of the younger men with no families to return home to stayed with Crixus. In total, the Gaul took about ten thousand men in his camp, which accounted for a quarter of the remaining slave army. Spartacus had no words for his longtime fighting partner. The two had already talked in circles enough on the issue, and it was clear neither man would budge in their position. This was where their stories parted. Spartacus slapped a heavy hand on Crixus' shoulder before he mounted his stolen white horse from the praetors, and the two men exchanged somber smiles. It was not a joyous divide, but more like one that had to be made. Spartacus could not satisfy the boys who desired Roman blood for the sake of blood, and Crixus could not be content with running north, away from Rome. Spartacus pulled a meeting together with the commanders that remained. Téadora did not attend as she was busy saying her goodbyes to some of the women leaving for the promise of motherhood in some nearby villages. Gannicus saw Spartacus' attention lingering on his partner, more than the commanders, but before the older ginger bearded man could say anything on the subject, his younger cousin Castus was struggling with an issue of his own. Gannicus couldn't help but intervene.

"What's the matter, Castus?"

"Oenomaus. He's insisting I'm not carrying my weight in camp."

"Oenomaus, what's the meaning of accusing my cousin of this?"

"Just because he's a healer doesn't mean he gets to back out of the duties that every other man and woman in this camp carries. He does not go hunting or foraging. He does not raid. He carries weapons but he does not kill. I gave him a pass on Vesuvius, but I watched him hide again in Lucania. That's *two* fights now, Gannicus, that he has not helped us."

"A man serves more purpose healing people than killing them. My cousin is pulling more than his weight by making sure we do not die of foolish injuries or pride. Leave him be, Oenomaus. The camp is shifting enough as it is. There is no need to go making enemies of allies. If his actions bother you so much, separate yourselves."

"Separation is the last thing we need right now. I know none of us were friends with Crixus, but the fact he just walked off with a quarter of our forces says something."

"What does it say, Oenomaus?"

"I don't mean to be critical of your decisions, Spartacus, but you should not have let him take so many."

"The will of man is his own decision. I am no god. I own no one. Everyone knows when they come here, they can leave at any time. I am sorry to see some of them go, but it does not affect what the rest of us have set our minds to do. We're going home. I made a promise to you and I intend to keep it."

"There's a lot of ground to cover between us and the Alps."

"I know. We have the Apennines first. Those mountains aren't so bad, and it'll help us get a feel for what the Alps might be like. After the Apennines we can march along the Adriatic coast. It should be fairly safe for us there."

"Marching along the coast will be risky. More people live along the water than the valleys."

"But Téa needs the water and I need Téa. So, we march the coast. Tell the Germanians my plans, Oenomaus. I'd like you to lead the march when we leave camp today."

"I'll make the rounds."

"And I'm going to need you to apologize to Castus before you go."

"I don't regret my words."

"I didn't think you would. But Gannicus was right about not making enemies of allies. There are only so many of us, and we need to trust one another. Without trust, we have nothing."

"Forgive me, Castus, for speaking harshly of you. My position still stands, but it was wrong of me to bring it to your attention."

"It's no secret we do not see eye to eye, Oenomaus. I doubt anything will happen to change that. But I do not see you as my enemy."

"Nor I you. Excuse me. I need to go rally my men. They will be excited to lead the march. I know I am!"

Oenomaus left the commanders with a smile on his face that revealed his foul, rotten teeth. Castus was renowned for his good hygiene and winced. When he looked up at his cousin for reassurance, he was scolded by the disapproving glare. Gannicus did not like having to handle things between men like they were children. Castus took off for his tent and began slowly breaking it down so nothing fell into the dirt. Gannicus sighed, and shared a chuckle while he stood with Spartacus. They were the only two commanders left in the huddle. In the distance the Germanians were starting to cheer at the task they'd been assigned. The excitement drew Téadora's attention for a couple seconds too as she continued to say her goodbyes. Some of her gladiatrix friends were quite pregnant now. There were promises made that if any daughters were born, they might bare Téadora's name, out of respect. Gannicus nudged Spartacus' shoulder, seeing the leader crane his head in an effort to eavesdrop.

"You working on a child of your own, are you, Spartacus?"

"I would be so lucky if the gods bestowed that gift. She'd be a good mother, wouldn't you think, Gannicus?"

"A mother in war, there's nothing more dangerous. But a battlefield is no place to be raising babies."

"I do not intend for this war to go on much longer. Crixus may do what he wishes. Let the fight continue with him. I have a home to get back to, and a lot of land to cover before I get there."

"Do you think you could give up this war so easily?"

"For Téa, I could give up anything."

"It's just, all you two know is fighting. I worry, a life of peace might bore you, Spartacus."

"I will have something else more worthwhile to keep my hands busy, trust me."

"But will she share your view on that?"

"You think it would be hard for Téa to give up this war?"

"She sticks with you now, but will she stick with you always? You knew the girl she was. I know the woman she's become. I saw her in every one of her matches for Batiatus. She's ruthless, Spartacus. She's too good at killing not to take some joy in it. She keeps herself occupied, either with bloody hands or a busy mind. You might be willing to give up the world for her, but…"

"You don't know if she will walk away so easily?"

"Have you talked to her, of a life together once this is behind us?"

"She wants what I want."

"Truly?"

"She is not just saying what I want to hear. If there's anyone willing to break my happiness, it is her. She will be honest with me, sometimes to a fault. She is like that. A life together is what we want, and she trusts that I know how to make that happen."

"Then it is *her* desires that push you north so hard, not your own?"

"Yes. If it was me, I'd stay in the south, barter passage on a ship, and be home within a couple months. But she does not trust the sea."

"The *sea* she trusts. Water has never hurt her. It's the people that run the sea that she has trouble with."

"Has she ever spoken to you of why she hates the Cilician pirates?"

"She has brought it up on several occasions, but not in great detail. I know they sold her to Batiatus. I did not ask why. I don't think *she* understands why she was sold. But this is just what Castus has told me. They are closer than she and I."

"I'd like to know what your cousin knows, but I don't want to go prying. She promised she would tell me when she was ready."

"But you are impatient?"

"There is a wall between us I can't seem to break down. There never used to be walls when we were younger."

"Walls don't have to be a bad thing. Everyone deserves the right to keep some things to themselves."

"I still tell her everything."

"That is good of you to do. She needs that. All of us commanders appreciate being well informed."

"Your eyes are saying more, Gannicus."

"Did Crixus give you any warning before his departure this morning?"

"No. He did not. But this has been a long time coming."

"He took a lot of men with him."

"I know."

"It will be hard for us to regain our numbers."

"We do not need to actively recruit."

"Our victories only came because of superior numbers. You do know that, don't you, Spartacus? Superior numbers, and experience. But sooner or later the Senate will wisen up and send somebody out to us worth fighting. Someone who knows their stuff. Not every military strategist is out at war right now. Some men are still at home. If this goes on too much longer, someone who matters will come looking for us, and we might not be able to stop him."

"I thought you were ready to die in battle, Gannicus?"

"I am. But that doesn't mean everyone is. You keep preaching the possibility of these men seeing home again. I don't want to see that ripped away because we got too comfortable."

"I am not comfortable with anything. If it were up to me Crixus would have stayed. Divisive or not, he's a good soldier, and he took many a good fighter with him this morning. It will be a difficult loss to swallow, but swallow it we must, and with a straight face too."

"You are a good man, Spartacus."

"I question that sometimes."

"Do not let Crixus' decision bother you. We will find a way to work around what he's taken from us."

"Isn't that what we always do? Work around? Steal. Manipulate. Make do. Adjust. Adapt. Survive. Struggle. It is tiring."

"But it will be worth it. To those who live, it'll all be worth it."

"And what about for those who don't? Do they die in vain? What happens to them, Gannicus?"

"Don't worry about the dead, Spartacus. Their troubles are over. Ours, ours are just beginning."

Gannicus raised his orange eyebrows and took in what remained of the camp around them. They had started this fight with only seventy-five people. If you looked at the thirty thousand from that perspective, this was still a glorified success story. It was all on how you looked at things. Gannicus left his leader to think, and went to pack up his things and make sure the Celts were ready to follow the Germanians out on their march for the mountains. No one was too thrilled about having to cross the Apennines, but there was the promise of good farmland to raise in the higher elevations. Camping in the cooler weather would make the upcoming summer much more tolerable. Crops would be coming into season. Everything was going to be alright. What remained, was the best of the best. Spartacus walked down to the river's edge and sat down on the muddy banks with his feet in the water. As he began twisting his mother's silver ring necklace between his fingers, he was quickly joined by Téadora. She invited herself to sit down beside him. He pulled her in closer to his side and kept his hand around her thigh. She could tell something was bothering him, and as easy as it was to assume it was the breaking down of camp, she did not think that was the true cause to his silence now. Crixus was bound to leave at some point. Everyone had been expecting his departure. Seeing so many men side with him was not anticipated, but it was far from a total loss. Less mouths to feed, less men to worry about getting into trouble. Smaller armies covered ground that much faster. Crixus would no longer be casting doubts into the minds of men. The other fifty or so thousand that left to go back to their lives, you couldn't hate them for wanting to go. Two good battles against the Romans, it was more opportunity to get revenge than most slaves ever got. Debts had been settled. Families were growing. Téadora was all smiles for the sake of Spartacus, but he could see tears welling up in her eyes as they sat beside each other. He let a fingertip trace up her cheek to get wet, and she laughed at her own expense.

"Age has weakened me, Spartacus."

"How do you mean?"

"I never thought I would be a woman who cried *happy* tears."

"You are *happy* right now?"

"By doing what we've done, we've given people hope again. One of the women I said goodbye to this morning, she's been with me for years. We've been partners in matches in the arena many a time. We thought alike, and moved alike. She's about five months pregnant now. A baby will be born before the end of the year, just as the snows come in. She's lost two children before this, but they were the product of rape. This child, this child will be born from love. We've given that to her, Spartacus, isn't that amazing?"

"I was worried it was going to be hard for you to let the women go."

"I couldn't be more thrilled for their lives they're going to lead. Back at the House of Batiatus, at night, we used to all gather up in circles and speak about what we would want to do if we had our freedom. Back then, it was just dreams, but now it is truth."

"And what of your dreams?"

"I'm sitting by your side. I need nothing more. I'm not greedy."

"But if you *could* ask the gods for more, what would you want?"

"When we were about fourteen, my tribe came from our island to your tribe in the mountains. Do you remember this trip?"

"I remember it fondly. I took you on a hike. I nearly slipped half way down a hillside because I was so nervous to show you my special place I used for hunting."

"You promised me when we were older, you would build us a home like the one on top of that hill. You said…you were so bold when you were a boy…you said I had to have all of your babies! And we would raise them in a home on a hill like that."

"Did I really say that to you when we were fourteen?"

"I remember your words as clearly as if you just spoke them to me. We were so young. I had never thought about having kids of my own, or who I might have them with. You were my best friend. When you said that, it changed something in me. Suddenly, I wanted to work for something in my future. I wanted to be the woman you were going to make a wife and mother out of. We never talked of children after that, not until just recently. I have thought about it often though. If the gods were to grant me my dream, it would be that house on the hill, with you, and our kids."

"No war?"

"No war, Spartacus. I do not dream of war or death."

"That's good to hear."

"Were you worried I had such dark dreams?"

"With everyone leaving, I just wanted to know our heads were in the same place."

"Never question me, Spartacus. You know me better than anyone. Some days, you know me better than I know myself. Oenomaus told me you plan to march us along the Adriatic coast."

"I know how important it is for you to see the water."

"You'd move an entire army to make me happy?"

"I'd move mountains to make you happy."

"I *am* happy. So long as we stay alive, I am in a state of bliss. The gods themselves could not upset me. I want this war behind us, Spartacus. I feel the farther north we reach, the better we'll all be."

"That means we'll have to pass Rome."

"I'm fine with that. We'll be quick about it."

"When do you think the Senate will send more praetors after us?"

"It takes them months to get anything decided. By the time they can pay someone well enough to come for us, we will be long gone. But the way we left Lucania was not the way we left Vesuvius."

"Tell me why you think that."

"We wanted Rome to know what he had done at the volcano. But this last time in the valley, we did not send anyone back to the Senate. Dacia is with this praetor. She will not abandon me."

"There is…something else? Look at me, not the river, Téa. Why was Lucania different than Vesuvius?"

"Oenomaus is a good man. I asked him not to tell anyone what he saw me do."

"What did you do?"

"When I was with the women, we were looting the Roman camp. I came across two men cowering in a collapsed tent. I gave them mercy and let them leave."

"We're not in the practice of taking prisoners. I don't fault you for showing mercy."

"Spartacus, it was Batiatus and Furius I showed mercy to."

"They were *here*?!"

"I let them live. With the legion in shambles, I didn't see the need to kill them. To stab a soldier is one thing, but to stab a Senator, I could never imagine the consequences. I could have doomed us all. Instead, they remain breathing while we run."

"Why didn't you tell me?"

"I didn't want to cause divide amongst the commanders. It was bad enough having to explain my decision to Oenomaus. When he saw Batiatus slap me he about…"

"Batiatus slapped you?!"

"Not like he hasn't done it a million times before. But this was his first time doing it to me when I had my freedom."

"I'll kill him!"

"Spartacus, no! I'm fine, and he's gone."

"We don't know where he is."

"He's not here. He's not with us. That makes it fine."

"I don't like hearing you've been hit. I don't want *any* man laying *any* kind of hand on you unless that man is *me*, in which case, there'd be *no* shred of hate in my touch."

"You can't protect me from the world, Spartacus."

"I can try."

"You are too sweet for words sometimes, you know that?"

"No one has ever called me sweet before. Men fear me. They've cried for their lives on bended knee, begged for mercy. I have been cursed at in more languages than I can count. I lead an army of some of the most intimidating people this empire has ever seen. But not once in all my years have I ever been called *sweet*."

"Then I suppose I will have to do that more often."

"I guess I can tolerate that from you. But it'll cost you a kiss."

"A punishment I will endure bravely."

XII

When Varinius bucked down and finally asked Rome for reinforcements, ships of soldiers were sent to a port on the Adriatic coast. Crixus and his men intercepted the praetor's runner and killed him for this information. The Gaulish slaves had no intention of ever letting Varinius reestablish his legion. Instead, they lied in wait on Mons Garganus, guarding a path from the countryside to the coastal peninsula. It had been nearly two months since the Roman defeat in Lucania. Varinius was as eager to make up for his losses as Crixus and his men were to kill them. Spartacus and his forces were steadily north of the region, making slow but quiet progress on their way out of Rome's reach. Crixus could hear his old fighting partner now, urging him caution and patience while baiting this battle. It had always been Spartacus' way to ask a million questions to the soldiers around him so as to avoid any careless mistakes when things intensified. Crixus was far more impulsive, always pushing limits and testing boundaries. He was inherently impatient, and that was not lost on him as he sat on his white horse alone on the high ground. No fellow commanders at his side for peace of mind. He did not need anyone else, but this was the first time in his life he could not share victory or blame with someone. Whatever happened today, it would fall on his shoulders squarely, and his alone. He gulped hard seeing the flags of Varinius rise over the horizon. In front of him was a small force. Behind him on the ships was the reinforcements he had to scare away. After a rousing speech to his men, it was clear this afternoon was going to be a fight to the death. Hopefully, not his, but if it came to it, he'd take as many down with him as he could.

The main ship coming into port had the Senate's latest and greatest minds onboard. To be truthful, these two men in charge of the reinforcements were young, dumb, and too arrogant to know what they were being put up against. They were as expendable as the praetors before them. The Senate was merely hoping throwing numbers at the problem might make it go away. They were tired of hearing about it from wealthy constituents and the raids were becoming a more widespread nuisance. Consuls Publicola and Clodianus could be spared from Rome. While back home the pair were little fish in a big pond, out on the prospective fields of battle they were mighty fish in a tiny pond. Their thin chests were inflated and their smiles unfounded. While docking, they stood on the bow of the boat and boasted to each other of their potential military prowess, how many slaves they were going to kill, and how fast they were going to do it. Both men were in their early twenties, seen nothing of life but privilege, and had been told no very little. They had no business confronting Crixus and his men today, but that's just what they were going to do. From the countryside, Varinius had met his obstacle at the mountain pass. The Gauls threw rocks and jeers down at the Romans to little avail. Ten thousand to two thousand, Varinius understood the defeat he would be handed if he were to pursue. Despite being heavily outnumbered, he did not falter at the entrance to the pass. Instead, he sat there, and bid his time, all the while the reinforcements amassed from the ships, and began to pinch Crixus on the high ground he was so proud of. Some worried Gauls from the coastal side of the pass tried warning their fearless leader of their predicament, but Crixus had a twinkle in his eye and a smirk on his lips that could not be extinguished. It was understood that this was the hill he was to die on. Today was the day. Word of this fear spread rapidly through the ranks. Some men trickled down the mountain crags and valleys to try and get away before a battle opened up and swallowed them whole. Crixus did not bark any orders or give any commands to stop them. Like Spartacus, he was only going to fight beside men who wanted to be there. He was no tyrant, no warlord. He was just a man with a death wish, and the gods were going to give him what he had been asking for every night since the Romans captured him and forced him into servitude when he was a teenager. The young men today were going to pay for what old men had done to him in the past. Crixus could not contain his excitement. He charged on horseback down the mountain pass, abandoning his high ground, and aimed himself for Varinius' position. The praetor did not waiver however, for he had the information of Dacia the seer on his side, who had already seen the battle play out before her eyes, and knew how the day would end. She stood beside Varinius in the middle of his haggard legion as he leaned over to whisper in her ear. His men were to hold their lines. Let Crixus be the madman he wanted to be.

"How far away did you say the reinforcements were, Dacia?"

"The consuls will arrive on the other side of the mountain before Crixus can reach us. But I warn you, Varinius, once Crixus realizes he's trapped, nothing will stop him from coming after you."

"But you said I will survive the battle?"

"You will, but no need to go taunting a man in his final moments."

"I would so like to humiliate that man. Spread him up on a cross for Spartacus to see. Make the slaves shake in their sandals. Let them know what they get for choosing to follow the wrong man. It didn't have to be like this. *They've* made it this way, not *me*."

"Perhaps it would have been wiser for me not to tell you how today was going to go. It has given you a confidence most unflattering. Forgive me if I don't want to witness what's about to happen. Seeing it once was bad enough. Do I have permission to move to the rear?"

"Of course. I will join you as soon as I can."

"Don't rush. The men need you here. Excuse me. My head is aching. I have to find some shade. The visions are plaguing me today."

While the seer removed herself from the ranks and file, Varinius was steadfast in his position. Crixus was halfway down the mountain pass now, wrapping back and forth across the steep hills of Mons Garganus. He was followed by a line of men as reckless as he was, all shouting in native tongues and raising weapons. Varinius had his archers up front, and ordered them to release their first wave of arrows. It took a couple seconds before a line of defense was cut into the mountain pass. Crixus and his horse trampled over a dozen arrows as they stuck into the ground, but the men behind him on foot started to slow. Screams were coming from their rear. The Romans had arrived from the ships. They were young and fresh, healthy, and unexperienced. There was no hesitation in their attacks. Publicola and Clodianus sat astride their brown horses in the middle of thousands of soldiers, pressing onwards like valiant generals of a bygone era. They praised each other, as if their swords had seen blood. The narrow pass was bulging with men. The Gaulish resistance was failing. What forces could scatter, did so in the most ungraceful of ways. Most of the time they were just hurling themselves down cliff faces, hoping for the best, and if not, suicide by falling was a better way to go than a Roman sword. The injured, dead, and dying were flung down the mountain as well. Those living and trying to escape kept getting caught up on their bodies. There were many shared regrets of leaving Spartacus now. With any luck, if the gods were listening or watching, the survivors would try and make it back to their former Thracian savior, and seek forgiveness for leaving so foolishly. Spartacus would take them back, because he was a good man. The trouble was getting to him.

Over the course of the afternoon the Gaulish lines surged and retreated with the pressure from Varinius, Publicola and Clodianus. Crixus had taken an arrow to the thigh, and twice broke pieces out and threw them to the ground. There was still a bulk of the shaft left in his leg though, and he could feel the blood draining from him in the unforgiving heat of summer. As he grew dizzy, he thrusted on his horse less, and just tried to lead his men around him. Three times Crixus tried to get off of the mountain, and three times he failed. His first two attempts were against the superior forces to his rear. Publicola and Clodianus wee coming up the pass now, eager for displaying strength at the enemy's defeat. They wanted a little dirt under their fingernails when they met up with Praetor Varinius. Consuls like them were anxious for a quick promotion and better post. Crixus' third attempt to break out from captivity was towards the legion he and his men had fought at Lucania. There was bad blood there, and many men fell. Seven thousand of the ten thousand were lost. Three thousand were injured to some degree on the mountainside, and a handful had run for Spartacus' help. Crixus would not surrender. Some of the Gauls had dropped to their knees in quiet resignation. They were killed for doing so. Varinius strode forwards on his white horse and made his way for Crixus. He was halfway up the mountain, resolute as a statue. He'd tied his hand to the saddle for stability, but when Varinius came up to surround him, the praetor cut the straps lose and Crixus fell to the ground. He was near death, but unwilling to die. He coughed dirt back into his mouth from the path beneath him, unable to roll over onto his back. Varinius jumped down, and kicked his body over. Crixus winced, then spit on Varinius' feet out of spite. His breathing was labored, but a curved Thracian dagger was still in his hand. Varinius smirked, crouched down, and pulled the blade away before tossing it down the mountain.

"Spartacus is not here to help you. You should have stayed with him. Now you die on this godforsaken pass with all the men stupid enough to follow you. Thank you though, for this afternoon's entertainment. I'll be taking Rome's horse back now."

"He will…avenge me."

"Who? Spartacus? He's nowhere around. My runners tell me he's a day's ride away if not more. He will not come for your body. You and he are nothing to each other. If you were, you'd be up north with him, instead of down here, with me. Look at *me*, Crixus! The last face you lay your eyes on will be *mine*. Look at *me*!"

Crixus worked up all the strength he had left in his body to spit on Varinius' face. The praetor had the Gaul by the chin, forcing him to awkwardly crane his head up off of the ground so they could look at each other eye to eye. Varinius thrust Crixus away in disgust to wipe the bloody spit off of his face, some of which had gotten onto his lips. By the time he had composed himself his enemy was dead. Crixus lied there, eyes wide to the sky above. On safe inspection of his body, Varinius could see Crixus had taken many arrows and cuts to his body this afternoon. It was hard to tell if any one injury could be to thank for his death, and not an amalgamation of the marks as a whole. Regardless, the battle had been won, and Varinius had his first victory under his belt. The signal was given to slaughter whatever Gauls remained on the mountain pass. Publicola and Clodianus looked at each other with uneasy stares, and took out their swords, which to this point, had remained comfortably sheathed. But to be a leader, one had to do the dirty work. The young men drew their weapons, and began to ungracefully make jabs at the Gauls beneath them. Many of the men were already dying, so to lay the final blow was really more of an act of mercy than spite. Varinius was already walking back down the pass towards his rear, where Dacia could be seen rocking on the ground, mumbling to herself in a language Varinius was not fond of. As he tapped the woman's shoulder she shuttered, but refrained from looking at him. The man wanted praise and acknowledgement. He got neither. When Varinius knelt down, to crouch before the seer, he could see her fingers were bloody where she had been clawing at her arms. Her eyes shook in their sockets. It scared Varinius to see her like this, and he bolted upright to ask the nearest soldier to her what was happening.

"How long as she been like this?"

"The whole time?"

"Why didn't anyone tell me? She's in distress!"

"You were busy with the Gauls."

"She is more important!"

Varinius hadn't meant to shout. When he did, he realized the weight of what he had just said, out loud, and it was not well received. The young soldiers around him all looked confused, and took a step back from the praetor. Varinius would have taken a step back from himself as well, if it were possible, but since it wasn't, and what he had said was unable to be unsaid, he rejoined Dacia back on the ground and tried to snap her out of her daze. He pulled her in close to her chest to try and stop the rambling but it just continued, albeit muffled by his armor. He squeezed her in an embrace, and slowly but surely, he felt her muscles ease under his pressure. She never hugged the man back, but she did accept his closeness, and begin to cry. Varinius' soldiers were called away by officers to tend to their fallen, and help make acquaintances with their reinforcements. The day moved on. There was a lot of bodies to handle. For lack of want or care, the Gauls were largely left in place. A score of them were tossed aside or heaped into piles for the means of transit on the pass, but if they didn't need to be moved, they weren't. Varinius was giving no formal orders. Any action had been left to lower officers doing their best in his stead. Publicola and Clodianus rode down to try and meet their leader, but seeing him on the ground with a seer in his lap, they did not know what to do. They had not been briefed on this relationship. In fact, no one in the Senate knew anything about Dacia, or Varinius' strong reliance on her. The two young consuls agreed amongst themselves that it would be up to them to set up camp tonight, but they were unfamiliar with the area and unquestioned authority they found themselves in now. It was nice, it was what they thought they had wanted, but now that they had it, they were unsure of how to go about exercising it. To ensure unity, the men would have to split up and cover more ground. Soldiers were a bit scattered up and down both sides of Mons Garganus.

"Clodianus, you take the left of the battlefield, and I'll take the right. We'll meet back at the ships. Regroup where we know we are safe."

"Good idea. Right."

"Right."

"Right, Publicola?"

"Right. Wait. Right like you're taking the right or right like you're taking the left?"

"I don't know. Now you've got me confused."

"Take the left, Clodianus."

"And what are we to do about Praetor Varinius?"

"Leave him be. You never interrupt a man when he's with a woman."

"Are we even sure that's a woman, Publicola?"

"Yes! I mean…yes. Yes! She's a woman. She's not the best-looking sort, but out in war, a man must make do with what he has."

"If I ever drag a woman like that back to my tent, kill me."

The men laughed with each other before parting. Varinius did not hear a word spoken around him, though the consuls were hardly subtle in their judgement of the seer. Dacia heard though, and spoke the first audible words Varinius had heard from her in hours. Publicola and Clodianus were destined to die together, as they lived. Varinius looked over his shoulder as Dacia said that, but neither consul wanted to give her recognition. They both glanced at each other as if they hadn't just heard some death curse placed upon them, and shook their heads at the ridiculous notion. Varinius was in no hurry to get up. Dacia wanted out of his arms, and she wished she hadn't wrenched herself away so quickly for the expression on the praetor's face was heartbreaking if the seer could have cared. She stayed cold, and wore a blank face as she stood up and dusted herself off. There was a single request made to bury the Gauls but Varinius cooly denied her and walked back to his two white horses. The way he was holding out the reins for her, Dacia knew she still held a soft place in his heart. The seer took over ownership of Crixus' white horse which had been stolen at the battle on Vesuvius.

"I don't need my own horse, Varinius."

"Yes, you do. We'll have a lot of walking in this war, and it won't do to keep you on foot. I'm on horseback, and you stay with me, so it only makes sense you have your own horse."

"White horses are reserved for praetors."

"If I want you on a white horse, you'll sit on a white horse."

"Thank you."

"You're welcome."

"Can we go to the ships now?"

"Yes. I need to get you out of this heat."

Varinius stayed on the ships in port for the next three days. He periodically sent runners out to check on the bodies of his enemy bloating on the mountain pass, getting picked apart by scavenging animals. It took two days for word to get to Spartacus and the army to turn back around for the south. Friends buried friends, or what was left of them, and the base of Mons Garganus was turned into hollow ground. It was tricky work reaching some of the men still hung up on the hillsides, but all bodies were accounted for eventually. Oenomaus was the one who found Crixus. While the commanders had never been close with one another, it gave the brutish Germanian no pleasure in seeing Crixus cut down with festering wounds all over him. Maggots were eating him without mercy, but Oenomaus still scooped the body up in his arms for a more proper grave off to the side of the others. A grave fitting of a leader. Téadora personally collected stones to outline the mound so Crixus would not be forgotten. Spartacus was uncomfortably silent during the whole process. For the most part, he sat on a boulder and watched Crixus' final moments in the sun. If he had fought harder against the separation, the two men could still be bickering back and forth with each other about moving north and escaping. Crixus got his escape alright, but this wasn't right. None of this was right. None of these men needed to die like this, trapped like rats between two Roman forces. During the burials the Celts were on lookout. Gannicus and his men sat on top the pass and took note of the Romans lurking just offshore, camping in the ships so they could leave at a moment's notice for somewhere safer. Castus was sent down into the peninsular town to see what the people were saying. He was as unintimidating as anyone in the slave army, and with his kind eyes, he could get just about any shop owner or small child to talk to him. Castus found what he was looking for in an old fisherman in the harbor. He was sun worn, old before his time, toothless, and not very fond of the Roman ships scaring away his catch of the day. Castus took a seat beside the man, commiserated on their lives, and returned back to the mountain pass where his older cousin was waiting. Gannicus then took that news down to Téadora. She was the only one brave enough now to go and speak with Spartacus, as he sat supremely confused on his boulder. She crouched down and placed gentle hands on his knees.

"Spartacus, the men have found out where the Romans are who did this. If you want to get even for this battle, there is a way."

"It's not in my nature to be spiteful. But for Crixus, it is what's most appropriate. How many Romans are there? And where are they?"

"Castus says there's several ships parked on the coast. Each of them has comfortably three hundred men on board. If we were to ambush them, we could make at least one ship pay for what's been done to Crixus. Give him the justice he fought so hard for. What do you say? Do we attack, or do we hold back?"

"Hold for sundown. We'll move at night. Send Castus back to port. I want him to find the ship where the officers are. I want them all."

"Spartacus? How are you? The commanders are all worried."

"I'll be fine. I need to make up for my mistake. Once I do that, we head back for the north. Nothing has changed."

"I'll spread the word then. And I'll go with Castus to the coast."

"Be careful, Téa."

"I will be. You should go and say something nice to Crixus. I'm sure he'd appreciate one last conversation between the two of you. Squash whatever argument you are fighting in your head."

Téadora placed a lingering kiss on Spartacus' forehead before she left his side. She wasted no time hiking up the mountain pass and taking Castus off for the shore. They worked well as a team maneuvering through the little fishing town and collecting pieces of information. This was not a place the Romans were welcome, but as small as it was, they were smart enough to keep quiet about their discontent for the sake of their lives. The soldiers were ravaging their shops and peaceful streets. Two local boats had been sunk by drunken officers. One shop owner said his daughter had been raped. This really got under Téadora's skin. She saw a young teenage girl cowering in her father's shop, chattering like it was snowing outside though it was the middle of summer. Castus talked to the father while the gladiatrix did her work, convincing the girl to trust her, and describe this officer who attacked her. She knew the ship he was on and everything, because it was parked right out front her best friend's home. It was the officer's ship, the one a man with white horses was on. Horses, as in plural. White, as in praetor. Before leaving Téadora hugged the girl like a mother would a child and locked arms with Castus to walk down the road. Castus admitted the man's wife had died the following year and he was in over his head raising his daughter. Before the slave army left, Téadora would be sure to get Spartacus to place a hefty bag of coin on that man's doorstep for his help. It was the least they could do after solving this Roman problem. Maybe not solving it, but scaring the living daylights out of them for sure. It was a good thing Spartacus was out of sorts, because if he had been in his right and stable mind, no revenge of such nature would have ever taken place. At sundown, the Thracians led the stealthy charge to the coast. Not all of the army went, just enough to send a message that Crixus' death would not go unchallenged. Oenomaus cut the officer's ship loose from it's mooring, and the Germanians commandeered the ship under Téadora's barking orders. All her time at sea with the Cilician pirates was really paying off. With her steering the ship she isolated the officer's ship. The Thracians kept most of the three hundred from jumping overboard and making a swim for it. All the other soldiers were forced to watch helplessly from their own boat, or from the shore, like Varinius and Dacia. The seer tried to keep from smiling too much, for she had seen this in a vision during the battle. She lied when the praetor asked her for an explanation, saying Spartacus must have decided to do this at the last minute, and that's why she could give no warning. Varinius was beside himself watching his own ship come under attack. His white horses neighed like wild when the Romans started dying. Less than an hour, was all it took. Spartacus ordered his enemy to fight to the death, like gladiators, until they were all dead. At first, there was hesitancy amongst the Romans. They would not submit. But after Gannicus sliced a man's neck and threw him into the center of the deck for all to watch him die, there was little in the way of resistance. It was either die by a friend's hand, or die by the enemy's, and the enemy was going to enjoy it too much. Castus stood behind Téadora at the ship's wheel. Neither of them had ever seen Gannicus so happy to draw blood before. It was unsettling. Then again, the entire night was. No one was themselves. They couldn't be. Crixus was as ornery as they came, and if he could be cut down so easily, then they all could. It was a group effort to pile the dead officers and soldiers in the center of the ship. Lanterns were broken, and the oil was used to drip over the bodies to make them more flammable as the torches were tossed in. The entire ship was lit aflame as it drifted out into the Adriatic. The slave army jumped out into the water and swam back for the shore, heroes of the little fishing village. Varinius and Dacia were seeking shelter on another ship by this time. The praetor could have done something against Spartacus. The two men locked eyes at one point as the slave army retreated to the countryside, but nothing was done. Dacia clutched onto the praetor's arm like Téadora clutched onto her Thracian. The women nodded to each other with stern faces. This was how it was going to be. There was no glory in war. No one had anything to be proud of. It was just a matter of who had the gall to endure more pain before the other gave in.

XIII

Varinius and Spartacus went back and forth with tiny victories all up the coast of the Adriatic Sea. The Romans kept to the water while the slaves marched along land. Sometimes it was Varinius who would reach a port town first, and leave the ragtag army of rebels and scorned fugitives to go raiding elsewhere for their food and supplies. Sometimes it was the other way around, and rough seas or unfavorable weather would keep the Romans at bay. There was an unspoken avoidance of one another. Varinius would follow Spartacus until he ran out of water, in which case the slaves would become someone else's problem, or, and the praetor was really hoping it was the latter, or Spartacus and his army would make such a costly mistake that Romans would be forced to take decisive action on land. The Senate had not sent Varinius more soldiers or ships to make up for what happened in the south. As far as they knew, their praetor was a military genius. What they didn't know wouldn't hurt them, and complaints were at a minimum. The politicians were more concerned with the wars in the Mediterranean, funding those campaigns, and seeking those victories. Slaves were a lowly matter, low enough to get swept under a rug when careful enough. Spartacus was trying to be careful too, mindful of his ultimate goal of going home, keeping his commanders in like minded territory and the morale of the army high. Their ranks were growing again. Oenomaus and his Germanians had freed a couple thousand slaves working fields in Consentia. Many of them had been Gaulish prisoners. Spartacus took the position of looking after the Gauls now that Crixus was gone. They worked well with the Thracians, with similar values and fighting styles. They could be a ruthless bunch those farmhands. They already knew they had nothing to lose, so death did not frighten them.

    A few weeks after the loss in the south, things got complicated in Picenum. The obstacle of Rome had now been surpassed, and the dream of reaching the Alps in the north no longer seemed out of reach. Spartacus had been pushing his army more hours to take advantage of the summer days, and kept up a strenuous pace. In his eagerness, his unspoken timetable with the Roman ships had been disturbed. Both armies arrived in Picenum at the same time, and neither was in a position to back down and let the other have their way with the town. The slave army was exhausted, and needed respite from travel, whereas the Roman ships had depleted all of their resources and had to make port. The fight they had been avoided for weeks had finally come to a head. Téadora volunteered to ease into the town with her women first. They would be the front line to try and quell any fires before they got too big. Soldiers would go easy on them, perhaps. If not, the women could more than defend themselves. Gannicus and Spartacus held high ground in the countryside to keep an eye on the Téadora's progress. It was slow going, street by street, but the women were moving towards the city center. Roman officers were already on their horses, rifling through crowds and upsetting everyone. Oenomaus flanked the women's position for intimidation factors, keeping people quiet as they raided from carts and open windows. Picenum didn't want any trouble, but since trouble had found them, they were going to defend themselves. A group of veterans approached Téadora in the outskirts of the city center. It was enough tension to cause her to draw her curved sica blades, and when some of the veterans saw the design in her hands, they charged forwards with a vengeance. Téadora did not signal for help, but Oenomaus and the Germanians plunged in to her aid anyways. The city was quickly engulfed in chaos. Streets were on fire, carts were burning. From the port, Romans were jumping from their ships to defend their supplies still being loaded. They couldn't move fast enough. No one could move fast enough. People couldn't get out of the way. A stampede of panicked locals in alleyways was becoming a death trap. The women were separated. Téadora found herself surrounded by angry veterans, blaming her for things men her father's age had done. She was elbow deep in blood and rage when strong hands gripped her from behind. It was only when she recognized Spartacus' matching seven dot tattoo on his forearm, did she stop to breathe for a second. The Thracian leader had to peel her sweat pinned strands of black hair off of her face just to get a good look at her and make sure she wasn't in trouble. He tugged her into a ransacked home so they could speak.

"You need to leave, Téa."

"My women are out there!"

"Gannicus and I have rushed the town. Oenomaus is in the city center. We will get what we need and get out."

"But the raids. We need food and…"

"We will get what we can. But you need to go back to the countryside. Set up camp. Give our army somewhere to run back to. Let me clean this up down here."

"No. I am no leader, *you* are. *You* go to the countryside. This army is nothing without you. You can't be injured. You are the face of this war. *I* made this mess; *I* need to be the one to clean it up."

"Are you sure?"

"It's *my* women out there. I have never left them before. I can't leave them now. I will finish this. But you should go."

"I don't like this."

"I know you don't, but it is the wisest thing to do. Fall back, Spartacus. I will find you in the countryside when this is over."

"You promise?"

"It's getting nasty out there. I need to return. You need to go!"

"I love you, Téa."

"I love you too. Now go! Spartacus, run!"

"You promise you will find me?!"

"Don't worry about me. Run, now! I'll catch up! I promise!"

Téadora jumped up on her tiptoes and grabbed Spartacus face with two bloody hands still fiercely holding onto her sica blades. Spartacus squeezed her body against his until both of them could barely breathe, and she wrenched herself away, right back into the thick of things. Spartacus could not waste anytime watching or worrying. It was like Gannicus had told him before, this was what she was good at, taking life. Almost too good. She was efficient, and uncaring. Every Roman she saw she stuck with her blades. Sometimes it was quick and easy, a gash across the neck. Sometimes the men tried to get a hold of her, use their superior strength, and she'd have to get messy, stab them in the gut, and twist her blade about like she was gutting a fish. She grew up on an island, gutting fish was like second nature to her, and really, a human man wasn't much different. Scramble about a bit, and tug with all your might. The eyes would go black, the body limp, and you moved on. And she did move on. She moved right through to the city center and reunited with Oenomaus who was livid with the Romans, but damn happy to be fighting by her side. The large Germanian had guts hanging on his arms, and Téadora could see a Roman officer barely recognizable as a human off to the side. Before the commanders could make small talk of what had happened, more soldiers ran up from the ships, and the fighting continued on the stones of Picenum. Spartacus was running for his life back for the countryside. He managed to pick up Castus and a few of the healers on the way, uncovering their hiding spot in a bathhouse above the town. Castus begged Spartacus not to tell Gannicus or Oenomaus that he had avoided yet another battle. His curly head bowed in shame, but Spartacus was not at all upset.

"Castus, the army needs you healthy. We all have our part to play here, and yours is not down there in the blood, it is back in camp. Come with me, and wait for the others."

"Wait! I found where the city stores their food. We can help ourselves while everyone is distracted. There're rooms full of jars. There's more food than I know what to do with."

"Perfect!"

Spartacus slapped an approving hand on Castus' shoulder, and the thin man winced at the force, but quickly bore a smile. It was the first time he'd done something praiseworthy for the army. He just wished Téadora had been there to witness it. But she was busy right now. Castus and Spartacus kept their eyes on her in the city center. She was easy to spot by the circle of avoidance that was growing around her. Oenomaus and his Germanians were howling like wolves. The women yipped and shrieked. It was over. Varinius had loaded what he could on ships and was setting sail for the deeper part of the sea. The slave army began the process of looting and sacking shops and homes. For the most part, there was no interference from the locals. Seeing the bodies of their veterans dead in the streets was a good enough reason to stay hidden and out of the way. Téadora led her women away first, running for the countryside like she had promised Spartacus, but when they made it outside of town, there was no camp to be found. There was however, a cache of jars. The women looked around and began to help themselves to the fruits dried inside. They were starving from the travel and the battle. Some of them went to the river to clean up, but most of them chose to sit in the grass and enjoy their spoils. Téadora was cleaning the blood off her blades in the river water when Spartacus came up with several large jars filling his arms. It was all he could do to set them down with spilling them and catch his breath. Téadora giggled at his expense while he was doubled over in the heat. She dried her blades off on her tunic and went to go shade his face with her hands. She ducked down to kiss his cheek and he just shook his head in complete disbelief.

"What took you so long, Spartacus?"

"Téa! How did you get here so fast?"

"Told you I'd catch up. Guess I'm still a faster runner than you are."

"I found food."

"I see that."

"Actually, Castus found it. I'm little more than a donkey hauling it back. Could you do me a favor, and start setting up our tent?"

"I'll get my women on it. Give the men something to run back to, right? Take it easy, Spartacus, please?"

"There's still a room full of jars to move."

"And you are not the only able-bodied man in the army to move them. Don't strain yourself. I have a victory to celebrate with you tonight and I don't need you falling asleep on me."

Spartacus grinned like a wild man, and tackled Teadora into his arms. She pretended to fail to break out of his hold, and hung there in his arms like a damsel in distress. He kissed her neck until she giggled so much neither of them could stay standing. Spartacus pulled her in close and they rolled together so he broke their fall into the long grass. It was brittle from the summer's heat, and nearly knee high. Lying on top of each other it was like their own little oasis from the world, the river water streaming behind them. Téadora got comfortable, lying on Spartacus' chest, and folded her arms to rest her chin on them. He couldn't stop smiling, and she couldn't remember a time when they had been this unapologetically happy. With one hand Spartacus wet the tip of his thumb, and began smearing away the charcoal that Téadora and the women had streaked across their eyes for the battle. It made her bright eyes glow even more than usual, but Spartacus preferred seeing her without battle regalia. There were long grasses like this on the island of Samothraki where she grew up. If he closed his eyes, Spartacus could see them now, running through the hills when they were kids. He could hear them laughing. They laughed now, but not nearly enough, and it sounded different, heavier. The world had darkened their happy moments, stained them red with needless bloodshed. Téadora could see Spartacus was deep in thought. She reached around and wrapped their fingers together on both hands, bringing them up together to hug on her chest. She sat upright, and pulled Spartacus up with her while she sat in his lap.

"Where do you go when you get quiet like this, Spartacus?"

"I go to the past where war has not ruined my memories."

"There has always been war though, even in our past, even if we were too young to be aware of it. There was war then, there is war now, and there will be war long after we are dead and gone."

"I do not want to think about us being dead and gone. I am not ready to lose you yet. I don't even want to think it is possible. I want you forever, Téa. Can I be so bold as to ask for that?"

"I will have you forever, so it is only fitting you will have me. The gods will know this to be true and make it so."

"Oh, the gods know this, do they?"

"Yes. I have spoken with them, and they have agreed to let me have you. You are mine as I am yours and that's all there is to it."

"You make me smile when I don't think I am able. How do you manage to always be able to light up my darkness?"

"It's a gift. Do not question it."

"I just mean to understand it. I hope to do for you what you do for me. I worry sometimes that I am not enough."

"Spartacus, you are more than enough. To thousands of people, you are everything."

"I do not care what I am to thousands of people though. I only care what I am to *you*. If I do not have your good words, I will have words from no one."

"Then let me remind you how important you are to me."

While Téadora was laying Spartacus down in the grass a man cleared their throat to ruin the moment. The couple looked up to see Oenomaus, bloody and smiling with his foul teeth and necklace fashioned from severed Roman fingers. Téadora chuckled in disgust, happy to have Oenomaus as a friend rather than an adversary. She had so many questions, but she was unsure if she wanted to know the answers. Spartacus wanted to hear, and wrapped a friendly arm around the Germanian commander's wide, tattooed shoulders. Téadora had to get the camp set up. Men had to collect the jars from the city. Castus showed them the way, and Gannicus helped guard the path in case any local got wise to interfere. In addition to fingers, Oenomaus had also stolen maps from the Roman officers while looting their bodies. Across these papers were port towns marked for future visits, and some sort of heads up as to what the slave army could expect on their move north. Spartacus and his commander sat on the river's edge, trying to make sense of what their next moves needed to be as the day faded into night. A push to the Alps was still possible, but there was a glaring obstacle marked up that no one had worried about until now. Oenomaus waited to get his leader's opinion on the subject before offering up his two bits of sense. There was a garrison of soldiers waiting for them in the city of Mutina. Varinius had marked on the map that there were two legions totaling ten thousand men. Spartacus did some basic math. At his last recollection the army under his command was towering well above a hundred thousand again. If it was one good thing to come out of losing Crixus, it was recruitment amongst the disaffected in the countryside. Their ranks swelled with the massacre on Mons Garganus, and only looked to continue trending higher as word spread of this victory too. Spartacus didn't want to smile and appear to arrogant, but Mutina shouldn't have been much of a problem to worry about. Oenomaus was fiddling with the severed fingers around his neck, matching Spartacus' sly smile.

"What do you think, Spartacus? One more go around before we hit the Alps. Then we're home free. A simple in and out. Those boys in Mutina don't stand a chance against us."

"Varinius is in contact with them though. That praetor has been humiliated by us more than once. No man in his right mind would take that sitting down. He might be planning something here. I don't want to walk us into a trap."

"There's no way we're getting to the Alps before winter if we don't go through Mutina."

"And Varinius knows that. By now, and with Dacia at his side, he has to know we are looking for our way out of the empire. I was hoping he'd just let us go, and not trap us here. What does he get by reinforcing Mutina with legions?"

"A politician is only as good as the pride he holds for himself. He's not acting alone. The Senate must be on to us as well. This is them trying to save face."

"You think?"

"Men know when they are about to lose. It's a feeling you get, deep in your gut. You know what I mean. You've been fighting too long not to know. There have been battles you walked into knowing full well it was going to be a disaster."

"You think we've scared Rome?"

"I think putting legions directly in our path screams fear. They are desperate to stop us, Spartacus. We are a threat. A *real* threat."

"And you said you got these maps off of an officer?"

"Yes. He was one of the men guarding Varinius. I tried, Spartacus, I tried so hard to get to that praetor for you, but he slipped right out of the town square. That seer keeps a close eye on him."

"What do you mean you were trying to get him for me?"

"He's *your* kill to take, not mine. I'd wound him for you, but I'd like the final strike be yours. It's only right. A leader for a leader."

"I have no desire to kill that man."

"He desires to kill you."

"You only think that. You've never spoken to him."

"That's not entirely true. I spared him in Lucania."

"I didn't know that."

"We were alone. I didn't think it right for him to die without an audience. The Romans have tortured us for so long in the public eye. Making us fight to our deaths for their entertainment. I want *him* to die in the public eye. I want *him* to hear people cheering as he leaves this world."

"I hope you get that chance, Oenomaus."

"I hope so too, but if I don't, make sure it happens."

"I'll do my best. But why wouldn't you get the chance? Since we escaped that gladiator school, you've always been the most confident man the army had to our name. And if you weren't, you've been putting on a good show."

"War is a game, Spartacus. You either play it well and die a hero, or play a fool and live. I have been doing my best to play well, but I fear I have been a fool too. I lie to the men to keep them going, but I have been living those lies so faithfully, I think I have begun to believe them."

"I know what you mean. There is a fine line between lying for the army's benefit, and lying for your own sanity. Lies make you happy, but you can't trust that kind of happy."

"When I see you with Téadora, I know that is the only part of your day when you are no longer lying, Spartacus. You are truly happy with her. She has that effect on men. On all of us. You can't help but want to make that woman smile. If she is smiling, then you know everything is going to be alright. And if she is not smiling, then you better watch out because people are going to die."

"She has been that way as long as I have known her. It is one thing I can say, this war has not changed her. She is still the same little girl I grew up with. She still keeps a piece of home inside of her. I wish I could say the same. I think I have seen too much and done too much wrong to be the same boy she grew up with."

"War changes us all, Spartacus. Téadora is not immune to that, she just hides it better than we do. For you, she would do and say anything to keep you happy. We all would. I am glad you listened to her today and got out of town when you did."

"I didn't want to go."

"I know. It is not like you to run, but it was wise. We had it handled."

"I am getting tired of running, Oenomaus."

"I am getting tired too, but we're almost out, Spartacus. *Almost*. We can stand to push a little more. If it means humiliating the Romans who have abused us, we can keep pushing. Even when one is ready to give up, there's still that little bit of fire that keeps us going."

"Fire. We will have to raze Mutina to the ground to get out of here."

"*That's* the Spartacus I've been waiting to hear!"

"Keep your Germanians at the ready, Oenomaus. I don't want the Romans to be getting too comfortable."

"Of course. We need to strike while the iron's hot."

"How far away is Mutina from where we are now?"

"According to the maps and the pace you've been setting, I think we can make it there in three days."

"Three days. And where would that put Varinius by sea?"

"Mutina's not on the coast. He'd have to dock and march inland."

"Romans only march eight hours a day. After sailing north and getting everything organized, we might be able to beat him by a whole day. Leave him to find nothing but smoldering ashes."

"I like the sound of that."

"I like the sound of that too. But if winds are favorable on the water, it might mean we hit Mutina at the same time."

"You think Varinius is heading to Mutina?"

"He didn't mark it on the maps for no reason. He's desperate for help. It's a godsend you got a hold of these, Oenomaus."

"Thank me after Mutina has been razed."

"This is just the kind of break we've been needing!"

"Well go kiss Téadora already and pick up where I interrupted. She's been waiting for you and I can't take her glare a minute longer."

XIV

Mutina was located in a region of the Roman Empire known as Cisalpine Gaul. It was a contentious border region between what the Senate held comfortably, and what it wished it held comfortably. For many men in Spartacus' army, it was nearly home. Languages and food changed this far north. The chilly air from the Alps could be felt in the early mornings and late evenings. Freedom was in that air. But that freedom wouldn't come without a price. It was clear on the evening of day three for the slave army that favorable winds had indeed occurred on the Adriatic Sea. Varinius had beet Spartacus to Mutina. Now in addition to the garrison of ten thousand soldiers, Varinius brought another couple thousand with him. Still, that was no match for Spartacus' one hundred and twenty thousand, of which every man and woman was worth at least three inexperienced Romans on a good day. It was unclear what kind of day tomorrow was going to be. Oenomaus volunteered the Germanians for sentry duty to stakeout the fortifications they'd be up against the following morning. According to rotation of duties, it should have been Gannicus and his men on watch tonight, but the ginger bearded man understood Oenomaus needed this patrol for some personal reason he was not so willing to share. The Germanian commander wasn't too sure he didn't know a man in charge of Mutina. A white bearded, older man who used to come see Oenomaus fight in his more northern reaching matches. Frequently, the man would be sitting front row in the arena, rather than up in the shaded boxes meant for the elite spectators and betters. Hefty bits of coin always sitting in his hand. Oenomaus wanted to know exactly who he was up against, so without even telling a single one of his own men, he climbed up the southern barricade to the city, and spied on the private quarters where Varinius and Dacia were sleeping that night. The governor, a man named Claudius Longinus, had just invited himself inside. Oenomaus was beside himself. It *was* the same man from his matches. A man his blood had made rich. The hulking Germanian perched on top of the wall, gripping the branches of an olive tree for support, while Longinus thanked Varinius for his impromptu visit. In the presence of a titled man, Dacia was merely to be seen and not heard as she sat in the corner of the room, pretending to distract herself with sewing, when in reality she was paying as close attention to every inflection of every word spoken, just like Oenomaus was.

"I just wanted to thank you for coming Praetor Varinius. The legions will be most excited to run exercises with your men in the morning."

"The pleasure is all mine, Governor Longinus. But I must be honest with you, I don't think we'll be *running exercises* in the morning. The slave army will be here soon. I anticipate a bloody fight with them when the sun rises. Our incessant back and forth up the coast has finally come to an end. A stand will be made on your lands."

"Am I to understand you brought war to my quiet towns?"

"War was coming to you whether I came or not."

"Had I known this I would have revoked your visit."

"With all due respect, you don't have the authority, Governor. I am on orders from the Senate. I can say and do what I please for the betterment of the empire."

"That's not how the empire works."

"You are new to your position here, yes?"

"A little under a year, but I am hardly new to politics. I have been working for this title longer than you've been alive and I will not let it go just because a bunch of brutes want to walk through my lands."

"Then you see, we're on the same side?"

"You said the Senate sent you here?"

"I said I act in accordance with the Senate's wishes."

"Then why has the visiting Senator not told me anything of which you speak of now?"

"What Senator is this? Perhaps he is ill informed?"

"Would you consider Senator Furius, ill informed?"

"Furius is here?!"

"He just got in two days ago. And in our meals together he has told me nothing of your war, only that he is chasing a woman who was supposed to be coming through here before the end of the year."

"So, he's been following the war closely since I last saw him. I half thought he'd been killed in the battle of Lucania."

"He did mention that mishap in passing."

"*Mishap*? Is that what he called it? I was nearly killed by a Germanian in my tent and he called it a *mishap*?"

"It is very unfortunate what happened to your forces, Praetor Varinius. But I will not have that repeated on my watch."

"I will not have it repeated either. I intend to kill that Germanian with my own two hands as soon as I get the chance."

"I thought you said you've been fighting back and forth all along the Adriatic. You pick *now* to kill this Germanian?"

"If I don't stop the slave army here, they're headed out of reach, and I will be made the laughing stock of the Senate. I will lose my power, my respect, my credentials. I will lose everything. I am not prepared to lose everything; hence, I make my stand here. It is unfortunate for you, yes, but for the empire, this will be seen as a fine victory."

"You are a proud man for being so young."

"I am wise beyond my years, I assure you."

"I have seen many a proud man fall in my day."

"I'm not like those other men."

"How would you know? They lived and died before you could take your first breath. I was their friend, their brother, their uncle, and son. I have sacrificed enough for my position in this empire. You will not run it all into the ground for your vanity project."

"Killing these slaves is hardly a *vanity project*, Governor."

"It is hardly in the interest of the empire you speak so grandly of either. What's so wrong with these slaves anyways?"

"Forgive me for pointing this out, but have you not made your fortune on the backs and broken bones of slaves?"

"I have frequented the arenas, and made a fine bit of coin, but I do not wish a life of war on any man. If these men are just looking for a way out, I say let them go. They've more than paid their dues."

"You're a hypocrite, you know that?"

"I have just lived long enough to see the error in my ways. That is all. If you are so lucky, you will be just like me one day."

"I will *never* be like you. Excuse me, Governor, but tomorrow is going to be a long day for me and I have been travelling many months. Allow me to retire with my advisor for the evening?"

"Of course, Praetor. Enjoy your woman. I have business with Senator Furious to tend to anyways."

"What business?"

"It does not concern you."

"If it's about the slave army, it most certainly concerns me."

"I thought you were going to retire for the evening?"

"Fine. Keep your secrets. But you will regret this conversation."

"So much anger for such a young man. Enjoy your time in Mutina."

There was a smug exchange between the two men. Governor Longinus looked pitifully over at Dacia on her chair, no further in her fake sewing project than she had been at the start of the men's conversation. The Governor couldn't tell if she was some sort of hostage, whore, or truly an advisor. Whatever she was, she was not happy here with Varinius, but she was oddly content. She offered up as sincere a smile as she could muster for the old man but it did not convince him of anything. Oenomaus crouched stealthily on the top of the wall, shadowing Longinus as he walked across the courtyard to another room illuminated by candles. This was where Senator Furius was staying, a ground level room built into the hillside. Oenomaus jumped to the ground to eavesdrop on this conversation, but it was brief, and guarded. He heard no useful information while he spied on the two men, but he was able to pick out Téadora's name a few times. The Senator seemed quite concerned about her, and this upset Oenomaus. Seeing Téadora in Rome was worth than losing her to this war. It would absolutely kill her to become that man's wife and lose Spartacus. And that's the only way Furius would get his way, if Spartacus was to be slain in battle. On his way back to his men on sentry duty Oenomaus grappled with the idea of what to do with what he had learned. Spartacus was his leader and deserved to know all the facts so he could make a proper and informed decision which could potentially impact the lives of over a hundred thousand men and women. But on the other hand, if no one knew Furius was here, and no one knew Varinius intended to create a legacy for himself by his actions in the morning, certain pressure need not be applied to an already tense situation. Oenomaus was not good at moral dilemmas. His moral compass didn't exactly point true north, but he knew one man's whose did. Besides, he owed Gannicus an apology for stealing sentry duty from him tonight, again. It wasn't like the ginger bearded man held a grudge, but Oenomaus was in dire need of a good talking to by the closest thing to a father figure man men in this army had. The Germanians remained on patrol around the walls of Mutina while Oenomaus welcomed himself to Gannicus' campfire. The Celt commander was thoroughly confused to see Oenomaus so early in the night.

"What troubles you, Oenomaus?"

"Is it that obvious something is bothering me?"

"Why else would you come seeking me out?"

"I was spying on Varinius while he talked to the Governor. That old man made a fortune off of my matches in the gladiator arenas. I almost feel bad being angry with him. He expressed regret, but still, I bear the scars of his fortune. He's only governor here because of men like me. And now, he sits in his walled cities, safe from the world, and allowed to live out his days. He tried putting Varinius in his place, but the praetor will not be scolded. He's acting like a spoiled child eager to please a parent who cares nothing for him. The battle will be fierce tomorrow morning."

"And what do you want me to tell you?"

"I spared Varinius in Lucania because I wanted Spartacus to have the chance to kill him in battle. Now I wonder if that was a huge mistake. Crixus was lost at Garganus because I spared Varinius."

"No, Oenomaus. We lost Crixus because he was blinded by hate. If you had killed Varinius in Lucania, we'd still be fighting Rome today, it would just be another man's name on our lips. You are worked up because a battle is coming up. That's all this is. Go back to sentry duty. Keep your mind busy with the task at hand. Do not let your mind go wandering into the shadows."

"There's something else. Senator Furius is also here."

"Has he a legion with him?"

"No. He's here alone. Varinius didn't even know he was here. The Governor let that slip."

"So, the Senate is not keeping Varinius informed. That is good news for us. Why are you so upset still?"

"The Senator is here for Téadora."

"How could he have possibly known she'd be here?"

"He's been tracking her. You know as well as I do how closely he followed her matches when we were in the House of Batiatus. He wants to make a wife of her and he will not be told no. For all of his mild manners, the man is persistent, I'll give him that."

"She won't go with him."

"I know. But should I tell Spartacus about this?"

"If you tell Spartacus, he'll tell Téadora. He tells her everything."

"I know. But do either of them need to know what's going on inside the walls of Mutina? That is why I have come to you tonight. I don't know what to do. I don't like the idea of lying to either of them, but there's over a hundred thousand men and women depending on those two to have the fight of their lives tomorrow morning. I volunteered for sentry duty. I have to tell Spartacus something."

"Tell him only what he needs to know. Mention nothing of the Senator. Nothing of Varinius either. Spartacus needs only the facts. Give him hard information, numbers, locations of the soldiers, where the gates in and out of the walls are, things of that nature."

"I haven't got any of those answers."

"Then I guess you better go out and get them, huh?"

"Thank you, Gannicus."

"For what?"

"Being the father I never had. I know you might not want to hear that from me. We're almost the same age, but it's true. You've helped more men and women in this camp than you realize. We are lucky to have you."

Gannicus sat there a little stunned beside his campfire. Oenomaus excused himself and ran back into the darkness to try and make himself useful, setting aside the gossip he had overheard. The Celt commander stroked his ginger beard and sat with the advice he had just given. Looking across camp he could see that Spartacus and Téadora were pouring over maps by their campfire. They were deep in discussion, as they typically were if they were not kissing. They did not need this information that sat on Gannicus' conscience. It would not help them if they knew, nor harm them if they remained ignorant. Morale was at an all-time high as Gannicus scanned the camp's numerous fires. There was no need to pretend to hide. Varinius knew Spartacus was here and vice versa. The men could not have coordinated this rendezvous any better if they tried. The stars aligned. It was the will of the gods. Gannicus wondered who the victor might be. The slave army only seemed to take their winnings in the dark. Tomorrow morning there would be the clashing of blades at sunrise. Whatever the case, the army had tonight together, to laugh, and tell war stories and reminisce. Gannicus sharpened his swords and knives. He'd collected quite an arsenal for himself by now, carrying twice that of any other man in the army. He took care of them well, cleaned them and maintained them. All of them stolen at one point or another. Some of them were fishing knives, hunting knives, curved knives. Some had busted blades, short blades, long blades. Some had sheaths, most did not. It was a good thing Gannicus was such a stocky man otherwise his waist would not have enough room to house all his weapons. Gannicus chuckled at his waistline. He used to be so skinny in his youth. By some accounts he was still young. He was only in his thirties, upper thirties. Oenomaus thought of him as a father, though there was only two years between them. And others thought of the ginger bearded man as a father too. He was kind words and tough love for them. It was all he knew. He wasn't trying to be a father figure. He was just being himself. It was good enough. Gannicus looked at his campfire, and thanked his long-lost lover Muire. He could see her smiling at him from the flames. He knew whenever he saw her image when he was awake, that he needed to close his eyes and shut the world away for a few hours. That was his sign that the day was done. He'd never disregard a message from his Muire.

  Dawn came almost impossibly too fast. Some men had been so worked up for the battle ahead they hadn't even slept. Oenomaus had been moving all night, from one gate to another so he knew Mutina like the back of his own tattooed hand. Gannicus woke early, as did Téadora. She was incessantly sharpening her sica blades by her morning fire as the soldiers rose for the day. Spartacus did not wake up for another hour or so. When he did finally crawl out of his tent, he wrapped himself around Téadora, and fixed her blades in their straps tied to her waist. She tended to his weapons as well, securing them and cleaning them. She straightened out his mother's silver ring necklace, making sure it shined in the morning light. Téadora was the only one allowed to touch that sacred little piece of home. Every soldier had their special little something that they carried with them, some trinket of personal value. They had rituals, routines, prayers to the gods that had to be conducted in a very specific way. It was heavy that morning, in the camp, as it was heavy inside of the walls of Mutina. The Romans were no more pleased about them being here than the locals were. But the quicker this battle got started, the quicker it ended, and the survivors could begin to process what they had to do to move forward. That's where Téadora's head was. She was hyper fixated on that night. Where would they be camping, how would they tackle the Alps. Spartacus did not share her sentiment. He could not see that far out. He just kept staring at the stone walls. He wished he could see through them, see the Romans scrambling to maintain order. They'd be in their nice, blocked up ranks and file. Men had their orders. Spartacus knew the drill; he'd been a part of it for years. He was not a part of it anymore though. His men were free. They fought as they saw fit. They scattered like ants, encompassing everything that they could as fast as they could. Commanders had some control, but that was also an illusion, to think anyone had control in war. Men were going to do what they were going to do. They were going to live or die or run. Varinius made the first move. At daybreak he climbed up to the top of the wall along the southern gate, and released his archers. Spartacus had the Thracians and Gauls with him in the south. Gannicus had the Celts in the west, Oenomaus the Germanians in the north. To the west Téadora had the smallest force with the women, and Castus with the healers. Everyone was fighting.

The Romans spent very little time shoring up the weaker defenses to the east and west. It was not the way the town was oriented. The pathways were too narrow to allow a large fighting force through. There was a lot of single file walkways and alleys. Gannicus and Téadora did meet up fairly quickly, and fairly unharmed to the surprise of them both. Gannicus and Castus hugged, but were unsettled by the sound of battle on both sides of them. Téadora lunged for the southern gate where she knew Spartacus was having trouble, but Gannicus insisted she go north because her force was smaller and the women fought better with the Germanians. There was no need to argue a proven point. The Celts had fought with the Thracians many a time, and Téadora was confident that Gannicus could help Spartacus with his superior numbers. While Téadora and Castus ran for the northern gate to reinforce the Germanians, they happened to pass by the room in the hillside that

Senator Furius was seeking shelter in. Crouching beside his window, he made the unmistakable identification of his desire running past him with her sica blades drawn, and charcoal streaked across her eyes. He half thought to make himself known to her, but he was too ashamed to think she would not positively receive him. He carefully ducked his blonde head back into the recesses of his room, and decided to wait the battle out for a more opportune moment. Many locals were doing the same. They had abandoned their streets, shops, and markets. The governor was also hiding in his private quarters. This was why Oenomaus had gotten caught up. He was consumed with a personal vendetta and he could not be talked out of it. Téadora spotted him on a second story balcony and called out to him, but the Germanian could not be stopped. Téadora climbed up, at the caution of Castus, to try and help her friend and fellow commander while the Germanians plowed through the Roman forces on the ground. Castus took shelter in an abandoned shop but kept Téadora in his sights at all times, praying to the gods for her safe return to him. The gladiatrix commander was good on her feet, and scaled walls as well as buildings as confidently as a cat. When she jumped onto the balcony where she had last seen Oenomaus, she was slow to speak to her friend. He was standing over a very bloody old man, neither gloating nor sobbing. Téadora was careful to come up behind Oenomaus, and startled when he turned to bury his face in her neck.

"I had to do it. I just had to! He begged me for mercy. He said he was sorry. I *had* to kill him. I couldn't help myself. So many matches. So many faces!"

"What's done is done, Oenomaus. Come with me. You are not in the arena. Let's leave this place. Spartacus needs our help in the south."

"I killed an old man in his home."

"We've all done things we're not proud of."

"I couldn't stop myself."

"Oenomaus, it's done."

"Who will be the governor now?"

"Succession of Mutina is the least of our worries right now. Varinius is at the south gate killing our friends. We need to stop him. Will you help me?"

Oenomaus stood up and dried his tears, nodding in agreement for Téadora's sake. She had never seen him so shaken up before. She felt like she was losing him and he wasn't even gone, but he also wasn't here. She tugged at his hand and led him downstairs. They regrouped with Castus and drove their portion of the army south, hoping to pin Varinius and the remaining Romans like they had pinned Crixus. It was chaos. Legions were slaughtered. Spartacus had been captured by several guards close to Varinius, and the Thracian had been knocked unconscious. While the army raged, the Romans died. Téadora panicked seeing Spartacus carried along an upstairs walkway. She tore at Castus' arm to get him to follow her because he was simply not moving fast enough as she hopped over bodies and walls and jars, and plants, and anything else that might have stood in her way. Castus could not keep up, but he tried his damndest to keep on her heels. When Téadora took an arrow to the shoulder it was Castus' arms she fell back into and screamed. Across the courtyard Gannicus locked eyes with Oenomaus. Gannicus shook his head no, but Oenomaus had already made up his mind. The Germanian picked up where Téadora had left off. He scaled the wall and chased down where Varinius had Spartacus carried off to. He ran into the little room, trapped, and had the door slammed behind him. Spartacus lied unconscious on the floor while Varinius sneered, sword drawn. Dacia was being held back by guards behind the praetor. She was trying to mime a warning to the Germanian, but he was not understanding. Oenomaus took a step forward to attack Varinius, but two swords came jutting into his back from behind. He dropped to his knees, unable to breathe. Varinius raised his weapon in a kill strike above Oenomaus' tattooed head.

"Any last words, *slave*?"

"For those about to die, we salute you."

XV

When Spartacus woke up, Oenomaus lied dead beside him. The Germanian commander had two gaping holes in his back, and a severed throat. Spartacus was warm and wet in his friend's blood. The room was otherwise empty, and the battle over. Rome had lost again, but the cost was great. As Spartacus carried Oenomaus' body down into the courtyard of Mutina, the first thing he saw was Téadora, with a bloodied bandage around her shoulder, sobbing at the sight of him. She crawled over bodies in pain to place her hands on Oenomaus' face, and close his eyes. Spartacus could see her hands were shaking as she tried to process the loss of her friend. She had been chasing Varinius because he had Spartacus. As if the potential loss of him wasn't enough, now he was alive, standing before her, but Oenomaus was gone. Oenomaus, the man who could never be beaten in a match in the arena. The man who struck fear in the hearts of men just by looking at them. It didn't make sense to see him dead, but Téadora could see the severed white strips of muscle in his neck, and there was no coming back from this. Spartacus laid his commander down in the courtyard with the rest of the dead being lined up. Castus was elbow deep in injuries, as were the other healers, trying to asses who was going to live past sunset, and who was not. The slave army had beaten back the Romans and taken the city, but it did not feel like victory today. Gannicus was posted up on the walls to keep an eye on the enemy's retreat. They were running back towards the coast where they had left their ships. It was anyone's guess where they would be going next. Winter was coming. The weather would be unforgiving soon. The Alps were within reach. Home was within reach. But it also wasn't. Spartacus sat beside Teadora on the stone floor of the courtyard, she was still mourning Oenomaus. She could not stop crying, or laughing. It was an odd mixture only Oenomaus would have understood.

"We will bury the men outside the walls in the field."

"Oenomaus did not want to go into the ground. He wanted to be burned like an ancient hero, with coins on his eyes. I will build a pyre for him. He was a commander. He deserves that from us."

"But your shoulder is injured."

"Oenomaus is only dead because of me, Spartacus."

"Téa don't blame yourself for what happened."

"*I* brought him to the south gate. *I* asked him to help me. That's all he was doing. It's all he ever did. Half the scars on his body came from punishments he took covering me in the House of Batiatus or one of the many arenas we were taken too. I would mouth off at a lanista, or a sponsor in the halls. I cut a spectator once at a match in Capua, nearly killed him. He deserved it though. He was being very crude. Oenomaus said if we ever crossed that man when we were free, he'd kill him for me. This war is going to be so hard for me without him at our side."

"I don't know how much of a war we have left to fight. We've taken the city. The Alps aren't that far off. We can be home by winter."

"I can't go home now. Rome must pay for what they've taken from me. Oenomaus needs to be avenged."

"But we've come all this way, Téa."

"And we can come all this way again. Spartacus, you have an army to think about. I understand. But I am not crossing those Alps until Rome knows what they have taken from me. Until Varinius knows. I want him to see the pain in my face. I want him to know. All Oenomaus ever did was look out for me. Now I need to look out for the memory of him. Once that is settled, then I can go home with a clear head. But if I crossed the Alps now, I'd never forgive myself."

"I won't go anywhere without you."

"Spartacus, think clearly. You can't move thousands of men just because of a decision *I* have made."

"We make decisions together, you and me. If you stay, I stay. Where you go, I go. That's not up for negotiation. If the men don't like it, they can do as they wish, just like it's always been."

"Thank you."

"I will try and help you through this any way that I can."

"I am so sorry to change your plans. I know how badly you've been wanting to go home."

"Going home would be meaningless if you were not with me. My dream is *you*, Téa. We can make a home anywhere."

"We will not make a home in the empire. Dream sweetly for me while I seek this revenge, please?"

"Of course. Take as long as you need. I'm going to take a walk, try and figure out where the men's heads are at. Will you be alright here with Oenomaus?"

"We'll be fine. I have a few things I need to thank him for before I start gathering wood for his pyre. I'm alright, Spartacus, really."

Spartacus hugged Téadora tightly before he excused himself. When she put her mind to something, there was nothing Spartacus could say to dissuade her. Injured or not, she was going to push herself to do right by her friend. As the Thracian leader took a tour of the devastation of Mutina, it was clear the consensus amongst the Germanians was that they were going home. Spartacus wished them well, and hoped for an easy crossing of the Alps. As for him, he had to explain that because of the loss of Oenomaus, he was going to remain in this war until debts had been settled. One look at Téadora was all the explanation anyone needed. The slave army hadn't suffered heavy losses in this battle, but many friendships had been severed. The idea of debt was heavy on the minds of the survivors. In total, about seventy-five thousand men, about two-thirds of the army, was going to stay with Spartacus. It might not have been the wisest decision to make, but it was felt right in their hearts. They were sitting in the ruins of a town where the governor had been murdered and the citizens terrorized. They would not stay in Mutina. Spartacus suspected Varinius would be sailing south for the winter, and the slaves needed to go south too. Once again, they'd be trailing along the countryside through river valleys and farmland to try and raid enough to get by. It was a hard way to go about things, but the army was hard, and not ashamed of it. To play it safe, Gannicus suggested the army make winter quarters in the familiar territory of the Bruttium peninsula, quite a travel from where they were now, but worth the time it'd take to get there. It'd be a few weeks, but no one was complaining when Spartacus made the official announcement that evening. He did so in the grave filled fields outside the stone walls of Mutina. Téadora lit Oenomaus' pyre aflame, and everyone stood quietly as they watched the fire flicker up into the starlight.

Rome did not wait for Varinius to return to them with bad news. The Senate received letters explaining the loss at Mutina weeks before the praetor could arrive to try and explain himself. An interim governor had to be appointed, and Varinius was relieved of his authority to control the issue of the slave revolt. Taking over the fight was an established, middle aged praetor named Marcus Crassus. There was hardly a man in the empire who wielded more influence. He was considered the richest man in Rome, worth somewhere around one hundred and seventy million sesterces. If anyone could stop Spartacus, it was going to be Crassus. The Senate also endowed the praetor with six legions numbering forty-five thousand men. As a personal favor to his younger sister, Crassus was bringing along his bumbling nephew, Mummius, as an aide in the war. Mummius was a simple boy of barely eighteen, and was not good at much of anything but complaining and pointing out obvious flaws that everyone else possessed enough social graces not to voice out loud. What one does for family never made much sense to the public but because Crassus' decisions were above reproach, the boy joined the legions with all the ceremony of the other young recruits. When Varinius arrived in Rome he had been humbled ten times over by his rising defeats, and the news of his replacement in command did little to add to his dwindling self-esteem. The young praetor proved himself useful though by directing Crassus to the Bruttium peninsula where he knew the slaves to have made their winter camp. Wanting to keep on top of things, Crassus quickly left Rome for the peninsula, and made his own camp a day's ride away. The elder praetor assigned his nephew surveillance of the slaves. This was done for two reasons. Primarily, it was so Mummius wouldn't mess anything up in the camp and degrade Crassus' nearly flawless reputation. The lesser reason was Crassus needed intelligence on the enemy. There were many more ways the elder praetor could have gone about this, but, even if the boy was blood, he was still seen as expendable. Crassus was not about to send any man out to the slaves who he would be upset to lose. Mummius did not understand his uncle's strategy, so when he was assigned to be a scout for the legions, it was one of the proudest moments of his life. Just to be sure his nephew wasn't a complete hazard to himself, Crassus also sent two centurions to guard the young man in case there was some sort of unforeseen threat out in the peninsular countryside. No one volunteered for the guard positions but Crassus was able to pay handsomely to compensate for the less than glorious job.

  Spartacus and his army arrived to their winter quarters without issue. They set up camp in the hills between villages and took to raiding on rotating schedules like nothing had changed. The only difference they had to make up for was the lack of intimidation they were used to holding with Oenomaus and his Germanians. Not all of them had left, but compared to the resounding force they used to have, now Spartacus was left with merely a handful. They were half Germanians, mixed with Roman or Celtic blood. They were also men of little allegiance aside from the debt they owed to their dead friends, and the respect they held for Spartacus. Some of them had married Téadora's gladiatrices. There would be babies born in the springtime. There was talk of kidnapping some midwives from the nearby towns when the time arose. Téadora would handle that though. Spartacus was not fond of families in his army. He wanted them to build a home, get out of the business of fighting. It was a good stance to take, but not necessarily all that realistic. For many misfits and rejects of society, this army had become their family. The escaped gladiators from the House of Batiatus had forged bonds that ran years. Even since their escape and the following recruitment, it had been over a year, closer to a year and half this winter. Téadora softened Spartacus to the idea of maintaining familial stability to their soldiers. It might have been dysfunctional from a Roman perspective, but a collective, more tribal dependence was what most of these people grew up on, including them. Gannicus and his Celts stepped up into a more permanent role as sentries, and would often look out for Castus and his healers as they wondered the river valleys and hillsides for herbs to keep up the health of the army. As the months grew on though, and the thick of winter was upon them, Castus found himself having to travel farther and farther to find what he needed. Some of the pregnant soldiers craved berries that only grew on distant hills. And some of the ailments to be treated could only be quieted with herbs from valleys a day's ride away. Castus took his role as a healer very seriously. He had no trouble riding out for these errands on a weekly basis. While his cousin Gannicus urged caution, the curly headed healer merely took that as paranoia. In winter, no one was hunting them. The slave army was enjoying peace in the cold weather, and it had dulled their battle readiness. Castus was naïve in trusting that peace, and that was going to cost him. Mummius might not have known much, but he did know the importance of a praetor and their white horses. Seeing Castus, foraging out all on his own, on a white Roman horse, caused more than just casual suspicion in the eager teenager. He really thought he was on to something when he brought this up to his centurions one evening while they were eating dinner around a campfire. Usually, the men just shrugged off what the teenager had to say, but the mention of a white horse caught their attention. The next time Castus was out collecting herbs, he was followed back to the slave camp from a safe distance by the pair of centurions. They watched as Castus hugged Téadora, and gave her the bundles of what he had gathered. Upon further inspection, the centurions were also able to watch Téadora go to her tent that she shared with Spartacus, and the centurions smelled a promotion in the air for the both of them.

    When Crassus was informed by his nephew that he'd taken a hostage of the slave army, it was understandable that the praetor placed little faith in this news. It was not until the centurions produced Castus, beaten, bloody, and tied like an animal, did the older man get a smile on his face. To add to this revelation was the return of a white horse. Crassus ordered the horse be taken to the stables for care while he intended to interrogate Castus personally. The curly haired Celt was hardly in the shape for conversation, doubled over on his knees, and refusing to hold eye contact, but Crassus could be persuasive. A couple swift kicks to his side and Castus raised his eyes to meet his enemy. His tears were mixing from the blood of his battered nose, and seeping into the gag in his mouth. Crassus untied the gag so that his hostage might speak, but all Castus did was spit on the praetor's feet and curse in Celt. No amount of pain would get the man to talk. Mummius stood worried in the corner of his uncle's tent. If Castus wouldn't speak, Mummius would make up for it with the information that he and the centurions had. But the teenager didn't know what he was talking about, or what pieces of information were important. He was giving half estimations on numbers of tents, and sentry positions. He did not know where the officers of the slaver army were, or how many of them were were. He did not know where they raided, on what days. He did not account for weapons, or how big the cavalry was. Crassus felt the need to slap his nephew for getting his hopes up, but the praetor took his anger out on Castus instead. When the healer rolled to the ground, he had fallen unconscious unintentionally, and the centurions picked up his limp body and hauled it into a cart in camp. Dacia recognized Castus from her dreams, and ran to tell Varinius something was wrong. This was the young praetor's chance to regain a little respect for himself and his time served in the war against the slaves. As the centurions pulled Castus out of the Roman's winter camp and back towards his own people, Varinius welcomed himself inside his leader's tent with a smug grin and began popping grapes from a gold bowl. Crassus was not amused by Varinius newfound confidence, and wanted an explanation.

"What is the meaning of this, Varinius?!"

"You're making a terrible mistake letting that hostage go."

"You know who he is, don't you?"

"I know who he is."

"Then tell me!"

"Castus is the main healer in the slave army. He's a cousin of the Celtic commander, Gannicus, a ginger bearded man. Your hostage just also so happens to be close friends with a gladiatrix commander named Téadora."

"I know that name."

"That's the same woman Senator Felix Furius has been chasing up and down the empire for over a year now."

"And why is this woman of any importance to me?"

"Téadora is Spartacus' woman. So, if you want to end the war and break the man, you must first be getting to her. And you get to her by getting to her friends. Ergo, that hostage you just hauled off."

"Should I call them back?!"

"You're the leader here, not me."

"Varinius, this is no time for games. You and I are on the same side!"

"Are we though? Because I have been treated as little more than a foot soldier ever since you and your legions stepped into this war. I'm not saying if I had the same resources you had that I'd be any further along, but I know if it were up to me, I'd never have let Castus out of my camp."

"You and I are two *very* different men."

"I couldn't agree more."

"You had your chance to stop this war. The Senate gave you a year. All you managed to produce in that time was three embarrassing defeats and a dead governor."

"That may be true, but my legion was composed of volunteers, veterans, and boys. The Senate gave you six times the manpower and you have enough coin to stop ten slave armies. Do not confuse your wealth for intelligence, Crassus."

"How dare you come into my tent and insult me like this!"

"How dare you overlook the sacrifices I have already put into this war! We *are* on the same side, Crassus. It's about time you understood what that means. I am no boy to order around. I am a praetor, same as you. I know the enemy. I have had their blood on my hands, and their voices haunt my dreams. You know nothing of what I have seen. Don't be so quick to dismiss me."

"How long have you been waiting to stand up to me?"

"Since I found out I was being replaced."

"I did not go asking for this job, Varinius. The Senate came to *me* with a problem and I promised them I could solve it. Can I count on you to fight with me?"

"I had no intention of fighting against you. Tell me, what are your plans moving forward?"

For the first time in weeks Crassus and Varinius sat down like equals to pour over maps and strategies for the upcoming season. Dacia watched the men's shadows through the tent and hoped this was not a one-time encounter. Before she could return to her own campfire on the outskirts of the camp however, she caught sight of the consuls Publicola and Clodianus lurking around Crassus' tent. Mummius was still pouting outside as well, waiting for the invitation back in so he could explain himself to his uncle. While the teenager had been warned time and time again not to engage or let himself be seen by the slave army, he was tired of waiting around for the opportunity to prove himself as a worthy member of this army. With like minded eagerness, Mummius asked Publicola and Clodianus for help to go an invade the slave army's camp under the cover of darkness. It was such a stupid idea that even Dacia did not see this coming. Within a couple of minutes though, many young men in camp had been roused from their campfires and were gearing up for some sort of half-baked ambush. They fled on foot with snickers and boyish giggles. Dacia could do nothing to stop them. No officers respected her from Crassus' legions. She was little more than a whore in many of the men's eyes. To go and warn Varinius or Crassus was certainly punishable by a beating and she was in no mood to be cold and sore. Perhaps it was better for her to stay silent, let the fools get their own comeuppance in due time. It would be long. A couple hundred young souls against an entire slave army, one which had a perfect record of victories when attacked at night. Dacia walked back to her tent and laid down. This was going to be a very ugly night indeed, and she just wanted to go to sleep.

Despite the two centurions having a head start in their walk back towards the slave camp with Castus in a wagon, the impromptu Roman war party overtook them and surpassed them with ease. Not wanting to miss out on the potential victory, Castus was abandoned in a wagon in the middle of the grassy path, and left to his own devices so the centurions could go satiate their blood lust. It took a couple of hours before Castus woke up, and that was only because of the familiar war cries of the gladiatrices ringing in his ears. In a dazed panic he was able to free himself of his restrains, wriggle out of the ropes, and start running back for camp. When he arrived, he was flooded with the memories of what had happened around the base of Vesuvius. It was just dead Romans everywhere. The survivors were few and scampering like rats across the earth. Armor and weapons were being looted. Spartacus' army had no warning, but they weren't in need of it. Gannicus and his Celtic sentries were enough of a barrier to keep the camp safe. Castus was limping and confused. He had left for a routine foraging expedition and returned with nothing but a beaten body and a lot of questions. He was looking for a sympathetic face amongst his friends and was having trouble finding one. He could see Téadora off in the distance but she was tending a cut on Spartacus' arm. Castus didn't want to interrupt, but he was caught staring by his cousin who was less than pleased to see him so disheveled. Gannicus gave Castus a slight shove on his shoulder and the curly haired man nearly dropped to his knees.

"Alright, alright. I'm sorry. Where have you been, Castus? What's happened to you?"

"It's nothing."

"It's not nothing. Who did this to you?"

"No one did this to me. I…"

"You what?"

"I fell off my horse."

"Where is your horse?"

"I don't know. Must have run off. I was knocked out. Lost a lot of time. What's happened here?"

"Bunch of little Romans thought they'd be smart and raid us at night. Bunch of little fools is what they are. *Were*. Most of them are dead now. I only saw a few run back from where they came. They must be close. They keep a poor camp if no officers got a hold of them."

"You don't think this was an organized attack?"

"The way they separated? No. This was little more than a child's prank trying to get a rise out of us. Well, we're awake alright, and they learned that the hard way. We've been looting the bodies. There were no men of rank here. They had no idea what they were doing."

"Did anyone ask about me while I was gone today?"

"Téadora did find it odd you were taking so long."

"Was she worried? Should I go talk to her?"

"And tell her what? You don't even seem too comfortable with the truth yourself. You just stood there and lied to me."

"I didn't lie."

"Castus, I have known you your entire life, and not once have you ever been able to successfully tell a lie. I also know you're one of the best men on horseback I've ever seen, so all that about falling off of your horse, I didn't believe a word. You were attacked, and you won't say by who. Maybe you're…embarrassed?"

"I was ambushed by two centurions. They took me hostage. I was in a praetor's tent. Not Varinius'. They have a new man, an older man with black hair. He kept kicking me."

"I'll kill him!"

"I blacked out. When I woke up, I was in a wagon, and I heard the women screaming. That's the truth of it. Don't tell Téadora. I don't want her to think any less of me than she probably already does. It's so stupid. I'd die for that woman, and she barely knew I was gone."

"Don't speak like that, Castus. You say you're willing to die for loving Téadora, but you don't know the first thing about what it is to take life or give your heart away. She is Spartacus' woman. Get that through your head before you get yourself caught in an accident you can't walk back from. Clean yourself up. You're a mess."

XVI

When Crassus found out about his nephew's impromptu attack on Spartacus' camp, to say he was outraged would have been an understatement. If not for the profound love for his little sister, Crassus would have slaughtered his nephew. Instead, he made Mummius suffer with the mistake of his insubordination. Despite Varinius' desire for the two praetors to make decisions about this war together, Crassus was above cooperation. It was not the way he had won his influence or his wealth. Sometimes, it paid to be the monster in people's minds. Dacia had seen terrible visions blurred by blood in the recent days. It was getting so bad she was sick to her stomach, and demanded Varinius move his camp away from Crassus, at least for the evening. The praetor was still granted a legion of his own. His men were loyal to him, and did not mind snuffing out their campfires or packing up their tents even though it was time to call it for the day. The legion moved under starlight, and in the cover of smoke. Crassus was so blinded by rage he did not pay his colleague any attention. Varinius rode out before the camp could get ugly, and it was about to get very, very ugly. Dacia couldn't hold back her emotions anymore, and rode out on a white praetor's horse, sobbing as she looked at the faces of the men she was leaving.

The Romans had a practice known as decimation. Due to it's cruel and violent, sometimes even barbaric nature, it had been discontinued for hundreds of years. Crassus was a modern man, well educated, and perhaps that was the problem. He knew about decimation, knew the carnage involved, but he also knew the effects and the aftermath. He gave a whistle, and gathered his legions. Some of the young men from Mummius' failed attack were still trickling in, a little beaten, bloody, and heavily embarrassed. Crassus was giving a speech on loyalty, the importance of unity and trust for an army. He preached of past military greats, Rome's finest moments. He knew them all, and captivated his soldiers. They felt inspired, and uplifted, albeit a little arrogant in thinking their names were about to go down in history as mighty heroes. Crassus then looked down at his nephew by his side, gripped him by the shoulders tight and pulled him in close with a smile full of gleaming clenched teeth. At first the nephew thought he was going to get praise for what he had just done, defeat or not, his heart was in the right place. Then his uncle began to dig his fingertips into his skin, and blood was drawn. Mummius could not wriggle away as Crassus forcefully held him at his side, and now the legions grew fearfully silent. The praetor was not pleased at all, his direct orders had been disobeyed and there would be hell to pay. Mummius was forced to identify the groups of men who had run out with him tonight. Whole battalions of men had gone. Out of the six legions, five now with Varinius' men trekking away to safety, there was only five hundred men that had run with Mummius. Five hundred. Crassus smiled, and had the men line up like they were going on a march in block formation. It was a little different though. No weapon, no armor, no flag bearer. The block was different. Not lines of two for narrow paths. Not lines of five for wider valleys. Fifty lines of ten. Crassus walked up and down with Mummius, confirming the men involved. Some could not stand upright because of their injuries from Spartacus' army. But they stood obedient to the best of their abilities. A couple were wheezing, having just run back. Mummius confirmed again these were the men loyal to him. The teenager was then placed at the head of these lines, as Crassus began to explain the ancient practice of decimation. It almost didn't seem real as the men began to slowly digest what was about to happen to them, and by who.

Decimation, as it's name suggested, involved ten men at one time. There were fifty of these lines of ten before Mummius. Friends he had made in the couple weeks they'd spent together. Friends from school, and his hometown. There were a lot of politician's sons here, veterans' sons, poor men's sons who needed the money and wanted a little world experience. A wife was always easier to get if you had a battle scar or two, a good war story. Mummius dropped to his knees when his uncle continued explaining what was about to happen. He didn't want to see it, but Crassus was going to make sure he did. Two centurions picked the teenager up and forced him to his feet, forced him to look forwards as the first line was ordered to fight to the death. Line by line, the ten men would take a democratic approach to who was going to die. They would come to a decision, either quickly or not. Nine would beat a man in their line to death, until all fifty lines had been gone through. Crassus paraded the outside of the block of five hundred the entire time, preaching loyalty, unity, and the importance of following orders. When a line had completed the act of killing a man, they then had to haul the body to the side, and make a pile. The nine men would dig a grave with their bare hands, and put their fellow soldier in the earth, cover him up then go back to their tents. Crassus promised, if anyone ever got the bright idea to act out on their own, or to disobey him, he would keep up this practice of decimation until he had an army completely devoted to him. There was no falter in his voice, no inflection he was boasting or bragging. The first line had taken their sweet time to come to a vote on who to kill. They had picked an already injured man succumbing to his wounds. The second line acted a little quicker. By the time the fifth line came up, and the first few lines were struggling digging graves, the men were becoming angry. They were picking fights with each other, yelling at each other on who had to be the one to die. Scraps were breaking out, wrestling matches. Crassus allowed all of it. It was death, and chaos, and sadness, and defeat. Such utter defeat and embarrassment. Mummius hung in the centurion's arms as he couldn't stand on his own two feet any longer. The teenager was mortified, broken to his core. Crassus came up, and firmly gripped his nephew by the chin.

"You disobey me again, and I'll put you in a line with the others."

Varinius had no intention of moving his camp all that far away from Crassus. He did not want to offend the older praetor or give him rise to suspect there was any sort or discord between the two men. Varinius simply moved to please Dacia, though she hardly seemed cured as the camp reestablished itself. He was not happy with the move; the timing made him uncomfortable. He felt like he was missing out on something so while his men pitched tents and tried to make a campfire or two, most were too tired to do even that, the young praetor marched off to the hillside where he could look down at Crassus in the valley below. It did not make sense to him what he was seeing. The older praetor was having his men kill each other. It seemed terrible counterintuitive to the war effort, but Varinius couldn't get himself to look away. He was hoping the more he watched, the more he might be able to understand. But there was no understanding this. It was just horrible from every angle. And the legions were watching this too. They had not been permitted to walk away or go to sleep. There was a lesson to be learned tonight, and that lesson was that Crassus was to be feared more than Spartacus and his army. Crassus was the man who held your life in the palm of his hand, and it was not a hand with a steady mind attached to it. Varinius saw his colleague smiling through the carnage, demanding the graves be dug faster, the pile of dead bodies was stacking up as line by line the fighting ensued. The block deformed. In the time Varinius sat there, he watched ten boys die. As the next line was about to come up, he was distracted by a sniffling behind him. He didn't even need to turn around to know it was Dacia. She had her arms wrapped around herself to try and keep herself together, but she was falling apart like water in a cracked bowl. Her hair was undone, flying about in the winds on the hills. Varinius got up to go to her but she stepped back from him. He was thoroughly confused.

"Why step back? *You* came to *me*, Dacia."

"Now you know why I asked you to move the camp?"

"This is what you saw in your visions? What even is this?!"

"Your people call it *decimation*."

"It's a massacre."

"It instills obedience by fear, which is apparently what your friend wants in his camp."

"Tomorrow will be a good day for the crows I suppose."

"You're a dark man, Varinius, you know that?"

"Thank you."

"It wasn't a compliment."

"To each their own."

"What's happened to you?"

"What do you mean?"

"You never used to be like this."

"Be like what?"

"Cold. Heartless."

"How am I heartless? Did I not listen to you when you came to me on bended knee and asked me to move the camp? Did I hesitate? Did I ask you one *single* question?"

"No."

"No. Because I trust you, Dacia. Whatever you need, it's yours."

"Whatever I need, so long as I don't ask for my freedom, right?"

"What is freedom anymore? We all serve someone. I am a generous owner to you. Do you deny it?"

"I do not deny it. But you have changed. You are trying to paint yourself in the image of Crassus, and it is most unbecoming."

"Crassus is the richest, most influential man in all of Rome. I should be so smart as to try and emulate that man."

"But I didn't fall in *love* with Crassus!"

"What?"

"Nothing! I said nothing! Forget I said anything. I should go."

"You said you were falling in love with me."

"I love *no* man! You are mistaken."

"I am not. I know what I heard. You love me."

"You know what you *think* you heard."

"I *know* what I heard, Dacia. Look at me. Look at me!"

"I *am* looking at you! I am *always* looking at you, Varinius. That is the problem."

"Why? Why am I a problem?"

"Your people have made a history of killing people like me."

"But I am not my people. I am me, and you are you. We are different than the rest of them."

"Are we? You keep me because I am useful. But I wonder, if I could not tell you of your battles before they happen, would you even want to keep me around anymore?"

"I love you, Dacia. Visions or not. That is not why I keep you. You have to know you are more to me than your talents."

"I do not love you, Varinius."

"I do not believe you. I know what I heard. I know what you just said. I felt it in my bones as you feel it in yours. There is no fighting this, what we have between us. Why are you so ashamed of it?"

"We are not good for each other."

"What is good? I mean after watching what's happening in the valley right now, I couldn't tell you anymore."

"Crassus will never trust you so long as you keep me around."

"Then I will not have Crassus' trust. To me, that seems like an awfully good thing. He's down there killing his own boys, and for what? Control? Pride? Ego?"

"I thought you wanted to be friends with him?"

"Before tonight, I *thought* that's what I wanted too. What I needed. But I *know* I want and need you more than anything. If I can't have his power *and* you, I choose *you*, Dacia."

"Really?"

"Really."

"What does this mean for the war?"

"I still want Spartacus' army to fall, he *needs* to fall, but if I can do that working more independently of Crassus, then I'd say that's quite a victory, wouldn't you?"

"What if he retaliates against you?"

"You will warn me."

"What if I can't see it?"

"I trust you, Dacia. I trust you with my life. You will not see harm come to me. Nor will I allow harm to you."

"It would be safer for you if I left."

"Where would you even go?"

"I don't know. But if it meant making you happy, getting the result you want in this war…"

"I want you with me."

"And I want to be with you, but it is not wise, and I am scared."

"Why are you scared?"

"I've never wanted a man like this. My concern for you clouds my judgement. I'm having trouble telling the difference between what will *actually* happen, and what my heart *wants* to happen. I've seen so many things come to pass, both horrible and delightful. I fear I'm losing my talent the closer I get to you."

"So, that's what it is all about."

"You will not keep me forever. My purpose is to tell you what you want to hear, and the second I can't do that…"

"I will still love you."

"You say that now, but you don't mean it. Not really."

"Don't tell me what I mean."

"I'm sorry. I'm just so overwhelmed right now."

"Come with me."

"Where are we going?"

Varinius held his hand out. It was clear he could talk until he was old and gray and Dacia might never believe him. She needed more than just pretty words from him right now, she needed hard proof. Something she could see. The seer was consumed with her fears, and so stuck inside of her head. She had convinced herself of heartbreak before anything had even happened. It was in her nature to prepare for the worst since that's what most often happened in her past. This was a fantasy anyways, to fall in love with a man who owned her. She knew this, she'd known this for years. She'd made mistakes in her youth she'd swore she'd never make again. But Varinius' blonde hair and blue eyes had her singing a different tune. He made her believe she was worth more than the intelligence she could give a man in battle or politics. To hear him say he'd keep her, talents or not, it was almost too good to be true. Varinius had Dacia by the hand, he was leading her to the tent she'd set up for them. He went digging through his belongings inside, pulling out the paper that said he owned her. It was her contract. He ripped it to shreds in front of her and she gasped, then he collected the pieces and threw them in the nearest campfire. Proof he was more than just pretty words. Proof she was worth more than the talents she had been cursed with. As the decimation continued through the last of the fifty lines in Crassus' camp, Varinius' camp was quite harmonious and peaceful this evening. Dacia was in a state of bliss, and in the praetor's arms, she was able to get the first quiet night of sleep she had had in years. And to think, all she had to do was be honest.

The next day Spartacus had his army on the move. He needed winter quarters to be further south, further out of reach of the Romans. If they were so close as to reach him in the middle of the night, then he was not paying close enough attention to his surroundings. More than anything, Spartacus viewed the little ambush as a wake-up call that he had become too comfortable as the months cooled. Gannicus needed to double the Celts' patrols, and leave no gaps in their lines, at any time of the day or night, in all kinds of weather. Gannicus too was a little embarrassed that the Roman boys had even been able to get that close. He prided himself on sentry duty and security. This was as much a mark on the leader's record as was his, maybe even more so because of the direct involvement of his cousin. Castus' injuries looked worse in the daylight. With a couple of hours passed, the swelling on his eyes had made him a useless navigator even though he was familiar with the southern peninsula's countryside. To keep him safe, Téadora took him with her as the female forces charted a new course for a campground. She was still keeping to the rive valleys for peace of mind, and held Castus' reins in her hand. He no longer had a white horse underneath him, but he remained on horseback, albeit propped and tied into position because of his injuries. There was an awkward slump in his body, and Téadora kept watching his curly head flop back and forth on the country paths. She tried to keep her friend informed of their surroundings, if they hit shade, what kind of tree it was, and if they passed a farm in harvest, what fruit was being picked. There were a lot of olives being collected right now. Many of the women helped themselves to wild trees dropping the fruit in the paths. Téadora stopped a collected a satchel full herself and paused the trek to eat a snack. She took Castus' hand in hers and dumped some of the black fruit in his hands. He was in so much pain he had no appetite, but he knew he had to eat, and for Téadora, Castus would do just about anything to please her. While the two sat in the shade beside a knee-high stone wall, Téadora took to carving an image of her tattoo in the ground where there was a fork in the road. Castus couldn't see what she was doing, but could hear her digging through the stones. She made a circle of seven dots, so Spartacus could follow her, then she slumped down beside Castus. He smiled, but it broke the cuts on his lips, and she had to reach up and catch the drips with her fingers. His eyes were completely black and swollen shut now. She grimaced, and was glad he could not see how uncomfortable she was.

"You're staring at me, aren't you, Teadora?"

"I am not staring. I'm just keeping an eye on you, Castus."

"That's called staring."

"You need to eat. I'm just making sure you put those olives in your mouth and don't dump them off behind you like the last time we stopped for a break."

"You noticed that, huh?"

"I notice an awful lot, but not nearly enough, I guess. Gannicus told me what happened to you last night."

"I told him not to say anything!"

"He was worried about you, Castus. And so am I. I don't need you running out trying to be a hero for this army."

"I wasn't trying to be the hero of this army."

"Good, because heroes die in war. They don't come back home. I don't want that fate for you."

"My death would upset you?"

"Greatly."

"Like you were upset for Oenomaus?"

"I will still avenge Oenomaus. He was a good friend to me, a good protector. But you and Oenomaus are two very different men. You are too kind for this war to take, Castus. You are too good at helping people to be cut down by a Roman. You should have just told them what they wanted to hear and come back to camp."

"They'd have beat me no matter what I said. Besides, if it had been you or Spartacus in my position, would you have squealed?"

"That's not a fair comparison to make. Spartacus is the face of our army; they want him dead. And *me*, they just want to make a Senator's wife of me. Breed me for exotic pleasure and brag to their friends. Carry me like a prize. You are not Spartacus. You are not me. You are Castus, and you deserved to be spared of this violence."

"You deserve to be spared as well, Téadora."

"Do I?"

"You deserve to be able to see home again."

"When we were in Mutina, and all the Germanians left to cross the Alps and go home, why did you not go with them?"

"I'm not a Germanian. The Celts stayed with Gannicus."

"And Gannicus stayed because?"

"I didn't want you to remember me as a coward who cut out on you. You were broken and in pain. You needed me to help you heal, and not just physically. I saw the toll it took on you to lose Oenomaus. But I was also the one who caught you when that arrow struck you on the wall as you chased Spartacus. I saw him. I thought he was dead too. I could only imagine what you must have been thinking. You couldn't lose everyone. I had to stay with you. There is no going home for me. I have no one aside from my cousin and you. He is determined to die in this war, be burned in flames and return to his Muire. I don't have anything to return to, in life or in death. You are all I have to look forward to. You are my best friend. I have no plans to leave you. If you go home, I would like…well, that is, if you would have me, I'd like to…"

"I'll show you where I grew up. You would love Samothraki, Castus. The water is the prettiest shade of blue you've ever seen. And it gets so warm in the summer. It almost never snows there. The fruit is the sweetest you have ever tasted in your whole life. Once you know life on Samothraki, you would *never* want to be anywhere else."

"It sounds wonderful."

"You are welcome to live out your days there. Spartacus and I have so many plans. If I knew I never had to say goodbye to you, it would be a dream come true."

"Then we shall never say our goodbyes. That is my promise to you."

XVII

To get some distance from Crassus for the winter, Spartacus had his army pushed into the tip of the Roman empire. It was his plan to gain passage to the island of Sicily where past slave revolts had experienced some victories. After witnessing how successful Varinius' travels had been by sea this year, it was enticing to think of the possibilities of the slaves not being land bound in the year to come. Téadora seemed to be the only one with apprehensions to this train of thought, and since she was overruled nearly unanimously, she kept her opinions to herself and remained largely silent as the army approached the coast. Where she was usually so happy to be in sight of salt water, now she was a burden to be around. She was uncooperative, untalkative, and very unlike herself. No one could cheer her up or get her to say more than two words. She answered every question with a head nod or shoulder shrug, and became close confidents with her white horse. The animal she would speak to. Gannicus insisted the mood would pass once the army reached Sicily. He tried time and again to get his cousin to speak to the gladiatrix commander, but she would not speak even to Castus. The secrets and pain she was guarding ran deep, and Spartacus had too many men behind him to go abandoning plans now. She didn't want to go north across the Alps and go home when they were at Mutina. She wanted to go south. Now that they were south, she wasn't happy here either. Spartacus was at his wit's end and would move forward however he could and just hoped she'd come around sooner rather than later. Téadora was far from abandoning him, but she had very strict opinions about sea travel, and it seemed none of that mattered to anyone anymore. While Spartacus went inside a taberna to try and barter passage to the nearby island of Sicily, Téadora busied herself with dangling her bare feet off the fishing pier. No man was stupid enough to try and sit next to her. Every couple of minutes she could be found looking over her shoulder into the taberna windows. Spartacus' shadow was illuminated alone. The man he was waiting for tonight was late, and she was not surprised. In the meantime, Gannicus had the army roaming the peninsula for any quick steals as opposed to an all-out, weapons charged raid. Téadora was never more than a stone's throw away from him. He was worried about her, and without being too overbearing, he knew he needed to stay close. She could be angry with him all she wanted, but he wasn't going anywhere.

    Spartacus was waiting for a man named Damanicus. He had never seen him in person before but the name was rampant around the southernmost peninsula as the man you needed to talk to if you needed to get away. His services came with a hefty price, but a year and a half of raiding meant the humble Thracian had more coin than he knew what to do with, and frankly it was becoming a burden to haul around with the amount of movement he conducted. Damanicus was the leader of the Cilician pirates. For Spartacus and his army, it was the only option available to get to Sicily aside from swimming two and a half miles across the water. Many of the men and women could not swim, so even if the motivation to escape the mainland was there, the ability was not. Spartacus would not lose thousands to such a petty thing as swimming if he had any hopes of avenging Oenomaus when the weather warmed. Peering out the window it was all Spartacus could do to make out the angry silhouette where Téadora sat on the pier. The Thracian leader was nearly ready to give up on the whole plan and go sit down to join her and apologize when a man walked into the taberna, with an unmistakable swagger to his step. He wore all black, like the

Bedouins on the other side of the Mediterranean, and had a face that looked like it was chiseled from marble. He appeared a real-life model of all those statues in Rome, distinct nose and jawline, perfect smile. Women swooned and men were jealous, and worst of all, Damanicus loved the attention. He frequented the peninsula often to take odd jobs and resupply. He had a special spot by the window where Spartacus was sitting now to conduct business. As Téadora over her shoulder this time, Gannicus could see the woman was crying, and she did not even attempt to hide it. No longer did she keep her back to the taberna, but faced it, with bold defiance. As Damanicus sat down he was trying to get a feel for who he was potentially going to work with. Big bags of coin sat at Spartacus' feet, but there was a circle of dots tattooed on his forearm that proved more interesting. Damanicus looked around, but did not see the matching tattoo anywhere in sight. It unsettled him, and he seemed distracted, loosing all of his cool as he sat down across from Spartacus. The Thracian leader assumed the pirate had become uneasy seeing that he was armed with a pair of sica blades strapped to his side. Damanicus' eyes were drawn downward, heavy set in his perfectly proportioned face. Spartacus cleared his throat, and pinched his mother's silver ring necklace for a bit of courage. He wanted to command the conversation from the beginning.

"To a Roman, a bend in a Thracian blade is an imperfection, but little do they know that it's the imperfections that make it work so well."

"I couldn't have said it better myself. I am quite familiar with what a sica blade can do in the right pair of hands. From one Roman reject to another, it is nice to meet you, Spartacus."

"You know my name?"

"The face of the slave war? Of course, I know your name. Your men have tapped all my usual haunts on the peninsula tonight, left me with scraps."

"My apologies."

"None needed. I admire a good challenge. So, what might I be able to do for you?"

"I am told you are the man to get a hold of for passage to Sicily."

"You don't want to go any further? I heard the Romans were making their way down south in a hurry."

"For now, that's all."

"How many men do you need me to move?"

"Seventy-five thousand."

"That's a lot of coin."

"That's not a problem."

"That's what I like to hear! How fast do you need to get off the mainland? It'll take my men a few hours to resupply."

"There's no rush, but I'd like to be out as soon as possible."

"Understood. Understood."

"You keep looking at my blades. Is there something wrong?"

"It's not the weapons. I know that tattoo."

"You do?"

"Where is she?"

"I don't know who you're talking about."

"Don't disappoint me, Spartacus. Téa! Where is she?!"

"How do you know about her?"

"That doesn't answer my question. Where is she?! I heard you traveled with a gladiatrix. It *has* to be her. She kills with sica blades, the very blades you wear before me. She had that *same* tattoo on her forearm. I've traced it many a time. *Where…is…she?!*"

"Outside."

"She didn't want to come in and see me?"

"I'm sorry, do you two know each other?"

"She didn't tell you about me. That makes sense."

"The only think I know is that she's angry with me for doing this."

"Of course, she is. Why wouldn't she be?"

"She said Cilician pirates couldn't be trusted."

"Ha! She's one to say such things. A pirate you can always trust to be dishonest, but a woman…ah, you never can tell with them, now, can you? At least not until it's too late."

"Is there something you need to tell me, Damanicus?"

"It's not my place to say. If she wants to tell you, that's *her* decision."

"Man to man, I'd like to hear what you have to say."

"Man to man, no you wouldn't."

"Did you hurt her?"

"It's not something I'm proud of. We were much younger, and if I had the chance to do it all over I would, but that's not the way things work. Yes, Spartacus, I hurt her. But I'd *never* do it again. Please tell her when you see her that I am sorry, and I still think of her often. Can you do that for me?"

"If you were any kind of man, you'd tell her yourself."

"If I was any kind of man, huh? Spartacus do you want to get your army to Sicily or not?"

"Yes."

"Then watch what you say to me. Give me two hours to resupply. When the moon begins to descend, meet me at the pier. Do we have a deal or not?"

"We have a deal."

"Good. I take my coin in advance."

"All of it?"

"How else am I expected to pay for my supplies? Anything worth stealing is in your men's hands already."

"Fine. Take the coin. What I brought should be more than enough to cover seventy-five thousand souls. I'll see you in a couple of hours."

"Pleasure doing business with you, Spartacus. And please, do try and tell Téa that I'm sorry."

"I can't promise you it'll be well received."

"Well, I can promise you it won't be, but tell her for me anyway."

Damanicus helped himself to the bags of coin on the floor and walked out of the taberna with two full arms and a wicked grin on his face. Spartacus couldn't help but feel sick to his stomach at the transaction, but the end result would all be worth it so he just had to push through. When the Thracian walked out to the pier, Téadora rushed up to greet him. She was a mess of silent questions as she studied Spartacus' face, her bright green eyes just darting all over the place. Her lips were parted but she still refrained from speaking.

She was up on her tiptoes, pressed into his chest. Spartacus held her there but his face was downcast. He could not pretend to be in better spirits around her. There was no use in lying. Passage had been paid for, and with any luck the army would be transferred in whole after a day or two. Spartacus said none of this though. He too had fallen mute in Téadora's grasp. Gannicus rested easy from his spying perch on the rooftop seeing them together, and went to join his men roaming around the peninsula. Castus was at another pier fishing when the pirates started loaded jar after jar of supplies onto the ships. They were jeering about their most recent pay, and Castus rolled his eyes knowing full well what the deal must have entailed. Spartacus probably overpaid to secure the army's passage because he was a good man and wanted good service. No one paid any mind to Castus or his fishing pursuits. It went this way for about an hour until the pirates started to board their ships, and Castus was getting the feeling something might be wrong. Out of about twelve vessels, the two at the very end of the pier had just untied themselves and set loose for the sea. None of Spartacus' army was on board. Castus abandoned his bucket of fish and ran for the taberna where he had parted ways with his cousin. Gannicus was still on a raid, but the curly haired Celt was able to find Spartacus and Téadora walking along the shore. He was nearly breathless when he intercepted them, and Téadora didn't even ask what the urgency was, she just immediately turned to Spartacus, and smacked his shoulder.

"Tell me you didn't pay the pirates in advance, Spartacus."

"You don't even know what Castus has to say, Téa. Why do you instantly go to the worst-case scenario?"

"Tell me you didn't pay them in advance, Spartacus."

"He told me that was the only way he did business! We were desperate to get off the mainland."

"No, *you* were desperate. *I* told you this was a mistake."

"What was I supposed to do? He seemed honest enough."

"He? He who? What did this man look like? Describe him."

"Why? Do you know *every* Cilician pirate out on the sea?"

"I bet I know most of them. I know all of them who would have been in the running to lead a fleet. What did he look like? Was he foolish enough to tell you a name?"

"He said his name was Damanicus."

"Of course, it was. *Of course*, it was!"

"What does that name mean to you?"

"It means…it doesn't matter what it means. What matters is that we find him and get our coin back. If you want to go to Sicily so bad, we will find another way."

"There *is* no other way."

"There is *always* another way!"

"Téa, what does that name mean to you? He recognized our tattoo, and my sica blades. He told me multiple times that he wanted me to tell you that he was sorry."

"Sorry? He's *sorry*?! Did he happen to say for what?"

"No. But can you?"

"Now is not the time."

"Téa, I've been patient with you, but it's starting to wear thin. I love you, and people who love one another don't keep secrets."

"People who love one another also don't sell each other to gladiator schools to save their precious ship either! But what do I know about love? What does Damanicus know?!"

"*He* sold you to the House of Batiatus?"

"I was worth my weight in gold, apparently. Damanicus found out Batiatus was on the hunt for a gladiatrix. He thought I'd be great, and he was in need of coin to repair his ship. We'd had a terrible winter raiding the Carthaginian coasts. He said he wanted to marry me. I was stupid enough to believe him. I never thought he could have sold me, but he did. And *that's* why I know a Cilician pirate can never be trusted. *That's* why I keep from the seas. My favorite place in the whole world. *He's* the reason why I wanted you to drag an entire army up through the Alps rather than save time and lives and just buy a ship and go home."

"Téa, if I had known that…"

"You didn't need to know, Spartacus. You don't need to know now. All that matters is that we get to him before he leaves and get your coin back. Castus, where did you say the Cilician's were docked?"

"Give me your hand. I'll take you right to him."

Téadora grabbed onto Castus and the two ran down the shore to get to where he had been fishing. In the time it took them to run, four more ships had left. Téadora knew though that Damanicus, as pirate king, was always the last ship to leave land. She found many a familiar face as she scanned the ships. Some old friends waved, and she smiled in return because they had not hurt her, but Damanicus, she had no smiles for that man. While she and Castus remained hand in hand, frantically searching the ships for their leader, Spartacus came up and joined them. He found Damanicus on the second to last ship moored at the pier, and whistled for Téadora. The Cilicians now knew they had been found out and started scrambling on the decks to unfurl the sails and get the ropes in order. Damanicus kept yelling orders, but all the while he kept his eyes on the shore. He couldn't help it. He hadn't seen Téadora in five years. He just wanted to see her, lay eyes on her. She was easy enough for him to find. Her long black braids trailing behind her in the moonlight. She was as gorgeous as he remembered. It's like he couldn't see anything but her once she was close. He cut the ropes on his ship to leave early. He knew that she knew he should have been the last to go but he couldn't risk her trying to board. He knew she could. She was as great a swimmer as they came and could climb anything she set her hands on. The rope slipped into the water just as she reached his spot on the pier and Castus held her back from jumping into the water. He could not hold her back alone, Spartacus had to intervene, and manhandle her from dropping to her knees. She jumped and hung suspended in Spartacus' arms.

"Téa, stop! No amount of coin is worth it. We'll figure something else out. It's no big deal. Téa! Please! Stop squirming!"

"How could he leave me again?!"

"You're upset that he left you?"

"Spartacus, I've watched that man sail away from me *twice* with tears in our eyes. I will not survive him doing that to me again."

"It won't happen again. I'll make sure of it."

"He didn't even speak to me. He had to have known I was here. I saw him in the taberna. Why didn't he speak to me?"

"A *real* man would have."

"He *is* a real man. You don't know him, Spartacus."

"I know I never could have walked away from you twice."

"You did it once."

"The Roman army took me. I did *not* go willingly."

"I watched you leave all the same. The heart cares not for what politics took you. *He* did this willingly. This was *his* choice! He should have apologized to me in person. I *deserved* that from him!"

"You deserve more than what he is capable of."

"I will get that coin back for you, Spartacus."

"Téa, no. You are worth more to me than *any* amount of coin."

"The pirates wouldn't hurt me. They were my family. If I could just get on that ship and speak to him, I know I could get the coin back."

"Téa, no."

"Why won't you let me do this?"

"It is not the closure you need."

"How do you know?!"

"I know what it is like to love you! Seeing you in pain is as good a punishment as a man can get. Do not give him the honor of chasing him. He is *not* worth your time. He *chose* to leave. Let him go, Téa."

"I don't know that I can."

Spartacus dropped Téadora from his arms. She caught herself on her knees and stared up at him with teary eyes. It looked like she had destroyed him. It's not what she wanted, but he didn't understand. Spartacus threw his hands up in the air and walked away. He went back into the taberna and sat in front of the window where he had made his foolish deal with Damanicus an hour earlier. Téadora looked for sympathy next in Castus' eyes, but he too was upset at her decision to give chase. He promised her he'd wait for her there on the pier until she came back, and took a seat on the wooden planks. Téadora wasted no more time. She dove into the sea and began swimming as fast as her arms would allow. It didn't seem fast enough, but the pirates on board had been watching her, and heard her splash into the water. Without telling their leader, they cast a rope into the sea for Téadora to latch onto, and help pull herself onboard. By the time she was on deck, Damanicus had retreated to the captain's quarters at the bow of the ship, and she welcomed herself in like old times. She and the pirate king had a patterned knock reserved just for the two of them, and when Damanicus heard it while lying in his hammock, he could have sworn he was dreaming. To see her on his ship again, he was overwhelmed. He couldn't wipe the smile off of his face. She couldn't reciprocate.

"Téa?!"

"Where's the coin, Dami?"

"Is that all you came back for?"

"It's all I'm worth to you, isn't it?"

"Téa, I…"

"I don't want to hear *anything* you have to say. Spartacus and our army busted our asses to steal that coin. I will *not* have you spending it on whores and wine. I'd rather see it at the bottom of the sea."

"Is that all you think of me now?"

"I'm trying to be polite because I know the crew are listening."

"I can't believe he let you come back to me."

"I'm *not* back, and I'm *not* here for you. The coin, Dami. Where did you put it? It's not in the usual place."

"You remember my usual hiding places?"

"I remember everything about you. That's why this is so hard. I should slice your neck open for selling me to Batiatus. But for some stupid reason my heart won't allow it. Where's the coin, Dami?"

"It's right here. I'll even help you dump it into the water if that'll make you happy. And thank you…for still calling me, Dami."

XVIII

When Téadora swam back to shore, Castus was sitting on the pier waiting for her, just where she had left him, only now he had a blanket with him to help dry her off and keep her warm. As the Celt wrapped his arms around her, they both watched Spartacus' slouched shoulder silhouette in the taberna window. Téadora had done the best she could to right this situation tonight. The coin was in nobody's hands, but the slave army was no closer to freedom than they had been in weeks since their victory in the north at Mutina. The Germanians might have been the wisest of them all to leave the war early and just go home. That was the ultimate goal here for so many of them, to get back to the life that Rome had ripped them away from. It was what Téadora and Spartacus wanted, though they just had different ways of going about getting there. Oenomaus needed to be avenged. But they were coming into winter, and there would be no battle worth fighting until the weather improved. Winter was for plotting and scheming, rebuilding, and redoubling efforts. Téadora had to go and apologize for her emotions getting the better of her. She wished she had handled herself before when she first learned of Damanicus return. In her head she had worked through that scenario so many times. She had speeches to recite, but when it all came down to it, all she could do was stare and seethe with rage at his downcast face. He was sorry. She could see that and feel that from him when she was on his ship. She knew those planks of wood like the back of her hand. He hadn't changed a bit, and maybe she hadn't either, but they were also no longer the same people they used to be. It wasn't like that with Spartacus. When they first saw each other again, after so long apart, it was like coming home. They had picked up right where they left off. They were always two smiling kids, laughing with one another. Castus gave his friend a gentle push towards the taberna. It wasn't like Téadora to hesitate doing something, but swallowing her pride and admitting she'd been wrong, it wasn't one of her strengths. Spartacus knew this too, which is why he was not expecting to see her again tonight. When she came slinking up to him in the taberna, taking the seat where Damanicus had sat a couple hours prior, he didn't know what to say. Her black braids were dripping wet on the table, and Spartacus reached across to push the puddles off into her lap, but her hand sprang up and latched onto his.

"Please, don't be mad at me, Spartacus."

"I'm not mad at you, Téa. I just wished you would have told me about Damanicus before I made a deal with him. I would have done everything in my power to avoid you having to see him again."

"That's sweet of you, but I needed this. It was important that I see him again in this light, seeing him for who he really is, and seeing what he is and always was capable of. When you're in love…"

"I don't…"

"I know, I know you don't want to hear this, but when you love someone, you become blind to their faults. You just accept them wholeheartedly and adjust. I had become a woman I didn't know when I was with him. He made me a fighter, yes, but he made me dull and hollow too. He took pieces of me that I am only now starting to get back. Tonight, I got a big chunk back. I'm sorry though about the coin. I could not lug it all back with me. I dumped it in the sea."

"Téa, how many times do I have to tell you, this was never about the coin. I am relieved it's not in his hands anymore though."

"He would have just wasted it all on Sicilian wine and whores. We did not raid for months for him to enjoy the fruits of our labor. He does not get to enjoy my hard work anymore. I do not owe him anything. I did at one time, but my debt has been repaid more times than I care to admit."

"Why couldn't you just tell me about him?"

"I was ashamed."

"Of what?"

"I feel like you have placed me high on a pedestal, Spartacus. You keep looking at me like I am gold. I don't ever want to disappoint you like I did tonight, but your expectations of me, they are unattainably high."

"I expect nothing from you but honesty. Everything else is just extra. I'm sorry if I've said or done anything to make you feel like you have to earn my attention or praise. I love you for who you are, Téa, messy past and all. We've all done things in our youth we are not proud of. But those acts don't have to define us for the rest of our lives. We can learn, and grow. We can be better. We *are* better. *You* are better."

"You are too lenient with me."

"You are too severe in judgement upon yourself. You always have been. You take other's burdens just to see them smile. It was *I* who was mistaken to have made this deal tonight. You were right, I *was* desperate to get off of the mainland. I wasn't thinking clearly. You warned me of the pirates. Gannicus warned me of hasty decision making. I should have listened and held back."

"We will think of something else."

"There is no solution in the sea. Crixus' voice is ringing in my ear. We must stay on the mainland. It is uncomfortable, but it is what we must do. We can't run away. We will winter over, and as soon as it warms up again, we will make our push north against the Romans. You will get your revenge for Oenomaus, and we can make our way to the Alps once more. Because no matter what happens, I *am* taking you back home, and I *am* building you that home on the hills."

"Perhaps it wasn't the worst thing in the world that I was sold to that gladiator school after all. If I hadn't been there, who knows how long before I would have gotten to see you again."

"There is a bit of light, in even the darkest times. Sometimes it just takes us a while to see that."

Téadora and Spartacus leaned into each other from across the narrow table, and rested their foreheads together, eyes shut, the world tuned out, just breathing one another in for a moment. He broke first, laughing as water from Téadora's wet braids began to dribble down his cheeks. She apologized with the most effortless grin on her lips, and began using her damp thumbs to try and dry his face. She had memorized every rise and fall in his cheekbones, the crease in his laugh lines, the dip of his lips, the strength of his jaw line as it gave way to his scarred neck. She traced the veins down to his collar bone, and Spartacus couldn't help but happily gasp, and pull Téadora in for a kiss. From that moment on, the two were inseparable. They walked arm in arm through the peninsular town in the dead of night. He was soaked from her wet clothes, and he did not mind. At camp on the outskirts of the villages, they didn't even bother setting up their tent. Unpacking was time consuming, so they took to lying in the dying grass and making love underneath the stars. Not a soul could touch them, and no one dared interrupt. In the morning, there was a bit of frost on the landscape. The weather was proving to change in a hurry, and it was a sign of the months to come. An early winter always promised to be especially cold and miserable. Emergency harvests were set out all across the peninsula. Preparations were being made to farms and vineyards. Fisherman took care to get extra rope for their boats. Rough seas ahead. The slave army raided with a purpose, moving to higher and lower ground to take advantage of caves where they could find them. Gannicus and the Celts took the coasts, while Spartacus kept the women and Thracians with him in the highlands. Some people could bear snow better than others. Spartacus was from a mountain tribe; he was well equipped with what it took to survive the elements. Téadora was from an island. She should have been on the coast, but she would not leave her leader's side if she didn't have to. They lived, raided, and worked together. They strategized together, but even sometimes, there was the need for temporary separation. Gannicus and his men still held sentry duty. There was word the Romans were undergoing some huge construction project. Gannicus himself was wary of the tall tales he was hearing, and asked for permission to go investigate during the daytime. Spartacus thought the ginger bearded man might be too easily identified. Someone else needed to go. Téadora volunteered impulsively, and her fellow commanders laughed at her.

"I'm serious! Gannicus, am I or am I not the fastest commander in the army?"

"Yes, Téadora. But you are too valuable an asset to go running across the peninsula in broad daylight. The Romans have a bounty on you for Senator Furius need I remind you."

"You need not. Spartacus, please, let me do this?"

"I don't see the need for you to be the one to have to go, Téa. We can send an aide, a local, a…"

"Gannicus says what his men tell him sounds too fantastic to actually be happening. Lower ranking men can't be trusted to come back with the facts. *I* can."

"What if something happens to you?"

"Nothing will happen to me. I'm too quick to be caught."

"You're overconfident in your abilities."

"Want to put me to the test then?"

"What are you getting at?"

"Want to race me, Spartacus?"

"I'm not racing against you, Téa. We're not ten."

"I beat you when we were ten. I can do it again."

"No woman can outrun a full-grown man. It can't be done. Rest on your past victories and leave it at that."

"You're just backing out because my victory would damage your pride in front of the army."

"More like *your* pride."

"I would not be embarrassed to lose a race to you, Spartacus. I mean, there's a first time for everything, right?"

"If I let you go scouting after this construction project, can we forget this race nonsense?"

"Maybe. Does that mean I have permission to go?"

"Yes."

"Thank you, Spartacus!"

"But if you are not back by sundown, I'm sending the search party of all search parties after you and it will be a bloodbath. I don't want to see you back in camp with so much as a scratch, you hear me?"

"Loud and clear. I'll be back before you know it! I'll go make sense of your men's tall tales, Gannicus. Wish me luck, boys!"

"That woman is going to make my heart stop one of these days, you know that, Spartacus?"

"You and me both, Gannicus. You and me both."

"Do you really think you could beat her in a race?"

"Not a chance. Besides. Why would I want to? The view is so much better from second place."

"I agree. But, Spartacus, on a more serious note, what are we going to do if she comes back and confirms these tall tales?"

"Are you really worried your men are telling the truth about this massive construction project?"

"What would they get for lying?"

"Maybe they're just eager to provoke another battle?"

"I don't think so. I think there's more truth to it than I want to admit to myself. I was so looking forward to a quiet winter."

"It would make sense that Rome would ruin that for you."

"It would. But if the tales are true, Spartacus, what are we going to do? We have to have a plan. The men will have questions and we'll need to give them answers."

"We'll have answers as soon as Téa comes back. Until then, we do not worry ourselves."

"And what if we're already worried?"

"Prepare for the worst. I mean, this is just a construction project. They could be building a camp. How terrible could it really be?"

"For as long as you served in their army, *you* should know better."

Gannicus excused himself, and left Spartacus alone with some of his worst memories as a soldier. For over fifteen years he had seen what the Romans were capable of building if they wanted to. It wasn't just winter camps. Spartacus himself had helped built traps that surrounded entire towns, and barricades that killed parents trying to get back to their children. It made him nauseous just thinking about it, and he slammed his fist down at his side. Instantly, the Thracian leader was pouring blood. He hadn't been paying attention to the rock shards where he was sitting. It was a simple accident, but the bleeding wouldn't stop. He pulled out the shard doing the damage and kept pressure over the wound, but he needed a healer. Spartacus looked for Castus but the man could not be found. The Celts said he was out on a walk today collecting herbs and such before the cold weather killed everything. While smart, and expected, it was bad timing on Spartacus' part. He bit his lip and cursed himself a bit before another healer offered to help. The bleeding slowed, and when he decided to go and try to speak to Gannicus again, he was amazed to find his commander riding out on horseback in the direction Téadora had run off to. Both of his best soldiers were now gone, and Spartacus didn't know whether to be pleased at their service to the safety of the army, or upset that they had left him behind. It was a bit childish to be upset, so he kept his wits about him and tried to keep distracted, but it was difficult. He kept finding himself looking out to the horizon in the east, waiting for some sort of sign everything was alright. He was well are the slaves did not hold a valuable position, being squashed down in the tip of the mainland, essentially trapped on three sides by water with only a narrow stretch of land promising them any kind of escape. Téadora was on a hillside, looking down at that stretch now. As far as she could see from north to south, Romans were crawling like ants upon the ground. They were busy for a stretch of thirty-five miles, from the Tyrrhenian Sea all the way to the Ionian Sea. A stone wall was going up, some twenty-five feet high in some places. Wooden palisades had been erected with guard towers at regular intervals. In front of these, on the slave's western side, was a trench filled with sharpened pikes jutting up out of the ground. The tall tales were all true. Téadora couldn't believe what she was seeing. She wished Spartacus had come with her.

While the gladiatrix commander was trying to process what this meant for the future of the army, the sound of horses drew her attention back to the ground below. She was confused. When she had left camp, she had no knowledge of Gannicus coming out to harass the Romans, but it was what he was doing now. He'd brought all the Celtic archers with him, and they only went so far as the reach the Romans while they worked. After a hail of arrows, the Celts retreated, seeing their attacks did little to stifle the Roman's project. Perhaps it was intelligence gathering of their own. Gannicus could be spotted easily from a distance with his ginger beard, and his white horse rearing up on its hind legs, neighing like a fiend. He was as angry as his rider. Téadora watched as the Celts ran back to the peninsular camp, and noticed they were one man heavy. Castus was riding on the back of an archer, no herb collecting satchel in hand at all. Téadora didn't even know her friend had been out today, and the reason for that was because he hadn't wanted anyone to know. That's why Gannicus was so upset and came out to pick up his cousin. There was something Téadora didn't know, and she safely assumed Spartacus was equally in the dark. Trying to piece together valid reasons for her friend's unusual actions, Téadora scanned the field below her again for signs of something off she might have overlooked before. It was understandable she might have missed some clandestine meeting in the shadows when there was a behemoth of a construction project taking place before her. She found it after a couple of frantic seconds, a young man running a pile of boulders. She thought him more a boy than a man, he was lanky and had yet to grow into his limbs fully. He wore nothing to signify rank or importance. He seemed not to know what he was doing, and had no one with him. He was alone, as Castus had been alone. But this boy was Roman, no doubt. He was welcomed into the construction project with ease, and she watched as his blonde head disappeared into the stone wall. Téadora tried to remember if she had ever seen that blonde head and lanky limbs before, at a match in an arena somewhere, or a visitor to the gladiator school. He must have been the son of someone important. A younger brother maybe. While she thought on this, she ran back to the slave camp to tell Spartacus what she had learned. She was eager for his insights so they could get to the bottom of this before her imagination got the best of her and started making enemies of allies. She laughed. Oenomaus had gotten in trouble for thinking such things of Castus before. Maybe he had reason? Téadora shook her head and kept running. Gannicus and his Celts had returned to their coastal caves long before she reached the highland caves. But Spartacus was at the entrance of his cave, on a cliffside perch, watching the Celts have no intention of telling him what they had just done. Téadora arrived breathless, hands on her hips, and Spartacus just waved her over to sit beside him on the perch, never breaking eye contact with Gannicus down below.

"What do you make of everything, Téa?"

"What do you know? And what happened to your hand?!"

"My hand is fine. My temper got the better of me, that's all."

"That doesn't sound good."

"Gannicus reminded me of what the Romans are capable of. For some reason, I had tried to forget that. I smashed my hand into a pile of rock shards, and when I went looking for Castus you could imagine my amazement to find him gone."

"Yes. I saw him out in the field."

"Doing what?"

"I don't know. But he was talking to someone from the Roman's camp. A young blonde man."

"Have you ever seen him before?"

"I can't say that I have. Whatever he was doing out there, I don't think Gannicus approved. He fetched him like a father would a son."

"Gannicus didn't tell me he was leaving."

"He took archers with him to cover their retrieval of Castus. This might have something to do with Castus' beating when we moved camp last time."

"This has something to do with a lot of things I bet, and as a leader there's nothing that should go on in my camp that I'm not made aware of. Even if Gannicus was justified in his leaving, he should have run it by me first. I wouldn't have denied his request to go and retrieve Castus. But what is your little curly haired friend up to, Téa? Speaking with Romans?"

"Castus wouldn't double cross us, Spartacus. I don't know what's going on, but he's a good man. I swear it."

"I trust you, but this still bothers me."

"As it bothers me. I will try and get to the bottom of this as soon as I can. But I fear we have bigger problems to worry about."

"The tales are true, aren't they?"

"The Romans have trapped us on the peninsula, Spartacus. From one sea to the other, they have walled us in."

"So much for Gannicus' quiet winter."

"Do we try and fight our way out before they finish?"

"What would be the point? The cold will kill us all if we're exposed. These caves are our only chance at staying alive right now. If we had made it to Sicily…"

"Let's not talk about Sicily."

"Understood. But it was my intention to make a winter camp there, in better conditions."

"We will make due here, with what we have."

"*You* may be tough, and *I* may be tough, but can we speak for the rest of camp? Winter has not yet arrived in full and already Castus is walking off without telling anyone, and Gannicus is leading search parties. I can't have men doing whatever they want without consequence. They are free, but there still needs to be some kind of unity, and order. We are a rough sort, but we're not animals."

"We will think of something."

"Will we?"

"Yes. We always think of something. If you are out of ideas, I will come up with something."

"Thank the gods for your confidence."

"Thank the gods for your patience, resilience, and level head."

"You always find a way to build me up when I am down."

"That is what a good team does. We take care of each other."

"I feel this army has forgotten that."

"They have not forgotten. Sometimes survival makes people do odd things. It is temporary. I promise. All of this is temporary. It might be difficult now, but that means we are headed for better times."

"You can say that with a straight face after seeing what the Romans are building?"

"We have gotten through tougher scrapes than this."

"I'll take your word for it, because my words are failing me. This war is slipping right through my hands like water, and there's not a damn thing I can do to stop it."

"Then I'll hold your hands. You know how good I am with water."

XIX

The snows fell early this year. It was unusually cold, and the white blanket of winter stretched all the way out to the coastal caves, much to Gannicus' grief. The Celts were familiar with the challenges that snow could bring, but many of them had spent so long under Roman control that they had forgotten their most crucial instincts. Necessity number one was keeping dry. Too many men had gone fishing in the morning for an easy breakfast and were rudely awaken by the fact that being damp in the snow was something of a death sentence. While Gannicus was busy scolding his soldiers, his cousin was sneaking off for another meeting with Crassus' nephew, Mummius. It had become a weekly habit. Gannicus was doing everything he could to keep tabs of his curly haired cousin but Castus was as crafty as he was persistent. He did not ever go at the same of day or take the same path out. The meeting place kept changing. Gannicus put up extra patrols at night, so Castus would leave in the morning. Gannicus started to get up earlier, Castus went midday. With thousands of men, it was impossible to keep track of every single individual every single day. With the temperatures dipping and resource stockpiles diminishing by the day, morale fell too. Spartacus had enough to worry about with the Romans and desertion that Gannicus didn't feel the need to worry him about whatever Castus was doing, but it did weigh heavy on the ginger bearded man's conscience. Because Téadora was one of the only friends Castus had to his name, Gannicus finally broke down this morning and went to her for help. He signaled her with his campfire, popping up smoke rings with a sacrificial blanket so she could see him from her highland cave. Spartacus was still sleeping, so she placed a gentle kiss on his cheek before slipping down to the coast. Gannicus was just eyeing this lone pair of tracks out through the snow as she sat down beside him to warm herself by his fire.

"What's wrong, Gannicus?"

"He keeps running away, Téadora."

"Who?"

"Castus. Why else would I bother you? Any other man walking off on a regular basis and I'd kill him for being a spy. But he's my cousin, he's blood."

"Castus is no spy. What do you mean *regular basis*? I thought he met the Roman just that once?"

"You and I both know that's a lie. You're smarter than that, Téadora. The night he was beaten, didn't I tell you something was off?"

"Have you followed him any of his times out?"

"Twice."

"Was he meeting a young blonde man?"

"Yes. Sometimes the boy has centurions with him, sometimes not. I've only been out there twice, so I can't say which is normal. What am I saying? *None* of it's normal. Castus isn't like this, sneaking off and lying. What could he be doing?"

"If you're asking *me* questions you really must be desperate."

"I thought I could handle this on my own. I've doubled the sentry duties, I've rotated shifts. He keeps slipping out of my grasp. It's like the harder I try to keep him here, the harder he fights to leave. He's a liability to the entire army for doing this."

"I know. I'm worried for him too. Acting alone like this isn't safe. I fear the Romans might be using him for information. He's too scared not to keep meeting with that boy. He might have been threatened with some sort of violent retaliation."

"This can't continue, Téadora."

"No, it can't. We have to tell, Spartacus."

"I've been avoiding that for weeks."

"Castus is my friend. Spartacus would never hurt him. But he already feels like he's losing control of this army, and the war. You can't keep doing things behind his back. It bothers him."

"I'm just trying to look out for my family."

"I know, and he knows that too. But this army is all family. We need to get Castus out of trouble."

"Is there any other way we can save my cousin and avoid angering Spartacus?"

"I don't think so. Now that you've involved me, Spartacus has to be involved too."

"Then let's hurry before new snow falls and covers these tracks. I've been watching the clouds, and it looks to be a difficult day."

"What day *hasn't* been difficult since we got down here? It's like the gods are testing us, and I'm getting awfully annoyed."

Téadora looked up at the gray skies with questioning eyes. It made Gannicus chuckle, and forget his problems for a couple of seconds. He was not in this struggle to help Castus alone, he never had been. The Celts were instructed to watch for Castus in case he should return, and keep dry until Gannicus got back. When Téadora had hiked back up to the highland caves, Spartacus was not yet awake, and she had to rouse him carefully from his slumber. Seeing Gannicus at his feet, the Thracian leader bolted upright, and scanned for further commanders. This wasn't an army issue waking him up today, but a personal one. He wasn't sure what was worse. Téadora appeared like she had bad news to share, and Spartacus flopped back down on his back, staring up at the rock ceiling above him. She rolled her hand over his shoulder, and he reached up to hold her there. She wasn't trembling, but resolute. If she had the strength to handle this, the least he could do was sit up and face the day's challenge with her. Gannicus crouched down so the three were eye level, and sunk his head so he faced the ground. This had to do with Castus. Spartacus reached over for his sica blades and began strapping them on. Then he reached for Téadora's sica blades and set them in her lap. She strapped hers on and the three leaders walked to the edge of the cave. Spartacus saw no uneasiness stirring, no frantic movements. He went to where the horses were corralled and mounted himself for a chilly ride. Téadora and Gannicus followed suit. The Thracian leader motioned for Gannicus to lead the way out.

"Don't you want to know what's going on first, Spartacus?"

"I'm assuming the issue is time sensitive. You can both fill me in on whatever it is you think I need to know while we head out. What trouble has your cousin gotten into now, Gannicus?"

"The trouble is we don't know what kind of trouble he's in. But there's a blond Roman boy I'm sure we can get some answers from."

"A *boy*? That's who we're after? Maybe I didn't need my blades after all."

"A boy who travels with centurions on occasion."

"So, it's an *important* boy then? Téa, is it the same boy you saw when scouting the Roman wall?"

"One in the same I assume. I can't imagine Castus having all that many Roman contacts."

"He shouldn't have any. One is enough to get him killed and put the whole army at risk. We already moved camp for him once, we can't afford to do it now that the snows have come. If someone needs to move now, it'll be the Romans."

"That's highly unlikely. They're safe on the other side of that wall."

"No one builds a wall that high because they feel safe. Rome knows we're a threat, and we might just have to remind them of that."

"You've got that glimmer in your eye, Spartacus."

"Never mind the glimmer, Gannicus. Let's get your cousin."

"What do you plan to do to him when we get him back?"

"Cousin or not, he needs to be punished."

"I agree. But don't ask me to kill my family, Spartacus."

"I didn't ask you to do anything, Gannicus. It's clear Castus no longer respects or fears you. It's complicated exercising authority over family members. That's why *I* will do something."

"Might I ask what that will be?"

"You can ask, but I haven't decided yet. The punishment will fit the crime. I just need to figure out exactly what crime he's committed, to what degree, and how many times. I won't kill him, Gannicus. Rest assured I will show mercy."

Téadora's eyes flickered back and forth between the two men as they talked. She feared for Castus as they walked further into the snows and away from the coast. As the men began to drift to topics like fishing as boys and misadventures while hunting, Téadora spotted Castus at a ravine with a shiny helmeted young man, and reared her horse into a full charge. Even on horseback, the men could not catch her. She went racing through biting windchill to catch this Roman before he could get into the safety of an archer's arrow from the wall. Regardless of who this boy might be, or who might be watching him, he was alone in no man's land now, and Téadora had her horse kick the Roman's feet out from under him. By the time he could roll over and catch his breath, Téadora had jumped down from her horse and was on top of the boy, straddling him with a curved dagger in each hand, poised to split open his neck from either side should he think himself clever enough to try and get away from her. Stupidly, he appeared unharmed. Castus came rushing out to try and stop this from getting messy, gripping Téadora's hands in his so she might release her blades. Spartacus and Gannicus were yelling for answers. Why had Castus run? Who was this boy Téadora had subdued? Castus was blushed fully red in his face. The gladiatrix commander sheathed one of her weapons and placed the other squarely on the boy's windpipe, drawing just enough blood to keep him from squirming. With her free hand she took hold of her friend's face, and made him look at her. This was not the face of a spy. She knew this man. He was her first friend in the House of Batiatus. The first one who made her feel like she had a life worth living when she contemplated suicide after killing a fourteen-year-old girl in her first match. This was Castus. The good guy. The healer. And Roman conspirator? It broke Castus watching his friend's face twist with her thoughts. By now Spartacus and Gannicus had arrived. Castus was picked up violently from his shoulders by his cousin while Spartacus took hold of the shiny helmeted boy on the ground. Téadora stepped aside, and flung the helmet off to get a good look at the face. It didn't seem strikingly familiar as he sniffled from fear.

"Who are you, boy? And don't you even think of lying to me or I'll make this snow red with your blood."

"M-my name is Mummius."

"My name is Téadora."

"I know who you are."

"I'd like to know who you are, and why you're talking to my friend."

"It's not what it looks like, I swear!"

"Then tell me what this is. Why do you two sneak away in no man's land to speak? What topics could be so important to risk your lives?"

"We seek information. That's all. I tell him the strength of our legions, and he tells me the strength of your army."

"And what do you do with this information? Whose good graces are you so desperate to earn?"

"My uncle's."

"Who's your uncle?"

"Praetor Marcus Crassus, the head of the Roman defense."

"Since when was Praetor Varinius replaced?"

"After his defeat in Mutina. He's still in the charge of one legion, but my uncle has the rest. The Senate was humiliated, so they sent us to handle the…slave situation."

"We're a situation now, Spartacus, did you hear that? Going on two years of war and the Senate calls us a *situation*. Mummius, can you do me a favor and hold your breath?"

"Um, yes, but what for?"

"I just need to do something really quick."

Téadora took the palm of her hand and smashed it up into the bottom of the boy's nose. The action was so quick and with such force that the crack almost assuredly promised a broken nose. Blood began spilling out all down his lips and chin. As Mummius cried and tried to wrench his arms out of Spartacus' hold, he was at a loss for words. Castus tried to avoid eye contact with the young man, feeling guilty for the injury even though his hands were clean. As Téadora stepped back to wipe her hands off she exclaimed that hit made up for the beating that Castus had taken at the hands of the Romans a few weeks ago. Mummius nodded like he understood, and that punishment gave Spartacus a wicked idea. He signaled for Gannicus to come over to him, and whispered something in the Celtic commander's ear. Téadora could not overhear what was being said, but the feeling in no man's land definitely shifted in that moment. Gannicus released his grip on his cousin, and ordered him to collect two pieces of wood, long ones, and to get the rope from his saddle bags. Castus was obedient, albeit clueless. Téadora silently asked Spartacus for answers, but he was avoidant until she came up and placed a hand on his forearm, right where their matching circle of dots were tattooed.

"No secrets, Spartacus."

"I'm going to avenge Oenomaus for you."

"What do you mean?"

"Do you trust me?"

"With everything that I am."

"Then know that I am doing this out of a place of love for you. The Romans took something from you that I can't return, so now, I am going to take something from this Praetor Crassus, that can't be returned. How are your knot tying skills?"

"Better than yours, I'm sure. What am I tying together?"

"Secure those two logs that Crassus brought back."

"Any particular way I need to tie them?"

"Yes. In the shape of a cross, Téa."

"A cross?"

Spartacus nodded his head in solemn agreement. Téadora understood, and she looked back at Gannicus who was stone faced. The men had decided. That was it. While Téadora wanted retribution for losing Oenomaus, she didn't think it needed to come at the hands of a boy. But sometimes, that's what it took to make the Romans understand what they had done. Barbarism. Trapping an army in the south, sending a spy for information. Mummius understood what was happening too. Castus had turned away. He begged his cousin to be allowed to return to camp but Gannicus insisted he was going to stay and watch this until Mummius took his last breath. That was his punishment for putting the army in danger for weeks. Mummius' blubbering only worsened. Not only was the pain of his broken nose the source, but now it was his imminent death. And all because he was trying to impress his uncle, make him proud for once in his short life. So short. He was only eighteen. He had seen nothing of the world. Done nothing. Mummius hung in Spartacus' arms as Téadora tied the logs together in front of him. Her fingers were getting slow in the cold, so she used her teeth to secure everything super tight. In the background Gannicus was digging the hole for the main log to be set upright. The dirt was soft from the snow on top, but hard from the cold below. No matter, the ginger bearded men was determined to make a worthy foundation for the crucifixion. The cross was set in, and the dirt packed back around for stability. Téadora took extra lengths of rope and cut them enough to fasten the boy's hands and feet. Gannicus and Spartacus hoisted him up. Mummius did not fight them. He was limp and useless while they tied him in place, sobbing all the way. Téadora's brows were heavily furrowed. She kept replaying the image of Oenomaus dead in her arms at the courtyard in Mutina. This death would please him, to know he did not die in vain. And with that thought, she was accepting of this act. It was the most painful thing they could think of doing. Killing the boy of the man who was trying to kill all of them. He might not have been a son, but blood was still blood. A nephew was close enough to get under the skin of Crassus. That is, if Crassus was any kind of decent man. He had great love for his little sister, Mummius' mother. But this boy was more of a scourge to his bloodline than anything, taking after his good for nothing, runaway father. Crassus was watching all of this from his position on top of the stone wall. Centurions had alerted him that there was an issue that needed his attention. Varinius had been alerted as well, and came running up with Dacia in tow. No Romans were sent out to save the boy, or punish the enemy. As Spartacus tied Mummius' hands and feet to the logs, he had one final moment of civility.

"Any last words, boy?"

"N-n-no."

"Then pray to your gods."

"The g-g-gods h-h-hate me."

"Hate them back, works for me."

The Romans watched quietly as Mummius drew his last, painful breaths. Téadora had been hoisted on top of Spartacus' broad shoulders. She took her sica blades and swiped them smoothly across the boy's neck. As it flopped down and he bled all over his own chest, she turned to lock eyes with Crassus in the distance. They were over half a mile away. No facial expressions could be discerned, but they knew each other was displeased, which was a certain kind of pleasure in and of itself. Even after Mummius was abandoned in the snow Crassus did not utter a single word nor show an ounce of emotion. The boy's body would not be retrieved, but would remain in the snow of no man's land as a stark reminder of what was to happen to any Roman or slave if they thought they could outsmart this war. Dacia took the crucifixion the hardest, and was absolutely disgusted with the whole bit. She fled from the viewing platform on top of the stone wall and ran for her tent that she shared with Varinius. She was done. She wanted no more of this. When the young praetor came down to try and console the seer, it was all he could do to wrap his arms around her from behind and calm her down before she set the camp in an uproar.

"He was just a *boy*, Varinius! A *stupid* boy, but a *boy* nonetheless."

"Spartacus only did this to send a message. That's all this was. You can't take it to heart, Dacia. Please. Control yourself."

"*Control myself*? As if that could be done."

"Please, Dacia?"

"You all just stood there and watched. A boy died for all of your pride today. Do you feel good about yourself, Varinius?"

"You act as if it was *my* hand that killed the boy."

"It might as well have been. Crucifixion is a punishment from *your* people, not mine, and certainly not the Thracians or the Celts. That is not the way people outside of the empire settle their debts. They do not crucify boys. This message was meant to be sent to Rome itself, and Crassus doesn't even care. That boy died for *nothing*."

"What does it matter to you?"

"This war has slipped into madness. When men disregard honor and logic then we become no better than animals. I can't see what's going to happen next. My dreams are as if they were in a fog. I am living blind with eyes wide open."

"You did not see this coming, did you?"

"I did not. Had I, Mummius would still be alive."

"In the grand scheme of things, he was unimportant."

"You say that now. But this deed will not go unanswered."

"But you saw it yourself, Crassus did not shed one tear. He cares nothing for his nephew. It's certainly nothing to fight a battle in the snow for. It was just *one* boy."

"Wars have been raised for such offenses. A fierce battle is on the horizon, and that boy will be avenged. Thousands of Spartacus' army will fall for this one act of defiance. They should have known better than to go after Crassus' own blood."

"How did they even know who the boy was? Perhaps, this was just a stunt gone wrong?"

"It's underestimating like *that*, that got you replaced, Varinius."

"Are you, are you *ashamed* of that replacement? I thought you hated the Roman army? Why would you want me leading it?"

"Nevermind. Forget I said anything. You're only hearing what you want to hear anyways."

"No, Dacia. Explain yourself."

"You don't own me anymore. I don't have to follow your orders."

"If you respect me, you still have to answer my questions."

"If Crassus doesn't even care about Mummius being crucified, what does he feel for you? I don't want to see you sacrificed for that man's pride. You are better than him in *every* way."

"You are...*worried* about me?"

"Why is that so hard for you to understand?"

"Dacia, I will *never* put you through the pain of seeing me die. If it's one thing you can be sure of in this world, be sure of that."

XX

Three days into a terrible winter storm and Spartacus had to make a decision to either help free his army from their barricade in the south, or risk dying in their cave camps. As it was, everyone had already moved down to the Celtic caves on the coast to try and rid themselves of the feet deep snow accumulating in the highlands of the peninsula. Even on the water's edge however, the temperatures were brutal and there was little in the way of warmth, or comfort. Food was scarce. Raiding was near impossible. Morale was at it's lowest point since the war had stared with the escape from the House of Batiatus. Spartacus couldn't take looking at the men and women's faces any longer. He and Gannicus had scouted the Roman wall for weak points. It was understood the most vulnerable points in the stone and wooden defenses were ironically where the watch towers were, because the Romans were too lazy to walk very far from their camps on the safe western side to the towers on the vulnerable eastern side. Doors in the walls were right by the towers. Trenches were also by these towers, great waste filled pits with wooden spikes jutting up. But feet of snow had filled those in a bit, turned them into surmountable depressions. With some compaction, throw in mud, rocks, any debris really, dead bodies, and the ground was now level.

Gannicus admitted it might be dirty, rotten work, but it would be a way out. While the army worked, some could act as defense against the Romans in the towers and on the walls. They could squeeze their thousands out through five doors. It'd take a while, but with the spread of the wall, only five doors were really doable for their need to maintain communication. Wouldn't want to spread out too thin and risk making a costly, and easily avoidable mistake. The army descended Vesuvius' hillsides on five ropes. They could get through this barricade in five doors. Their size then was the size they were now. Only on Vesuvius it had been warm and summer. Men had a different kind of motivation behind them when they were at risk of freezing to death. The anger was more desperate, less likely to give up in the face of a challenge. And this would be a challenge.

The slave army waited until it was later in the afternoon, when heavy winds, fog, and snow drifts were making visibility nearly nothing. It was white out conditions, and perfect for moving an army without being detected. Roughly seventy thousand trekked out on foot or horseback, or makeshift boat. The five doors to be selected would be the ones closest to the Ionian coast, on the southern end of the barricade. A straight shot out to familiar eastern lands where the army had camped before. Fruitful, plentiful hills for raiding. The possibility of a life worth living again. Men moved faster than they had in weeks to get to that stone wall. The platforms in the watch towers, and the stone wall were too high up at twenty-five feet to even see the army until it was too late. They worked carefully, shoving snow into the trench depressions with heaps and slabs of icy snow and slush. Dead Romans who'd been discarded provided nice fodder and easy work to build up the trench. Mud, sludge, whatever was there was all thrust into the depression until it was flat ground, and compact enough to take the weight of thousands running across it. Spartacus, Gannicus, Téadora, and two other Celts positioned themselves at the five doors. Castus stayed behind his cousin for good measure. Spartacus gave one final look at the no man's land behind them that they had crossed. You couldn't see Mummius' decaying body on the cross of logs from here, but on a clear day you could have. Just knowing the boy still hung there was validation enough that the Romans had this coming for them. It wasn't even about an attack or a slaughter today. This was no battle.

The slaves just wanted out. Whatever Roman was stupid enough to get in their way would be cut down, but no one was going to stay and fight. Run in, run out, and keep on running until the snow melted into the grass and the sun was in the sky. Run until th eland gave way to the sea if they must. Run, and take as many with you as you could. It was a simple plan, not a lot of things to remember. Spartacus was at the middle door. Téadora was to his left, Gannicus to his right. They were spread almost too far to see each other well, but when Spartacus gave the signal, a deep, trembling war cry, there was no going back.

Téadora and her gladiatrices made themselves heard first. They drew attention away from the men with their wolf howls and whistles. Archers quickly dismantled whatever Romans were up in the watch towers. Getting the soldiers on the walls took a bit more finesse. The slave army rolled over that barricade like water rolled over pebbles on a beach. They climbed the wooden towers from all four sides, twenty-thirty of them at a time. They got onto the top of the stone wall and began bloodying any Roman they could find. Down on the ground the defenses were weak at best. Because of the storm the force to protect the barricade was scant at best, and slow to respond and pull away from the warmth of their fires. The Roman camp as a whole was not prepared for the ambush. But it wasn't even really an ambush. The slave army was not raiding, not tackling anyone they passed. Romans were shoved out of the way as they trickled through the lines of tents and makeshift homes for the officers. They ran in, and ran out for the countryside, only to disappear in the white fog just as they had appeared. Crassus attempted to order his men into action, but they were more interested in watching the spectacle. Desperate gladiators. The fiercest men in the empire, running and retching like skin and bones. Some stopped briefly at a campfire or two in a more protected shelter, growling and hollering at it's inhabitants to leave. Some pots of stew were overrun with hasty mouths and dirty hands braving the scalding temperatures for some relief. It was mad, like nothing anyone had ever seen before. Varinius' camp was set further west than Crassus' who was position up against the barricade. He had time to come out with Dacia and observe what was coming at them. They heard it first, a steady yet muffled tremble. It was deep, and widespread, as far as the eye could see. One big wave of desperation. Gannicus was in the lead, forcefully dragging his cousin behind him who was struggling to keep up. Horses mixed in with the people. It had been such a hard winter, and the season was not yet over. Dacia urged Varinius to do something by tugging on his sleeve, but he was at a loss for words, mouth agape at the sight and sound of it all. They were barely humans, running through the snow, trudging in the knee deep white. It was so hard to do. People fell, grumbled, got run over, rolled, stood back up with white all over them. Always moving forward, tugging each other along. Varinius kept his men in their positions, no weapons drawn, and to only draw when drawed upon first. None of them were drawn upon though. Téadora ran through with her women. They were in the middle of the pack now. Dacia wanted to speak to her but the moment came and went as fast as Dacia could think of it. She was more alert when Spartacus ran through with his Thracians, and was able, out of their past cooperation with another, to grab his attention, as well as his arm. Varinius had gone to Crassus' camp for orders, but he went slowly in the hopes the situation would pass before he had to be the jerk that killed people struggling to escape dying in the snow. There was no honor in that kill, and Varinius wanted to try and retain what little dignity he had left to his name. Spartacus was reluctant to go with Dacia into her tent, but he could oblige her a couple of minutes so he could catch his breath and warm himself with her fire.

"Do you need food, Spartacus?"

"I'll take a mouthful of whatever you have, but I'm not staying long. I need to get back out there with my men."

"No, I know you do, but it brings me no pleasure seeing you like this. You were once such a proud man."

"I'm still proud, just desperate."

"Still *useful*, too?"

"You need me for something, Dacia?"

"My visions have left me. I am no longer the seer you once knew. I do not know what this war will look like anymore. But what my talents left me was a troubling sight, regarding Téadora."

"You have my attention. Explain yourself."

"The bounty Senator Furius has put on her head is enough to keep a man happy for the rest of his life. Spartacus, men have come out to the camps in recent weeks, in the dead of this winter, to come after her. She is no longer safe."

"She is safe with me."

"I urge you to reconsider."

"Are you asking me to turn her over to you?"

"A surrender now might prevent ample bloodshed in the future. Spartacus I've seen some of these men. Not that I'm not confident in your abilities, but these men…"

"I get it. They're bad news. But Téa is my life. I love her."

"And sometimes you need to let go of what you love to keep it alive. Her best chance of keeping air in her chest is to go to the Senator willingly. Deny the payment of this barbaric bounty. Varinius and I think it is a good idea if…"

"You've let the praetor get in your head."

"He's not a terrible man, Spartacus. There are far worse out there."

"There are far better too."

"Beggars can't be choosers, and I am a begging woman anymore. Without my talents I am useless to society. They'd just assume kill me as tolerate me. He protects me. He would never lie to me. He'd like to see Téadora in the Senator's hands. She'd be safe there."

"She'd be miserable."

"Is miserable and alive better than happy and dead?"

"Neither are suitable options."

"Spartacus what if I could assure you she was safe *and* happy?"

"You promise the impossible."

"With the right payment, I could promise such things."

"*Payment*?! I'm *barley* alive right now and you ask me for *coin*?!"

"Not coin, but something else of value?"

"What did you have in mind?"

"The silver ring around your neck would do nicely."

"That's my mother's ring."

"And it means the world to you, yes?"

"Yes."

"Does Téadora mean more?"

"Don't ask me to choose between my mother and Téa."

"Then don't choose. Live with the *memory* of them both."

"The necklace for Téa's life? Is that what you're saying?"

"I can go with her to Rome, explain everything."

"She hates you."

"We could come to an understanding. I've been looking out for her for years."

"She doesn't see it that way."

"She *can* see it that way. I can be very persuasive."

"You swear you'll keep her safe?"

"No harm will come to her. Senator Furius wants her very much alive and in perfect condition. Not a bruise or scratch. If she goes willingly, it'll be easier on all involved. Spartacus, please, I know this is difficult but…"

"Take the necklace."

"You'll see in time that I am right about this."

"How will you even get your hands on her? She won't surrender herself and I won't hand her off."

"I have seen her in custody. I'm not sure how it happens, but I have seen it. You have just made it so."

"Can you tell me one thing?"

"Perhaps."

"Will I ever see her again?"

"I don't know. My visions left me with the sight of her. I don't know what becomes of any of us. But if she does go to Rome, and she doesn't kill herself in the process, she will be Senator Furius' wife. You might be able to go to town and see her that way."

"That is a punishment worse than death."

"That is the world we live in."

Spartacus was offered a bowl of stew. It was steaming and full and tempting beyond words, but now the Thracian leader felt sick to his stomach. He had nothing. His mother's necklace was in the hands of Dacia, and Téadora was promised away. Promised to be kept alive, but for how long was anyone's guess. Spartacus flipped the bowl in the seer's hands and scalded her. She began to scream in pain as he left her tent to rejoin the run to the countryside. Upon seeing this, men in Varinius' camp assumed they had been drawn upon, or at least Dacia had, a rape perhaps judging by her screams. They drew swords and attempted to catch Spartacus but he disappeared into the stampede of the slave army. From up on high some of the army had reached the salvation of a cave to catch their breaths. Gannicus had corralled Téadora in there with him, alongside Castus. They were waiting for sight of Spartacus. Téadora had spotted him in the Roman camp and lost him in Dacia's tent. She could not be pulled away from the edge of the cave for anything. Strong gusts pushed Castus deeper inside more than once, but she remained in the windbreak of a boulder, angrily, seething with curiosity. It wasn't until Spartacus was seen running away did her imagination get the best of her. All the possibilities that could have taken place. She was bitter, and full of adrenaline and conflicting emotions. Castus kept tugging on her to come in to the warmer parts of the cave. They were far from warm, but less freezing than the chill in the air outside. He was rubbing his hands up and down her arms to try and keep her calm, but she just kept muttering more and more under her breath, faster and faster until she could barely focus. Castus snickered, and it was about enough to set her off.

"You think something's *funny* right now, Castus!"

"Don't stab me, Téadora. I'm not the one you're upset with."

"I'm sorry. But what do you think Spartacus could have possibly been doing for that long in Dacia's tent? I mean, what could have been so important he stopped running for her?"

"If I didn't know any better, I'd say you were jealous."

"*Me*?! Jealous of Dacia the Seer?! Don't be ridiculous. That woman is dangerous, that's all."

"You forget, Téadora, my days are filled with jealousy. It's nearly all I feel anymore. Watching you and Spartacus every day, it's almost unbearable."

"Oh! Castus, I…"

"Please, don't say anything. Just know I understand what you're feeling right now. Spartacus is a good man. Quiet your head. Whatever you're thinking, it's not what just happened."

"I heard her screaming."

"He probably told her something she didn't want to hear."

"I'm going down to speak with her."

"I don't think that's a good idea."

"I know it's not. But I'm going anyways."

"We have to keep moving forwards, Téadora."

"Stay with your cousin. Follow his lead. I'll catch up."

"Are you sure? I'd feel better if we waited for you to come back."

"I know that's what would feel better, but I don't want anyone waiting for me. I don't know how long this will take. I've been needing to have a conversation with Dacia for a while now."

"And you've decided *now* is the most opportune moment?"

"Now or never, Castus. One or the both of us might die soon. If you happen to see Spartacus before I do, don't tell him what I'm going to do. He won't be happy about it. I'm sorry. I have to go."

Téadora hugged her friend before forcibly pulling herself out of his grasp. He did not make it easy on her. When Castus turned around for advice from his cousin, Gannicus was speechless and offered no wisdom. He just shook his head, bundled up, and braved the cold once more. They'd taken enough of a break already. Castus couldn't stay in the cave alone and wait to see what happened to Téadora. She was having a hell of a time running against the crowds of her fellow men and women struggling to get away. It made no sense why she was doing this now, going back into harm's way. It was surely a death sentence, and Spartacus was nowhere to be seen. Gannicus was barking orders at the front though. He'd found a horse, and got him and Castus up in the air for a bit of clarity. He was giving the army direction in the absence of all other reason. Spartacus was in the thick of it, trying to help those with difficulties and snow weakened injuries. He had a heavily pregnant gladiatrix he was carrying in his arms. The father to be was nowhere to be found, but she was adamant he was still alive. She was trying desperately not to deliver the baby in this snowstorm and escape, but Spartacus felt warm blood on his arms as he carried her. He'd never helped deliver a baby before, and had no idea what he might need to do. The woman said not to put her down, so he didn't, and just kept moving with the flow of traffic, up the hillsides and out to the country. Visibility was improving. The fog was rising and the snow lightening up. The flakes were smaller, and no longer clumped on his eye lashes. They were going to make it. They were going to survive. Téadora felt this shift as well. The trickling through the Roman camp was becoming weaker. It was the tail end. She was sure of Dacia's tent as she pushed into the crowds. She'd kept an eye on it, only losing sight for a couple of minutes when she got tumbled to the ground by a frantic Celt. He didn't mean nay harm, she knew he didn't, but he was so apologetic. Téadora was working up a fiery speech for the seer, wanting answers for years of harassment and tension, but when Téadora walked into the tent, Dacia was not alone. Varinius had returned. Worse yet, the seer was putting Spartacus' mother's silver ring necklace into the palm of the praetor's hand. As Téadora reached around for her curved sica blades, Varinius was in a panic. He didn't mean to, but he also wasn't sorry about it as his instincts kicked in. He flung a fist, knocking Téadora unconscious.

"Varinius! What have you done?!"

"It's alright, Dacia. It'll be easier to get her out of camp now."

"She needs an explanation for what's going to happen to her."

"She's a smart woman. She'll figure it out."

"I'm going with her."

"I don't think that's a good idea."

"She'll need someone in Rome with her. She'll never survive the city alone. I can be her handmaiden, servant, something."

"But you two hate each other? And I need you here with me."

"Nothing is happening in this winter camp. I'll be back before the weather warms and the battles continue. Téadora is more important right now."

"Oh."

"Varinius, do you honestly think anyone is going to be paid a bounty if Téadora figures out she's been sold to the Senator and kills herself before she ever even makes it to Rome?"

"So, you're going to make sure she stays alive?"

"She will listen to me."

"And you will ensure I get paid?"

"You will have enough money to retire from the army and be free of orders for the rest of your life."

"We could runaway together. Be happy."

"I'm doing this for *us*, Varinius."

"Then you should be quick about it. I don't want word getting into Crassus' camp of what we're doing."

"He doesn't know?"

"I didn't tell him."

"I thought you had?"

"And risk our freedom? Here, wrap her in something before I get the wagons. Pack some food for the travel."

"When I'm gone, keep good track of that little necklace."

"Why?"

"It's very important."

"Then maybe you should just hold onto it."

"Are you sure?"

"I trust you with everything important in my life."

"I'll see that this is settled as soon as possible."

"Be sure you meet with the Senator directly when you get to Rome, Dacia. Do not give in to the pressures of any soldiers, guards, or centurions. Avoid the Senate and city center if you can."

"Don't worry about me, I have more than enough experience talking my way out of undesirable situations."

"Just be careful. You're a free woman now, *my* free woman, and I want you to stay that way. I'll carry Téadora out to the wagons for you. Take her blades so she's unharmed. She'll be waking up soon."

XXI

It took over a week to travel by wagon from the southern peninsula up to Rome. It was also the start of a new year, 71 BCE, though with nothing positive to look forward to. On the trip from the Roman camp to the capital, Dacia had kept Téadora heavily sedated with a concoction of opium laced wine. The last day of travel Dacia let Téadora sober up so she could have her wits about her in the city. The gladiatrix commander was a mess when she finally woke up for the first time in nine days. The first thing she did was reach for her sica blades around her back, and finding them gone she startled herself into panic which was instantly meant with a searing headache. As she sat up, she was trying to understand why she was in a wagon with pigs and hay if she was not injured. There was no blood anywhere on her, and she did not recognize her surroundings. She'd never been to the city of Rome before. She'd been to matches on the outskirts, in smaller feeder towns. The trees looked bare but possibly somewhat familiar. After throwing off the cloth over the back of the wagon in it's entirety she was able to see the seven hills of Rome coming upon her, and Dacia driving the wagon. The seer had taken up possession three days ago, stranding the derelict man who had previously taken her that far because of his repeated unwanted sexual advances. A glint of a silver ring necklace hung around her neck, and Téadora's memory was all coming back to her now. The breakout in the snow, the impromptu tent meeting she'd watched from the cave with Castus. Spartacus and Dacia. The scream. Téadora rubbed her temples, and climbed up from the back of the wagon to the steering seat with Dacia. The seer was quick to take the necklace off and give it back to the gladiatrix commander. Téadora pulled her tangled black braids to the side and put it, careful to tuck it underneath her clothes.

"Why are we in Rome, Dacia?"

"I'm delivering you to Senator Furius."

"Why do I feel like I've been run over by this wagon?"

"Cretic wine. Touched with opium. I drugged you to get you this far. Now you're less likely to kill the both of us."

"The thought has still crossed my mind."

"I bet it has. But will you hear me out first?"

"Why should I?"

"I gave you back Spartacus' necklace. Isn't that proof enough I am on your side?"

"You tracked me for years. How can I possibly trust you?"

"Your father paid me to return you to him. I disobeyed him to keep you safe. I tracked you to keep you from going back home and ruining your life the way so many other young, obedient girls do."

"I suppose I should thank you for that."

"I've always been on your side, Téadora. Despite what it may have looked like, I am a great supporter of women."

"Then why are we in Rome about to surrender all our efforts to a Senator who wants nothing more than to make a domestic servant and trophy of me?"

"You and I both know that will never happen."

"Dacia, I am still confused."

"The wine will wear off by the time you are in the Senator's company, I promise. Let me explain. Rome has a bounty on you, enough to set a man up for life. Hunters had come out to the camp in the south. It wasn't enough for the army to be after you. I knew it would be one massacre after another if this was not settled."

"You brought me here to save Spartacus' army?"

"I take no pleasure in senseless deaths. If we get you to the Senator now, before the war opens back up again in the warmer weather, if you refuse him properly, end this search for your love, you could be a truly free woman with Spartacus."

"I must reject the Senator in a way he understands? How do I do that? I don't have the social graces that it takes to refuse a man so far above me in society. He has *everything* and I have *nothing*."

"That's not true. You have me."

"What does that mean?"

"You've rejected this man once already in the House of Batiatus. Of this encounter I was made aware of by my visions."

"And what do your visions say about the situation now?"

"They have unfortunately left me. All I was left with were foggy bits and pieces of the future, but I will do my best to see them through. I have poison in my possession. Poison and an antidote."

"You want me to kill a Senator?"

"Death is the only thing that stops a man from pursuing a woman who has already told him no."

"I don't want to kill the man. He's just kind and misguided."

"You've killed many a man before. Don't back down on me now."

"Slicing with my blades is much different than the underhanded use of poison."

"Well, I don't need you charged with the murder of a Senator because it will mean death for the both of us. Poison is the way women handle things in this city. Your blades are for the battlefield."

"A place I am eager to return to."

"Soon enough. Soon enough. If all goes according to plan you and I will be back in this wagon and headed for our men by sundown."

"Where *are* my blades, by the way, Dacia?"

"Safe from you. Until we leave the city that's all you need to know."

"Spartacus stole those for me."

"I know. He'd steal the world for you if that was possible."

"When you two were in that tent, is *this* what you talked about?"

"You have to know how difficult it was for him to allow this."

"Did he hurt you?"

"What?"

"I heard you scream."

"He threw boiling stew on me. All things considered; it was the least amount of harm he could have made me endure."

"But he knows I'm coming back to him, doesn't he?"

"I could not promise him that."

"So, he thought he was going to lose me forever?"

"If I could prepare him for the worst, if anything else better happened, then it would be easier to accept than if I had been cruel and promised your return and you never came. To be honest, I wasn't sure if the opium wine was going to work on you, but since you never drink your body is inherently weaker to the effects. Drugging you was the only way to travel. You'd have killed us both to try and get back to Spartacus, and everyone knew it."

"*Everyone?*"

"I promised him I'd do everything I could to keep you safe. But we have to go into the wolf's den in order to protect the flock. You do understand this, don't you?"

"I have fought more than one battle in the arena that I thought I would never survive. For me, this is just another match."

"Except Batiatus isn't profiting off of you anymore."

"Tell me about this poison, Dacia."

"It will take some finesse to distribute. You will need to get close to the Senator. *He* will be none the wiser, but for *you*, this may prove to be uncomfortable."

"What do you mean, *finesse?*"

"This is an oral poison and antidote. It's the fastest way to get in and out of Rome before anyone even knows we're here."

"Oral?"

"By the mouth."

"I know what oral means! I'm just…you're being indirect. You could have just said I'd have to kiss him."

"Forgive me. I didn't want you to strike me."

"I'm not going to harm you, Dacia. We're in this together now whether I like it or not. We need each other, because without me, you have no protection. You're the sort Rome burns for pleasure."

"I know."

"And yet you came anyway?"

"Without the pursuit of you, the Senate will lose interest in chasing the slave army. The war will effectively stalemate and be over. People will dissimilate into the countryside and return to their homes. There is no extra funding in the government for this. The real war is out in the Mediterranean."

"Stop Furius, stop the hunt for me, stop the war?"

"Exactly."

"And we're all free to live our lives again?"

"Yes."

"You've never really had freedom before, have you, Dacia?"

"Being used by men is all I know. It would be nice to know something else."

"Get me to the Senator's door. Let's end this."

"Are you sure you're ready?"

"As ready as I'm going to be."

"Alright. At the door, slip the antidote into your mouth and let it dissolve under your tongue. From that point you have half an hour to slip the poison into your mouth and kiss the Senator without the risk of you getting sick at all. *Half an hour*, Téadora. That's it. Do you think you can do that?"

"Do you think I can get an obsessed Senator to kiss me in half an hour when I've scarcely seen him in two years? Dacia, it's like you don't know me at all. I could open the door and kiss him right there without a single word spoken. He's funded this war to keep me in his sights. I'll give him what he wants and he'll never be sorrier. Get my blades out. I want to see them in the wagon as soon as I'm back."

The tattooed seer cowered a bit on the bench of the wagon, reins tightly gripped in one hand. Téadora was unusually good at taking life. The ethical dilemma didn't seem to bother her too much. It crossed her mind only briefly when she weighed the pros and cons of what one death might mean. Senator Furius was a good man, not too corrupt or politically active. He didn't deserve to die, but if his life meant saving thousands of slaves, then it was a life worth taking. His money could be distributed to half a dozen families and keep them well off for years. Téadora could do this, and she would do it with a smile on her face. The smile was for Spartacus, and the thought of what he might look like when she returned to him. She'd jump up in his arms, and he would be shocked beyond reason. Téadora pinched his mother's silver ring necklace as it dangled beneath her clothes in secret. Dacia had parked the wagon in a nearby alley so she could see the apartment in Rome where Senator Furius was known to stay. It was right off the Via Appia, a main thoroughfare, stoned up nice with heavy foot traffic from all over the empire. So many different looking faces. The gladiatrix commander absent mindedly went tugging for her sica blades on her back again as she went knocking on the turquoise painted door. A servant answered. A young boy of maybe twenty. Téadora hadn't prepared for what she might say to a servant, so she just insisted to tell Furius he had a gift waiting for him. She stayed there, and as the door half closed, she stuck the antidote under her tongue as instructed. It tasted foul, like garlic which had rotted, but she was obedient, and let it swirl around her mouth while she struggled to manage a straight face. Over her shoulder she nodded to Dacia. The seer could barely breathe as she watched the Senator come to the door and welcome Téadora inside. His pale skin turned fifty shades of red in anxious anticipation. The gladiatrix did her best to maintain intimate spacing from the blonde man as he backed up into a wall, and she pressed him in place.

"Téadora! What are you doing here?!"

"You've been chasing me for nearly two years. Well, I'm here. Time to do something about it. Claim your prize."

"I'm confused. Has something happened to Spartacus? I thought you'd *never* leave his side. Have you…have you finally accepted my offer to become my wife? Is this really happening?!"

"It's really happening."

"I can hardly believe this!"

"Me either."

"You're not…you're not here…*willingly*, are you? I've not heard anything from the war. Spartacus lives, doesn't he?"

"If the gods are merciless, he still lives."

"I must know, what is that slave to you, Téadora?"

"Everything you're not."

"Then why are you here?"

"You wanted me for your wife. Don't you usually get what you want, Felix? I'm right here. Ripe for the taking. Congratulations. You've won."

"I didn't want to win like this. Something doesn't feel right."

"Just wait a second, and see how you feel. Kiss me. Let's celebrate. Before the moment passes. Come here."

Before the Senator could object any further, he was overwhelmed by the gladiatrix commander's hands on his neck. It was an odd mixture of firm and gentle touch. When her tongue parted his lips, he fought her no further and embraced her whole heartedly. She was everything he had ever wanted, and he just needed to stop questioning and accept what was right before him. Téadora felt the man's pulse under her fingertips as she held his neck, and when it began to slow, she let his body go limp between her own body and the wall. Carefully, she slumped the Senator down to the floor, and propped him upright with a nearby jar. His head bowed. He was not dead yet, but his breath was shallow and only getting worse the longer she hovered in front of him. Téadora bolted for the front door, refusing the servant's questions from the other room. She ran for Dacia and the wagon. A pair of sica blades gleamed on the front bench. The women nodded to each other as the servant boy began to ring out that something was wrong with the Senator. He needed help. There was minor stirring on the street. Téadora jumped into the back of the wagon and shoved the pigs onto the path to disturb the public and lighten the wagon so they could move faster. Dacia wasted no time getting out of the city. She wanted Rome far, far behind her, and if she was a lucky woman, she'd never have to see it again. The women exchanged pleasant smiles, with uneasy eyes. It was no laughing matter to kill a Senator, but there was no going back now. Dacia insisted they might get off the main path of the Via Appia after a day or so to cover their tracks. It might take longer than nine days to get back to their men, but they were at least headed in the right direction now. Forward progress. Téadora had Dacia pull over once by a river so she could wash her mouth out of the poison and foul-tasting antidote. Other than that, she was physically side effect free. Mentally, she was still a bit upset about killing Furius, but if it meant she got to spend her life with Spartacus, she'd kiss and kill a hundred Senators. The gladiatrix had to bite her lips to keep from smiling too much as she bounced along in the wagon through the countryside. If only her expression and hope could have been matched with that of her other half. Spartacus was in a deep depression, having gone nine days thinking he might never see Teadora again. Half the slave army had deserted, despite desertion being the main reason so many of them had become slaves and gladiators in the first place. Even the Celts were parting ways with the army. Gannicus and Castus were finally going home. They couldn't stay any longer. Their revenge had been sought, and they needed to move before the weather warmed and the war started back up again. There was a lot of regret for not following the Germanians after the victory in Mutina. Spartacus would never hold a man against his will, but was sorry to see his camp dwindle down. His Thracians remained steadfast and loyal to him, as did many of the female forces. Before Gannicus made his final exit, he met with Spartacus on a snowy hill overlooking the valley where fifteen thousand men sat ready to march. The ginger bearded man hugged the Thracian leader with tears in his eyes.

"Do not be sad, Gannicus. You're taking your people home. You should be thrilled."

"I wish you were coming with me, Spartacus."

"I have no will to fight without Téa beside me."

"You have to *find* a way to move on for the army."

"I won't let them die. I promised them they were going home. One way or another, I'll get them there. But this war, it is over for me. We had a good run, Gannicus."

"That we did. But all runs stop eventually."

"What way will you be heading?"

"To the coast, I think. Marching up the Adriatic seemed to work well for us before. I figure we stop off near Cantenna. Raiding was always good there. Stock up for the push north. Castus also thinks if we stay by the coast, we might be able to catch word of what's happened to Téadora. I told him not to expect anything, but the boy is heartbroken."

"Aren't we all?"

"You two have taken her disappearance the worst."

"It feels like there is a gaping hole in my chest that won't close. Will it ever get easier, Gannicus? Or will I always miss her?"

"Talking as a man with that same hole in his chest, no, Spartacus, time will not heal this wound. She will be with you always, haunting you. Your Téadora is my Muire. One day soon we'll be together again. Until then, we have to make them proud."

Spartacus' shoulders started to shudder and shake. He was silently crying at the realization Téadora was not coming back. Gannicus held the mighty Thracian in his arms for a bit before departing for the north. Spartacus remained on that snowy hill overlooking the valley for hours, even after the Celts had left it empty. No one was brave enough to talk to their leader that day. It had become something like a day of mourning, with everyone just keeping to themselves and tending campfires or collecting kindling. Some men went hunting, some women went fishing. There wasn't much food to be found in the winter, but spring would be fast approaching. At least, it's what everyone was praying to the gods for in complete desperation. An early spring. The Celts would appreciate that. Less snow made raiding easier. Crops were planted in the spring, more food for the army. Gannicus was not sitting well with the low turnout in Cantenna. He had low expectations marching up to the town, and even still he was left disappointed. It was almost as if it'd already been run through. Because it had. The Romans under Crassus had been through that morning and took what little was left to be taken. They were still there now, on the northern side, watching the Celts creep trough from the south. Crassus wanted to slaughter the raiding party. Varinius thought it almost a crime to go after them, claiming it'd be too easy, too one-sided of a fight. After Crassus accused the younger praetor of being soft out of the misery of his woman Dacia leaving him, Varinius wanted to prove just how dedicated to the war effort he still was. Flanked by his loyal, misguided consuls Publicola and Clodianus, the Romans swarmed the Celts from both sides of the city, pushing the weary army back against the icy banks of Lake Lucania. Some of the Celts attempted to break out of the surrounding maneuver, but they were all killed without a shred of mercy. The Romans outnumbered them three to one, and the slaves had never not had the superior numbers before. Gannicus himself locked eyes with Varinius in a hate filled tirade. It reminded him of his youth, what he had done to the Romans when Muire had been killed. It was a cold day like this. The ginger bearded man gazed up to sky as an arrow struck him in the chest and knocked him off his horse. Castus gasped in horror, in utter disbelief that's all it had taken to kill his cousin. Gannicus had cracked his head open on an icy rock, and blood was pooling into the mud. The Celts were dying, and when they looked to Castus for help, all the curly haired man could do was stumble into the lake for security. The water would never hurt him. It was so good and kind to Téadora. He asked for her help now, as he walked waist deep, chest deep, neck deep. The water was frigid, and the surface crunched with ice. Slowly, the Celts all found themselves dipping into the water of Lake Lucania. Not all of them could swim, but it didn't matter. Dying from the cold, or drowning, was better than a Roman sword. Crassus couldn't believe what he was seeing, and sneered at the sheer lack of will of his enemy. They were exhausted. Varinius barely had any blood on his sword, and took no pleasure in this victory. The lake had stolen his glory. Slaves had outsmarted the Romans yet again. One slave revolt after another. Death before dishonor. Varinius walked to the banks of the lake and dropped to his knees, screaming loud enough for the gods to hear him, grabbing bloody fistfuls of the mud and his blonde hair. This wasn't the way it was supposed to be. If Dacia was here, she'd have tried to stop this. But Dacia wasn't here, and now there were thousands of Celts bobbing in the lake like icebergs with dead, cold eyes while Varinius was burning with rage.

XXII

As Dacia and Téadora continued heading south, the war was coming north towards them. The defunct seer was able to seduce a young runner in the countryside who said the Romans had encamped on the outskirts of Campania. In an effort to try and save the Celts running up the Adriatic in the east, Spartacus had moved his small portion of the army to the west. If it was Rome where Téadora sat miserable, then that's where Spartacus was going to go. While he and his thirty-five thousand strong band of misfits, rebels, and rejects were en route to Campania, word had come to him by two barely surviving Celts about the massacre in Lake Lucania. This stopped him dead in his tracks. He was losing everything. For the first time in the war, he was no longer leading the hunt, but the one being hunted. He was tired of running. If Téadora were at his side, she would claim swift revenge for the loss of her dearest friends. Spartacus found himself clawing at his chest to try and speak to her, or his mother, any kind of reassuring presence. He voiced out loud his discontent at having received this news, and addressed the army while they were on a break midday. Spartacus put it to a vote what they were to do. It was about as unanimous a vote as one could ask for. They were to run to the Roman's camp with all haste, and kill as many soldiers as they could before they were struck down. There was this kind of suicidal euphoria shared amongst the ranks. They had bled and fought together. They had cried and won together. They'd been up and down the empire, giving everything they had and then some. In the back of their heads, it was all for those who had fallen before them. All the poor souls who never got the chance to get Roman blood on their hands. As the army cheered and redirected their marching, Spartacus was left standing with no one by his side. All his friends had fallen. Crixus. Oenomaus. Gannicus. Téadora was gone.

In Campania, Crassus and Varinius were in a heated exchange when the unmistakable thunder of an army approaching had them running outside of their blood red tents. Thirty-five thousand screaming voices. Half a dozen different languages crying out for justice. Wolf howls, whistles, clicks, jeers. The armies were somewhat equally matched. Crassus had lost little in the victory against the Celts. He still sported nearly forty thousand men at his disposal. Spartacus' men and women were comfortably worth more than a soul a piece. They may not have had the number advantage, but they had the heart of warriors who knew no cost when lives had been unduly taken. Crassus was amused, and didn't even put his armor on for this show. Varinius was allowed to ride out on his pretty white horse and lead the legions. The young man seemed anxious to die anymore, and wanted it to be at Spartacus' hands. Just when the Romans started to get within arrow shot however, the Thracian lost his nerve and pulled back. He ordered a retreat, and routed Crassus' position around the town. He could not follow through. There was hesitation, something stirring in the air. While deeply confused, the slave army pulled back, and continued their taunting like all of this demonstration had been intentional. Varinius was unsatisfied and went chasing after the retreat alone, ordering his centurions guarding him to stand down. He wanted an audience with Spartacus personally. The Thracian was alerted by his officers he was being sought out, and made it easy for the young praetor to reach him. Spartacus rode away from where his army would camp in the river valley, and firmly sat atop his stolen white horse with a little bit of pride at Varinius' expense. Spartacus kept a clenched grip on the sica blade at his side while the praetor flashed his sword. Before the men could do anything to each other though the dust of a wagon moving at full speed interrupted them. Dacia and Téadora crested the final hill into Campania. It was hard to say whether Varinius or Spartacus jumped off their horse first, but both men dropped to the ground and started running as fast as their feet would carry them. The young women shared a muffled giggle in-between them before Dacia stopped the wagon. She waited for the praetor to reach her, and jump up to the bench to smother her with affection. Téadora was much more impatient. The gladiatrix commander leapt from the wagon and ran impossibly fast for Spartacus. As they smacked together, they nearly knocked the wind out of their chests. Téadora had jumped up and wrapped her legs tight around Spartacus' waist, and let her fingers get tangled up in his short hair. They clanked teeth they were so happy to see each other. As Spartacus needed to take a breath, he set Téadora down on her feet, and she looked back to Dacia. The women nodded, and took their men their separate ways. With any luck, they would quiet this war for good. Téadora and Spartacus were walking hand in hand but the Thracian leader stopped short of getting back into camp. Téadora was confused, and could see tears welling up in his eyes. Spartacus never cried, so she knew this had to be something terribly serious. She reached up and tapped the corners of his eyes with her thumbs to try and relieve him, but he wouldn't let go of her waist. His fingertips were leaving indents into her skin. Carefully, she cupped his face, and forced him to look her square in the eye.

"These are not happy tears. Spartacus, what is it?"

"This morning I got word that the Celts had been massacred."

"I…I don't understand. The Celts were with you. Gannicus and Castus were with you! They were safe. They were…"

"They left a couple days ago. Most of the army deserted. No one thought you were coming back. I thought you were gone forever. I wasn't strong enough for them. Gannicus was going to take the Celts home. I don't know what happened, but Crassus surrounded them. Pushed them into the lake. Most of them chose to drown in the ice."

"Gannicus and Castus…they're…"

"They're gone, Téa. They're both gone."

"I…I need a minute."

"Téa, that's why I'm here. To avenge them. I know it's what you'd want. But I backed out today. I couldn't do it. I'm sorry."

"My chest hurts."

"Téa. Téa, come here. You're shaking. Téa, come here, sit down before you fall down. Téa!"

"He promised me we would never say our goodbyes to one another. He *promised*!"

"Who promised?"

"He promised me! Why would the Romans kill Castus? Castus would never kill a soul! He killed in the arena, but only because he *had* to. They were animals. It was kill or be killed. Never a human. Not ever. He was so kind. So good. The *best* of us! He *promised* me. *NO* goodbyes. Why would he go back on his word?! I *trusted* him! I told him…I told him all about how pretty it was back home. He was going to come with us, Spartacus. Back to Samothraki. He was going to live! He was going to live! He *deserved* to live! Why would Crassus take him from me?! Why?!"

"I don't have the answers you're looking for."

"I have something for *you* though."

"My…my mother's necklace?!"

"Dacia gave it to me in Rome. Proof she's been on my side the whole time. We had these grand delusions of ending this war when we got back to you and Varinius. So much for that idea, huh?"

"Keep the necklace."

"But…"

"My mother always said that her ring would be yours one day."

"I can't…"

"Yes, you can. Keep it. It looks better on you than it does on me anyways. This way, you two can be together. She's been giving me strength for years. But it wasn't until I thought I lost you that I realized *you* are my strength, Téa. I'm going to make this right for you. I'm going to make Crassus pay."

"What are you going to do?"

"I'm going to get even."

"I'm going to help you."

"I'd be insulted if you didn't. Let's get you back with the army. We could use a good morale boost. Let me dry your tears."

"Let me dry yours."

Spartacus had dirty hands as he smeared Téadora's cheeks dry, but she didn't care because she was streaking charcoal across her eyes for next battle around Campania. Strike while the iron was hot, just like Oenomaus used to say. Those who had stuck it out this long in the army were more than pleased to have Téadora back, and healthy in their ranks. She rallied them around her with a formidable speech about the cowards it must have taken to massacre the Celts in Lake Lucania. For the revenge of their friends and fallen commanders, Téadora made a personal request to go head hunting for officers. Any rank would do, any soldier really, but the closer to the praetors they could get they better. But not the praetors themselves. There was an exception. Téadora wanted them alive, to be able to sit with the mistakes they had made. Death would be a mercy to them they did not deserve. After making fast friends with Dacia on the trip to Rome, there was a bit of leniency given to Varinius right now. The seer really sang his praises as a redeemable man. Téadora did not see such traits in the young praetor herself, but would take Dacia's word for it. An agreement amongst women was not so casually broken. Nor did it need to be common knowledge. Let the men fight, conduct their battles, while the women pulled the strings in the background, or foreground. Téadora was not sitting back for this one. She was on the front lines with Spartacus, leading the violent charge on top of their pair of matching white horses. The Romans were not at all prepared for this second wave. They thought they were done for the day, victorious, and had driven the slave army back with ease. Crassus miscalculated, and was left desperately scrambling to maintain order while the outer rows of the Roman camp were destroyed. Campfires were strewn about, and grasses lit ablaze. The fires did little damage because everything was so snow soaked and saturated, but the damage was still ever present as row upon row of slave soldiers laid waste to their Roman enemy. Crassus led an embarrassing retreat from the river valley and up to the inner workings of proper Campania. He was not leaving altogether, but needed a safe place to regroup. Varinius was left behind with his lone legion to cover the main forces fall back. Téadora searched for Dacia but could not find the seer anywhere. Varinius himself, did not seem to know where she was either, which may have contributed to his somewhat erratic maneuverings. Some might have called it strategic genius, but really it was frantic luck. While the young praetor eventually did run for the hills with his neck still intact, it cost him his two faithful consuls. The gladiatrices lured the naïve young pair of Publicola and Clodianus into a trap, knocked them off their brown horses, stole the horses, and then bound and gagged the consuls for their crimes. The women drug the men to Téadora after the Roman camp had been left abandoned and the slave army was allowed to loot for food, armor, and weapons. Téadora was most pleased with her spoils, and planted a taunting kiss on each of the young men's cheeks as Spartacus came over to see what was going on. Publicola and Clodianus were pleading like desperate fiends for mercy and surrender, but Téadora had jars of water from the river poured on them until they could barely breathe.

"Perhaps you should go a bit easy on them, Téa?"

"No, Spartacus. These boys don't deserve your pity. Do you think they celebrated in the deaths of our friends?"

"I do."

"Then we will celebrate in *their* deaths tonight."

"What will we do with them until then?"

"I need some logs."

"For a pyre?"

"For a pair of crosses."

"Crosses?"

"Crosses. And I want them set up right here on the edge of the valley, so the Romans can see what we think of them."

"I don't think the Romans care what our opinion is of them."

"I don't care if they care. This is for Gannicus and Castus. Varinius loses his men. If Dacia can't talk some sense into him now, then I give him no more chances in this war. She has hopes for the man. After everything she's done for me, I owed her this chance. But I owe her nothing else. Go get the logs, Spartacus. I need rope. I'm sure I can find some in this Roman trash heap. I'll string the boys up myself. I have a blade for each of their necks. A pair for a pair. It couldn't be more fitting if I tried. Rope! I need rope. Can anyone get some rope into my hands, please?"

Spartacus grinned like a madman as Publicola and Clodianus cried themselves nearly into suffocation. He kissed Téadora hard while she beckoned for rope and took charge of the looting. Spartacus may have been the face of this war, but she had always been the backbone of it. Without her, everything had gone to shit. But with her, there was reason to to fight. Ten different hands threw rope at the gladiatrix commander. She was in no shortage of help or support. Multiple crosses were built from the surrounding tree timbers, and erected on the edge of the valley camp. Publicola and Clodianus were strung up before dinner, and then campfires were made to allow them to suffer with the guilt of their poor life decisions. Crucifixion wasn't the slave way of doing things, and after the lack of message sent with Mummius' killing, it was difficult to say if this would get a rise out of the Romans or not, but it made the army feel better about losing the Celts, so it was not a killing done for the sake of killing itself. Just before sundown Téadora was hoisted up on Spartacus' shoulders, and torches were lit so the Romans on sentry duty could see what was happening to their consuls. Téadora took her sica blades out, sliced their edges up and down against each other and then leaned to the right and cut open Clodianus' throat with her left hand. Before Publicola could make his final cry heard, Téadora was already leaning left, and cutting with her right. The boys both bled out at the same time, dying mere seconds apart from one another. It was like Dacia had said when she met them, that they were doomed to die together. She had seen it then in flashes, as she was seeing it now in person. She was up on the outskirts of Campania with the sentries and Varinius. She was the only thing holding the praetor upright on his feet. His consul duo may have been incompetent and nearly useless, but they had made for good company over the winter. More unsettling was the ease at which Téadora could be seen slitting their necks, and eyeing up at the Romans, as if to promise they were next. Varinius rubbed his intact neck, and gulped hard. Dacia reached up and pulled his hand away though from the phantom injury, and held it in both of her hands over the steady beating of her heart.

"She will not touch you, Varinius."

"How can you be so sure? I know what I've done to hurt her, and now I know *she* knows too."

"She won't touch you. She respects me."

Varinius wrenched his hand out of Dacia's hold and stomped back to camp. He needed wine, and lots of it. Enough to drown his sorrows and make him forget today had ever happened. It was just one jumbled mess of highs and lows. The highest of highs and lowest of lows. He was humiliated and confused. Dacia went after him to try and console him, explain why she had left for Rome and not returned with the coin, the bounty she had promised him. That had all been a lie. She wasn't being malicious about it. He would never understand. He was not a woman. He didn't know what the lack of freedom felt like day in and day out for years upon years with little to no promise of ever getting better. Dacia implored on her hands and knees as Varinius kept her shut out of their tent. He cried inside while she cried outside. Emotions were increasingly better amongst the slave army down by the river though. While Téadora was taking care to clean her blades and wash the Roman blood off of her arms, and the charcoal off of her eyes, Spartacus was watching her back, in more ways than one. He kept looking at her, so peaceful in the safe space of the water she so adored, and kept looking back towards where the Romans were now going to be sleeping in Campania. Crassus had come out with the sentries. Spartacus could identify him by the purple robes he wore, adorned with ridiculous golden tassels. The man must have thought himself the caesar of the battlefield. Spartacus was neither impressed, nor intimidated. He was lost in thought though, and was somewhat jumpy when Téadora came up to curl herself into his side. Crassus smirked and returned to the lights of his camp, while Spartacus held Téadora tight, and furrowed his brow.

"Tell me what you're thinking, Spartacus."

"I'm thinking, I didn't like the way Praetor Crassus was looking at you just now."

"He's too far away to do any harm tonight. Two battles are more than enough for one day. Besides, it's just fear making you think he was looking at me. I'm of no interest to him. Dacia and I handled that problem."

"Just what did you two do exactly? You were gone for weeks."

"We went to Rome, and I killed Senator Furius."

"You did what?!"

"I'd have killed a thousand men if I thought I could save you, Spartacus. This war was being funded by his fascination with me. With no more coin being thrown at the praetors, they will leave the countryside, and we can finally go home."

"I can't believe you killed that man. The punishment for killing a Senator must be…"

"Nevermind the punishment. I'm in your arms right now and that's all that matters, because this is where I'm going to stay."

"You killed a Senator for me."

"Does this amuse you?"

"I just never thought I was worthy of such an act."

"You *are* worthy. Don't let this cold weather bring you down. You are more than worthy. Spartacus, you are more than these collections of battle scars on your skin. You're my best friend, my peace of mind, my strength, my safety, the holder of my future, guardian of my past, keeper of my heart. You are everything a man could ever be to a woman and then some."

"I'm all of that, huh?"

"You're all of that."

"I feel sorry for the Romans."

"You do?"

"They will never know a love like ours. There is not a man or woman in those legions right now that could say they have what we have. And I am sorry for them. They are without."

"Don't feel too sorry for them. There will be consequences for what we did today."

"Like there were consequences for tying that boy up in no man's land? I'm not afraid of what might be headed for us."

"Really?"

"Are you, Téa?"

"I have a home to fill with children on an island very from here, and I need you to come with me to build that home. I had a very long time to think about that on the wagon ride from Rome. I don't want anymore obstacles between us and our happiness."

"I am happy right now."

"But we could be happier."

"I am not a greedy man."

"Nor I a greedy woman. But we can only ever be so happy being in each other's arms if we have Romans breathing down our necks. The crucifixions will not go unanswered."

"You know, I felt nothing when you cut their necks open. I was upset that the war had pushed us to do that to Mummius, but tonight was different. These boys didn't have to die. They were hollow deaths."

"The Romans didn't have to massacre the Celts either. But they chose to do that, so I chose to do this. Thank you for backing me up when I asked for the logs."

"You backed me up when I asked that of you."

"Hmm. Dacia said something to me when were in Rome."

"What did she say?"

"You'd steal the world for me if it were possible."

"She's not wrong. I'd do anything for you. And you for me. Even the enemy knows that."

"Dacia is not our enemy."

"She sleeps with our enemy. That means she can't be trusted."

"*You* once trusted her."

"I once *employed* her. My tolerance ends there."

"I don't know that I could kill her if the war brought me to it."

"It won't come to that."

"What do you think it *will* come to? When will enough be enough? When we will all be able to lay down our weapons and walk home without having to constantly look over our shoulders?"

"Soon. I promise."

"Don't promise me anything anymore. Castus promised me we'd never say our goodbyes and now he's dead in a lake."

"But I'm not Castus. I'm not dying on you. The gods themselves could not pull me from this earth unless you were in my arms."

"We die together or we don't die at all? You can make such a request from the gods? Spartacus, you're as bold as the day I met you."

"Well, you're prettier than the day I met you, and smarter, stronger. I can't wait to see what we'll be capable of in the future."

XXIII

In the Roman camp there was a clear divide between the four legions devoted to Crassus, and the sole legion loyal to Varinius. Crassus' camp paid little attention to the crucifixions of Publicola and Clodianus as they had been members of Varinius' inner circle. What the soldiers had trouble ignoring was Dacia the Seer. The woman was in an altered state this evening, chanting in her native tongue. Some officers appealed to Crassus to have her killed for the safety of their camp. They believed the war was being cursed as she stood atop the hills in the light of her campfire, all alone. She had no tent, no possession, but bundles of herbs were smoking in her hands, and she danced naked in the firelight, exposing all of her tattooed conglomeration of markings up and down her body. Everyone was too afraid of what she might be capable of to go out and talk to her in person. Some emissaries from Crassus' camp went into Varinius' camp to try and urge the praetor to go and speak with his advisor. Formally that was the position she held, informally it was understood she was a prostitute. The position of seer never really resonated with any of the men. Crassus let Varinius have his fun while the war raged in the countryside, but there were unspoken understandings that Dacia was not welcome back to Rome when everything was said and done, which at this point seemed inevitable. Varinius would have to make a break with his lover at one point or another. The young man was grappling his sense of duty with the will of his heart. He loved Dacia, but he could not have her, but he did have her. He didn't know what to do, what to say, or how to go about moving forward. He had been humiliated today in Campania, and all he wanted to do was hold Dacia, but he couldn't continue to show his dependence on her for his own sanity. The woman had her freedom now. Her visions had left her. She was far from stupid in the ways of the world and she had no desire to ever see Rome again, not alone make it her home. Varinius' future was in Rome. She was at peace with that, for the most part. She wrote Varinius a letter since she had been shut out of their tent this evening and he was refusing to speak to her. Before she walked off into the darkness, she left this letter secured with a moss-covered rock at the tent entrance. Varinius saw her petite silhouette and nearly crawled out on his knees to beg for her forgiveness, but the steady chatter of men outside had him paralyzed in seclusion. Dacia waited too, for a good handful of minutes, hoping her lover might come around, but she would not wait for him forever. On her gifted white horse, Dacia left the Roman camps, never to return.

From the river valley Spartacus and Téadora had been watching Dacia's spectacle up on the hills with quiet reflection. After the seer disappeared into the darkness, Téadora went to sleep with the sound of the river babbling to keep her happy. Spartacus snuck out with his body riddled with tense anticipation at the meeting he was hoping to secure with Praetor Crassus. After both men had taken a victory and defeat today in Campania, Spartacus thought it might be a responsible move to see if there was any way that they could end this war without the need for more senseless bloodshed. Spartacus just wanted a promise that the slaves could get home, like he promised. No more raiding. They had enough coin to buy things legally and outright if they needed. It had been nearly two years, and everyone was tired. Rome didn't want to continue funding this slave hunt with bigger wars going on in the Mediterranean. Spartacus had really been encouraged by the news that Senator Furius had been killed. It was as if a giant weight had been lifted off of his shoulders. He was no longer in fear or competition that Téadora was going to be taken away. The threat of war though, and the way the praetor had been looking at her tonight, it made him uncomfortable. But if Téadora had the courage to go all the way to Rome and kill a Senator to try and protect Spartacus and his entire army, the least he could do was have a talk face to face, and man to man with Crassus as they shared the land around Campania. To try and avoid alarm, the Thracian leader carried a hidden sica blade on his person, and a shield above his head. It was the Roman way to announce he came in peace. A Roman centurion on sentry duty personally escorted Spartacus to Crassus' tent. The elder praetor hid his shock well from his face as Spartacus lowered his shield to reveal his tired face. The centurion was beckoned to leave so the men could talk in private. Spartacus was offered the chance to sit, but remained standing. He was comfortably a whole head taller than Crassus, but the praetor was old enough to be the Thracian's father. Spartacus noted how clean everything was here. The man's hand hadn't seen dirt in years, and Spartacus couldn't tell if it was mud or blood, or both caked under his own ragged fingernails.

"So, *you* are the mighty Spartacus I've been hearing so much about. I must say, I'm a little unimpressed."

"I'm not mighty, I'm just a man."

"And who I wonder is the fool who gave you such a name? An idiot father, or the sorry whore of a woman who birthed you?"

"My mother was a wonderful woman. My name was her choice. It was in honor of her father. A great warrior of the Maedi Thracians."

"Then she was misguided like the rest of your people who think a lowly peasant tribe such as yourselves has any right to invoke the name of the might of ancient Sparta. You know, I must have run across a dozen men named Spartacus in my line of work. All of them a *filthy* disappointment just like you."

"I'll make sure you remember *me*, Crassus."

"I'm sure you think you will."

"From this day on, *my* name is one that will make your blood boil."

"Is that some sort of promise your people make?"

"I don't make promises anymore. That was a threat."

"That's a bold move to make in the middle of my camp."

"I've been told I'm a bold man."

"You're a fool."

"I've been told that too, but it's never stopped me."

"Why have you come to me tonight?"

"Our men are equally matched. Our armies equally sized. You had your victory today, and I had mine. We both just want to go home and end this war."

"Are you surrendering?"

"I am asking for peace and safe passage for my army to leave the empire. Is that possible?"

"Your army has committed atrocities across this empire, and for that they must pay. None of you are free to leave."

"I am sorry to hear that."

"*Unless*…you have something worth bargaining with?"

"I have a feeling I know what you're hinting at, and my answer *is* and *will always* be *no*."

"Is one woman *really* worth your life and the lives of your army?"

"This one woman is. Téa is not some object to be traded for politics. Besides, I have it on good authority she's no longer of interest to Rome as Senator Furius has been killed."

"Your authority is wrong."

"I don't know that that's possible."

"Senator Furius is currently sitting in a tent in my camp. Would you like to go lay eyes upon him yourself?"

"He lives?! How?!"

"An attempt on his life *was* made in Rome, but he came out to Campania as soon as he could to rectify that. He arrived just before sundown, while you were busy crucifying two of my consuls."

"The Senator is *here*?"

"Has all this fighting made you hard of hearing? Yes, Spartacus, the Senator is here, alive, and well. He's come for his woman and I intend on giving her to him as quickly as I can."

"I can't let that happen."

"Regardless of what you think you can and can't do, I *will* see her made the Senator's wife. I've been promised a seat in the Senate if I can secure this marriage and I want nothing more than the political security that position affords. You will *not* stop me in my ambitions to rise to the level of society I was meant for."

"You're so blind for power you can't even see what you're doing is terribly wrong."

"I care not for the ethics of what I am doing. I am in this for the end result. The ends justify the means, Spartacus. You're a leader, I thought you would understand the difficult decisions and sacrifices which much be made to secure victories."

"I understand war and struggle, hardships and the like, but I will never understand greed, politics, and Rome."

"That's why you will never be a great man."

"I don't want to be a great man if that means being like you. I just want to be a good man to a good woman. And I have a good woman. She thinks I am a good man. I am content if not for this war and my ability to take her home like I said I would."

"Oh, Spartacus. You really are a fool, aren't you? You and Téadora are never going home. I simply can't allow it."

"Can you allow me to speak to the Senator in your camp?"

"That I cannot."

"May I ask why?"

"You may ask, but you already know the answer. My kindness has it's limitations and you anger me at this late hour. I must ask you to leave my camp now. Leave quietly, or I will have you killed and you'll never see your precious Téadora ever again."

"If you *ever* so much as *try* to lay a hand on her…"

"I'll do whatever I like to get her to the Senator. As much as I've heard about her, you can be damn sure I'll see what all the fuss is about before I'm rid of her. Should be a good ride. I'm quite looking forward to it actually."

"You foul creature!"

"Careful, Spartacus. You're in *my* camp now, you must play by *my* rules. Wouldn't want yourself to have an accident, now, would we?"

"It will be no accident when you are killed, Crassus. There will be great intent and pleasure when your blood is spilled."

Spartacus marched out of the tent and shoved the nosy centurion to the side. The Thracian leader drew much attention to himself as he grumbled and cursed in his native language which sounded incredibly violent and vulgar to the Romans as they ate their dinner around their campfires, musing over their morning victory and shameful afternoon. Spartacus happened to overhear one man muttering something to his friends about Téadora being a whore, and with one forceful shove Spartacus had that man rolling in the flames of his own campfire. His friends helped him out quick enough and no permanent damage was done. Crassus saw this but ordered nothing be done about it. He was amused by his rival's angry reactions. Because of the burning man's screams, Senator Furius carefully poked his head out of his tent and saw Spartacus leaving the Roman camp. Eager to set his sights on Téadora, the still weak bodied Senator had the bright idea to follow the Thracian leader out into the darkness to see where his prospective bride and attempted murderess was camping. He was sure it had all been some sort of misunderstanding. He wanted to talk, if she was willing. They hadn't really done much talking back in Rome. The slender man still had guiltily fond memories of her pressing him in-between the wall and her own body. But before he could get carried away, he had to keep an eye on Spartacus. The hulking man was incredibly upset at how his conversation had gone with Crassus, and rightly so, but such a disastrous result should have been better anticipated. Despite everything he knew, Spartacus still had high hopes for peace. It was admirable, but foolish, and Crassus had called him out for that on more than one occasion. Spartacus didn't want to wake Téadora up and have to explain to her what he had just done, so to cool himself off he went for a walk downriver to try and clear his head, process what move he needed to make next when the army came looking to him for answers come sunrise. Senator Furius saw this as a somewhat golden opportunity to get Téadora alone as her and Spartacus' tent always sat a bit aside from the rest of the camp. Unlike Roman tradition, where the leader was protected in the center, the slave army was much more scattered and free flowing. No rhyme or reason to where the tents poked up in the valley. As the Senator slunk down into the shadows, preoccupied with facing forwards, something else was creeping up behind him.

Varinius was having a rough night. He could not sleep without Dacia, and the screaming man in the fire was about all he could take not to go outside and beg for some peace and quiet for his troubled mind. He argued with himself for a bit before finally opening his tent. He stubbed his toe on the moss-covered rock Dacia had left behind to secure her goodbye letter to the praetor. Varinius' eyes scanned the paper frantically seeing tears ruining the scribbles before him. He could not and would accept her departure without a fight. Dacia simply stated that if Varinius could not choose her over this war, that she would choose her freedom over him. It did not say much more than that, where she was going, or if she'd ever try to see him again. She apologized for not being able to speak to him directly, but his lack of cooperation had made it impossible. Varinius crumpled the letter in his fist and threw it in the embers of his dying campfire. Sword in hand he marched, barefoot, armorless, into the dark. He wanted to speak to Spartacus directly. He wanted to end this war. He might not have had the authority to try and do this, but he was marching all the same, determined to get something done. He would stop this madness, stop this fighting, and get his woman back. In his anger, he was not able to discern the two very distinct shadow differences between Spartacus' bulky frame and Furius' slender one. A man was a man, and when Varinius kept frustratingly repeating Spartacus' name to get the shadow's attention, Furius did not turn around. Téadora's tent was fast approaching. Varinius did not want to have to involve the woman if he could avoid it. He tried running up to Spartacus, reaching out and grabbing his shoulder, but he slipped, sword hand forward, and plunged the weapon into the shadow's back, gripping a shoulder with his free hand as had been intended, and then falling on top of the shadow and riding it into the ground. On closer inspection the man was identified to be thin, and blonde, and clean. The man was also found to be Senator Felix Furius, and he was dead. Varinius climbed off of the body in horror. He couldn't even get himself to retrieve his own sword. It just jutted up awkwardly from the man's back, shining in the starlight. In hushed whispers the young praetor stumbled back on all fours, desperate to get away from what he had just done.

"I'm a dead man! I'm a dead man! I'm a dead man! Dacia, help me!"

Téadora woke to the sound of a man crying, and Spartacus not beside her. She crawled out of her tent quickly, and searched the grasses for sight of her beloved, but he was nowhere to be found. What she did see however was a sulking shadow, sitting beside a sword. After lighting a torch from the embers outside her tent, she walked up to reveal a drunk Varinius, sniffling and apologetically looking up at her like a lost child. She knelt beside him to try and figure out what was wrong but the man could not speak. His lips trembled, and he was quite pale. She could tell he'd been rifling dirty fingers through his light blonde hair. She had already recognized Senator Furius lying in the grass face down with a sword in his back. The sight should have jostled her, but because she thought she had already killed the man, seeing him dead outside her tent now had very little effect on her. There were questions of course, but ones that only Furius could have answered, and seeing as how he was no longer amongst the living, there was no need to go asking those questions. Téadora reached over, and removed the sword, swiping it back and forth in the damp grasses to clean off the blood. There wasn't much, and it smelled like the rotten garlic antidote tasted. She shook her head and got chills, but then returned the sword to the praetor. He still couldn't touch it, so she decided to take it for her own. Someone in the army would be more than happy to swing it in the battles to come. Seeing Varinius so shaken bothered her. She should hate this man for his part in this war, but there was no glory in hating the broken. After some strong, albeit silent urging, the gladiatrix commander was able to tug the praetor down to the river's edge where she had to physically wash the Senator's blood off of Varinius' hands. The man had fallen into this kind of pathetic daze, just barely mumbling something unintelligible. Téadora had no idea what she was going to do with the man, but before she could get too lost in thought and worst-case scenarios, she heard a sloshing coming towards her from down river. The water was about thigh deep here, but she could identify Spartacus' figure from a mile away. She bolted up to her feet, and then clasped both hands over her mouth. Dacia's tattoos were quite visible on her naked body as it dangled lifeless in Spartacus' arms. Téadora tried to reach down and shield Varinius' eyes but the man was already staring, and cried out loudly now, waking up some of the slave army.

"Varinius, control yourself! Spartacus, what happened?"

"I couldn't sleep. I went for a walk, and I saw something in the water. She was gone long before I got to her, Téa. There was nothing I could do."

"Does she have any visible wounds?"

"Not that I can tell."

"I bet it was poison. I *knew* something wasn't right with her when we left Rome."

"Why is Varinius here?"

"I don't know. He's been inconsolable since I found him."

"Varinius?! Varinius!"

"You can yell all you want, Spartacus, it won't change anything. I've tried being kind, being a brute. He, uh, he killed the Senator."

"Wait, I'm confused."

"I know I told you I had killed him in Rome. I thought I had…"

"Crassus told me he was alive in his camp."

"*Crassus* told you? When did you speak to Crassus?"

"Nevermind."

"No, Spartacus. When did you speak to Crassus?"

"Can this wait, Téa?"

"You have a dead woman in your arms and we have a dead Senator outside of our tent. Varinius' is unresponsive except for the occasional scream. By all means, if there was ever a time for you to be honest with me, *now* is the time. Did you sneak away from me tonight to go speak with the enemy?"

"Yes."

"Spartacus, you could have been killed!"

"I was careful. I was just running a fool's errand apparently."

"Romans do not negotiate. You *know* this."

"I got excited when you told me the Senator was dead tonight. I thought for the first time in a long time we were really going to get to go home. I was going to get you out of here. We were going to be safe. Our future was so close I could taste it. I wanted it too much. I wanted *you* too much. I was hoping if I could speak with Crassus man to man, we could end this war, the way you and Dacia wanted."

"Oh, Spartacus, you sweet, sweet man. Why didn't you just tell me? I would have tried to help you."

"I wanted to do this on my own for you."

"Wars are not started or finished by single men in single actions."

"There's always a first time for everything."

"We will get home, and this war will end. But first, we have a couple of things to take care of."

"Like two dead bodies?"

"We should burn them. Burn the evidence."

"Why can't we just dig a hole and shove them in there?"

"I don't want to risk the Romans finding Furius' body here."

"Téa, need I remind you we crucified two consuls earlier? I don't think it matters what we do to a dead Senator."

"He was a nice man. Misguided, but nice. We'll burn him. I'll get a fire going, collect some more wood. I'll find something dry in this godforsaken valley. Set Dacia down beside Varinius. Let him say his goodbyes. Whatever they were to each other, the man deserves that opportunity."

"He can't stay here, Téa."

"Well, we can't very well escort him back up to the Roman camps either. They'd just kill us. I won't die for that man. He's hardly a man at all right now. Look at him, Spartacus. He's broken."

"If you want me to feel sorry for him, it's not going to happen."

"You don't have to feel sorry for him, but feel something. A lack of emotion makes you like the Romans. Even if you feel hate, keep feeling, Spartacus. Don't be like them."

"The army will kill him if they see him here in the morning."

"Well, if he's still here, then we'll just have to make sure that nobody sees him."

"We're going to hide a praetor now?"

"I'm good at hiding things."

"Not from *me* you're not."

"Don't be so sure."

"Are you hiding something from me right now, Téa? Téa?! I know that grin anywhere. What is it? What are you keeping from me?"

"I'm with child, Spartacus."

XXIV

As spring began the slave army had moved out of Campania, and to the east near Apulia. They stayed along the Silarius River because it was important Téadora keep near water. It was not a vital fact, but Spartacus had been treating her so carefully since she told him she was carrying his child. Now more than ever, this war needed to end. The Thracian leader was bound and determined for his baby to be born at home, amongst family, and not anywhere near the Roman empire. The gladiatrix commander was barely showing with a slightly swollen stomach, but for Spartacus, he was ecstatic at the prospect of finally becoming a father. He was never found not to be smiling, or preoccupied with what he was going to have to do to make sure the little family's home was built before the birth. Many soldiers volunteered their services for the job, everything from stoneworkers to midwives. Not everyone had a home to go back to, but there was always the option of going back to Samothraki with Spartacus and Téadora. The object of the Romans following them was an annoyance rather than a priority. Crassus stayed in Campania for many weeks before moving out towards Apulia. Slowly but surely, he'd camp a legion out over the hills. Gradually another legion would join them, then another and another. Crassus shared responsibility for his actions with no one anymore since Varinius' disappearance. For all the elder praetor knew or cared, and all Rome or the Senate knew or cared, the man had been killed. Varinius was not murdered or sacrificed for the war effort, however. He was serving as an intelligence advisor for the slave army. Téadora had granted him immunity for his services. It gave him purpose again, to be needed and asked for. He was not useless, but he was not all that helpful aside from what dirt he had on his former colleagues. He was no good at hunting, raiding, or fishing. He could not weave, sew, or mend. He was no healer. He was a politician though. What he lacked for in physical skills he excelled at in mind games. Today was the first really warm day all year, and while Spartacus was busy trying to figure out how much coin the army had, Téadora was pouring over maps of the countryside with Varinius. It was the Thracian leader's plan to rummage enough money together to buy a ship for passage to Samothraki. With the baby coming that accelerated his needs to get out of the empire the easiest way possible. No longer was traversing north across the Alps an option. He didn't want that stress put on Téadora. Despite the mother to be's protestations about sea travel because of her past with the Cilician pirates, she was eager to get home before the baby came too, and swallowed her pride to allow for the planning of securing a ship. Even while Varinius and Téadora talked about the maps, the self-exiled praetor could not help but focus more on the baby.

"Is it kicking yet, Téadora?"

"I'm not that far along, Varinius. Now, as I was saying, if we were to stay in this river valley, could we get all the way to the sea without interference by the Romans? What towns in this area are most loyal to the empire?"

"What?"

"Varinius, you're not paying attention! I've asked you *three* times about the loyalties of this countryside and all you can do is stare at my belly with this odd smile on your lips."

"I'm sorry. I'm just jealous of Spartacus' good fortune."

"Be jealous when we've made our escape."

"He's going to be a good father. I can tell from the way the people surround him in camp. The army loves him."

"We're a family here. You're supposed to love your family."

"It's not that way in the Roman camps. Everyone is separated. There is very strict hierarchy. Foot soldiers with foot soldiers, officers with officers. No mingling. No community. No trust. No care for one another. You all look out for each other. This war is personal to you."

"How else should a war be fought?"

"It is a job to the Romans, an order which must be fulfilled. A soldier is a number on a list, a mindless body in the formation. It matters not who is there, just so long as the position is filled."

"That sounds awful."

"Most men don't know any better. They just think that is the way of it. They want battle scars, war stories. Many want promotions, promises of political careers, big sacks of coin to drown themselves in. I know. I was one of those men for most of my life."

"What happened to change that?"

"Dacia."

"You still miss her, don't you?"

"Every waking minute of every day. I can't sleep without her next to me. Just looking at her made breathing easier."

"The separation will get easier in time."

"It has been weeks. I still feel numb."

"On the bright side, being numb means you're not feeling pain."

"Why are you so nice to me, Téadora? Everyone else in this camp would just assume slit my throat as talk to me, even Spartacus. But you manage to tolerate me, keep me entertained and involved."

"Dacia and I had a lot of time to talk on our way back from Rome. She made me realize you were more than your title and political ambitions. It was easier to hate you when I knew nothing about you. But she was quite fond of you, and I guess some of that admiration rubbed off on me. That, and the news she was with child."

"What?!"

"Oh…I thought she told you?"

"She was with child?! *My* child?!"

"A couple months along. She was further than I was. She really didn't tell you?"

"Maybe she tried. After you two got back, I was in a bad way. I shut her out. She tried talking to me, more than once. I was battling myself. I didn't want to hurt her."

"She told me she had seen a vision of herself dying in childbirth. She had never known who the father of this baby might be until you came along. That's why she always stayed away from men, to try and avoid what haunted her dreams."

"She never told me any of that."

"She said she never told anyone but me. She was trying to make me feel better about being with child. I was very nervous. I didn't know how to break the news to Spartacus, what with everything that was going on in winter. She was so happy for me."

"I wouldn't have made a good father."

"Don't say that, Varinius."

"It's true. I don't know the first thing about what it takes. My father was never around, except to make more siblings for me. My mother was always pregnant. When she died, he remarried, and kept her pregnant too. I was always taken care of by servants, or trained by masters in schools. I had no warmth or family to call my own. No one cared what happened to me. Dacia was the first person in my life who ever showed genuine concern if I lived or died at the end of the day. Dacia, and now you."

"You will have a life worth living now, Varinius. You can make up for all the wrongs of your youth once this war is over."

"There is nothing for me without Dacia. I am a deserter from the Roman army. I can never return to the empire. No other people will take me in."

"Spartacus and I would take you. A whole bunch of us are going to Samothraki once we get to the coast. You can find a place on the ship too. Start a new life in the east."

"I wouldn't even know where to begin. I've never been anywhere but the empire."

"There are a lot of nice girls where I am from. I'm sure one of them would be more than happy to teach you a new way of life."

"You think so?"

"I do."

"Maybe I'll do that."

"Maybe we could get back to talking about this map too? Now, are the towns around the river all that loyal to the empire, or not?"

While Téadora got Varinius focused on the task at hand, commotion was starting to stir on the far edges of camp. The westward edges, closest to where the Romans were. Crassus was going to take advantage of this warm weather. When Spartacus ran into his tent, Téadora could tell just from the look in his eyes that something was wrong, something big. She instinctively put a hand on her stomach and shook her head no. Spartacus nodded in agreement that her worries were true. Crassus was moving the legions towards them, and this was going to be their last chance to make a stand. One more day and they would have been able to make a march to the coast. One more day and they would have been spending time shopping for ships on the shore. All that hope was ripped away in an instant, clawed right out of view. Téadora began rolling up the maps to get them out of the way. Varinius had never seen what it looked like when the slave army prepared for a fight. The women rushed the campfires and streaked black charcoal across their eyes. Many men were starting to do it too, in different patterns along their cheeks and arms. There was a lot of wolf howling, whistling, cheering, and growling. It wasn't mean spirited, but uplifting, motivational. The Romans were always so stoic and dark. They made bets on how many kills they were going to make. The slaves did none of that. They were still talking about building houses on Téadora's island in the Aegean. Their heads were in the future. Crassus bringing this battle to them was just moving things along. They welcomed the black-haired praetor to their camp in Apulia. They begged the legions to move faster. Come so they could get this over with. By this time tomorrow they could be in the sea. Varinius wasn't so sure the slaves would win this battle. Their advantage had always been night attacks, or having superior numbers. It was broad daylight, and they lacked a couple thousand men. Not that the slaves couldn't make up for that, but they were at a disadvantage. For the first time since the young praetor had killed Senator Furius, he held his sword in his hands. Téadora had dropped it there like she had done this a million times with him. She got Spartacus ready, tied his blades on him, secured his leather armor. He did the same for her, careful to watch her belly. His hands lingered while she double checked her sica blades were in a good place on her back. Varinius liked watching them together, seeing their closeness.

"Spartacus stop worrying. I'll be fine."

"I just don't want you to push yourself too hard today. Be careful up on the horse."

"I'm a better rider than you."

"But more Romans will be chasing you than me."

"Don't be so sure. We've both got a target on our back. You be careful out there. I mean it. No hero stuff. The coast is so close I can smell the salt in the air. I want to bring this baby of ours home soon."

"Crassus won't get the better of us today. We've got too much to look forward to."

"How close is he?"

"The archers have reached the horse barrier."

"That's closer than I thought. Alright, Spartacus, what do you say, want to go for a run?"

"Mind the baby, Téa."

"I'm minding the baby. I swear it's all you ever think about anymore. I'm with child, I'm not helpless. And I'm still faster than you."

"You sure about that?"

"Be a man and race me to find out."

"One last run before we go home. I'll take you up on that."

"What does the winner get? Bragging rights?"

"Something better. Winner gets to decide which way the house faces when we get home. Ready?"

A wicked smile flashed across Téadora's face. She bolted out of the tent first and ran through camp, jumping over campfires like they were barely even there. The gladiatrices followed their commander without question, howling and whistling, and screaming. The men followed soon after. The entire charge was on foot. Varinius attempted to keep up with Spartacus but he was soon left behind by the Thracian leader. The horses had been sacrificed about a week ago. Due to the harsh winter the grasses weren't what they usually were and raiding was poor. With food scarcity the horses had been killed for meat, their bodies laid out in a barrier on the western edge of camp. Crassus took note of the white horses in the center of the barrier as he led the legions out across the hills of the river valley. Snow melt had caused rising waters, segmenting parts of the landscape. This did not affect the praetor's plans to squash the slave revolt once and for all today. He had had enough of camping in the countryside. He wanted the luxuries of the city again, servants, and women's flirtations. There had been an order for no mercy today. All of the officers were to push to the coast at all costs. Retreats were punishable by instant death. There were reminders of the practice of decimation. Crassus threatened to do it again to anyone who disobeyed him today. As the sun beat down on the valley it was rumbling chaos in slow motion as the two forces approached one another. It seemed like it took forever for them to meet each other's blades, but once they did, there was no turning back.

The Thracian men composed the front lines. They raised their shields to block the Roman archers and thrust forwards through swords, daggers, axes, and javelins. The gladiatrices placed themselves in the second lines, moving forwards with ease thanks to the Thracian blocks. There was no forward progress to be had by either side. Bodies fell, and became barriers of their own right beside the felled horses. Feet stuck through the animal's exposed ribcages for traction in the blood slicked grasses. Many a dead man came at the hands of poor footing. Varinius was one of those who had fallen many times, but had been granted undo mercy by his former soldiers that had at one time been in his command. They even went so far as to offer a helping hand up before going their separate ways. Because the young praetor had spent so much time on the ground already, he looked as though he'd been in ten battles this afternoon. Many men's blood was splashed on his body from head to toe. Some had gotten into his mouth and made him vomit. He felt better after losing his breakfast though, more unburdened. As a promise between men, Varinius had sworn his life to protect Téadora at all costs in whatever battles the slave army might face before they got to their freedom. The gladiatrix commander knew nothing of this deal, but Spartacus had made that his condition for keeping the Roman in his camp. Varinius was clever about the way he had been going about it. He couldn't outright join the women in their fight, but he could be near them at all times, always behind, always shadowing. If Téadora turned, he turned with her. If she ran, he did his best to keep up. When she fought, he supported her efforts. Spartacus frequently cut across her path, making sure her obstacles were taken care of. Many others in the army naturally looked after her too, not just because she was Spartacus' woman or with child, but because they loved her. It was hard not to.

    For the first surge in the attack Crassus did his best to stay out of the main vein of the fighting. He watched from a safe distance at the horse barrier, and tried to see the way the battle would go. He was upset it didn't seem to be going in his favor. There seemed to be a concentration around the gladiatrices, and the praetor pointed that out to his officers, and sent them to try and go break it up. Ever so gradually, the battle seemed to be shifting to the east of the valley. There was this unconscious pull to the sea. The women kept pulling that direction, one lunge forward, two lunger back. They tugged the Romans into their swords by taunting. The young men in the legions were too green not to bite the bait each and every time. Crassus was annoyed, and while he was deciding how to go about making his entrance into the fray, he noticed the familiar face of Varinius, actively committing one treasonous act after another. He was working in tandem with Téadora, and Spartacus was never that far away. It was almost too easy. Crassus pointed this out to his centurions keeping guard around him. He had six, two in front, one on each side, and two behind. They rode brown horses while he was on a white one. The Romans spared no expense for their protection. Some of their horses were better armored than many of the slaves, and better fed too. Crassus pressed into the battle when it was apparent both forces were getting tired. It had been a couple of minutes. The larger Thracians were winded. The women growing hoarse from their cries and howls. Spartacus made a sweep to the left, and caught a white horse in his line of sight. He moved away from the gladiatrices in the east, and shifted his forces west, uphill. It was steeper for tired legs than it looked, and the men decided to wait for the Romans to come to them. Téadora had her back to Crassus at this point. She seemed safe enough in her maneuvers and well-guarded. Her two sica blades were soaked in blood so bad that she sprayed it as she made her swings across her body. Varinius made the decision to reinforce Spartacus and the men from the rear. He'd keep the women in his sights, never too far away, but it was clear Crassus and Spartacus were headed for one another, and if Varinius could, he'd like to prevent a catastrophe. Spartacus picked up an ax in a Roman boy's body where it had been left by a Germanian soldier, and flung it at the centurion to the right of Crassus. While the praetor was overtaken by the splash of blood on his cheek, Spartacus threw one of his curved sica blades at the centurion in front of Crassus, and this time the praetor let out an audible scream. The centurion's body fell awkwardly backwards from his horse, revealing a Thracian blade protruding from his right eye socket. Crassus held a hand over his mouth to keep from screaming again, and ordered his four remaining centurions to pull in tighter to his position, and protect him for the sake of the empire. The men shifted and Spartacus no longer had a clear striking path. He did however have one more sica blade in his hand, and was poised to fling it when a javelin came flying in from seemingly out of nowhere, and pierced his thigh. It made it's way all the way through, and Spartacus fell. Everyone around was so busy fighting for their lives no one seemed to notice what had happened to the mighty leader. Varinius clawed his way, pushed, pulled, rolled, and crawled to get to Spartacus, dropping his sword in the process. He wasn't even worried about going back for it. He picked Spartacus' head up in his lap and was in a sheer panic.

"I don't know what to do!"

"Get that piece of shit out of my leg! I'm not done yet!"

"Get it out?"

"Pull it out, Varinius! Pull it out!"

"Which…do I go forward or…"

"Break it in half! Pull the pieces out. Just do it!"

"I, uh, maybe someone else…"

"I don't have time! Help me, Varinius!"

    The young praetor swallowed hard. Spartacus was in epic amounts of pain. He kept writhing on the ground, twisting back and forth. Varinius laid the slightest bit if pressure on the javelin in Spartacus' thigh and he groaned so deep it felt like the earth shook beneath them as he slammed his fists down. This had to be fast. Whatever Varinius did it had to be fast. He winced, and jiggled the javelin back and forth. It was thoroughly in Spartacus' thigh, poking through the back. Because of the angled metal tip, it had to be broken in two. Varinius got up and tried to steady himself on his feet, then up on one. With his free leg he bent his knee, and forced the handle of the javelin across his own thigh, busting it in two. Spartacus wailed again, and this time it drew attention. Men were surging back to protect him. It wasn't what he wanted. Varinius tried to push the army away, fight the Romans, but they weren't listening. The women were down in the river, making a crossing. Téadora was occupied, safe and occupied. The Romans could not get to her. Someone placed a gag of cloth in Spartacus' mouth to help him with the pain. Varinius tugged on the main shaft and pulled it out, tossing it aside. The Thracian leader was rolled over so Varinius could get the shorter piece out now. This one was much easier and faster. The praetor threw the javelin into the bloodied grass to get lost. If he never saw it again it'd be too soon. Before he could bend down and ask Spartacus how he was doing, or take pride in his minor accomplishment, Varinius was seized from behind and drug backwards. The pale hands in armor signified Romans. Romans loyal to Crassus. No matter how much Varinius struggled his could not break himself free. The sight of Spartacus vanished as the battle ensued. Thracians swarmed their leader's body, trying desperately to get him bandaged up and back on his feet. Crassus was in retreat with his centurions. Varinius could see them running outside of the battle on the empty hillsides. The young praetor was being drug that way. Out of the battle. Over bodies. He saw familiar faces from both sides of the war, cut down in their prime. He was feeling sick to his stomach again when tossed out onto clean grass. Before he could scramble away and get his wits about him, he was seized by Crassus' centurions, all four of them, one per limb, and carried to the sight of the elder praetor on horseback. Varinius craned his head to see what was becoming of the battle he'd been carried out of. Romans were slaughtering everyone near the hillside where Spartacus had last been seen. Anything that moved was being hacked to bits.

"Just what do you think you're doing, Varinius?"

"Making up for my mistakes."

"And do you think dying with the slaves will redeem you in the eyes of the gods?"

"It couldn't hurt."

"Stop being foolish and come back to camp with me."

"I'm a deserter. A return to camp is certain death."

"Like your chances are much better if you stay here."

"I would rather die amongst friends than beside you."

"Varinius, you hurt my feelings. Do you not consider me a friend?"

"Let me go!"

"What's the point? You have nothing to go back to. Any *friends* you might have made are dead. Even Spartacus."

XXV

Two-thirds of Spartacus' army were cut down in the valley of the Silarius River. Twenty-thousand souls. Four thousand managed to cross the river under Téadora's lead, and make a run for the Adriatic coast. For those six thousand that could not, or would not cross the river, they became prisoners of Crassus. But the praetor was not interested in taking them back to Rome. With rope he had the men and women tied together in single file chains like animals, and marched them back to the main camp in Campania. Téadora waited until nightfall to go back to the battlefield and see what remained. She hadn't seen Spartacus or Varinius in hours. Friends and family were severed in her ranks. There was a makeshift camp on the coast. The survivors sought shelter on the warmed Adriatic sands, and waited for their orders. The slave camp had been abandoned earlier that day so supplies, food, coin, it was all left behind. Téadora was acting as scout. In her mind, Spartacus and Varinius had men with them packing up camp, collecting their things and getting ready to meet her on the coast. This had to have been what was happening. It was the only logical thing that could be happening. She was not expecting what she saw. No part of her had accepted defeat. Keeping in the Silarius River the gladiatrix commander waded knee deep through the water, and followed the stars until she heard a man sniveling on the muddy banks. Téadora had heard those sounds before, and her heart leapt realizing Varinius was nearby. His blonde head glowed in the moonlight, making him easy to see. But something was wrong. Téadora gripped him by his sullen shoulders and bent down in front of him, urging him to raise his head and meet her eager gaze.

"Varinius! You're a sight for sore eyes. Where is Spartacus? It's been hours and he's not come out to the coast. Has he gone back to camp with the others?"

"What others?"

"Other survivors."

"Téadora, the only survivors ran with you. Anyone left here was taken prisoner by Crassus. Thousands of them."

"But…how are *you* here then?"

"I told him no."

"So, Spartacus is a prisoner then? That…no. He'd never let himself be taken by Crassus. Varinius, where is he?"

"He's…here…*somewhere*."

"You just vaguely gestured to the battlefield. I don't…Varinius I don't understand, where is Spartacus? I need you to tell me."

"Téadora, I've just told you. Why aren't you listening to me?"

"Spartacus is…*here*? With the…*dead*? No. That can't be. He…"

"He belongs to the gods now."

"NO!"

Téadora dropped into the river bottom, splashing Varinius as she lost her footing. It was as if her body was failing her. She felt instantly sick to her stomach, and all the blood was rushing from her face. She felt dizzy. Varinius took hold of her hands and pulled her up onto the banks. She was in a daze, and started to breathe heavy. As she muttered under her breath she started to slip back into her native tongue and ask the young praetor questions he could not answer. He just kept looking at her with his blank expression on his face. There was nothing there. Téadora stood up, and rifled wet hands through her tangled mass of black braids, trying to make sense of this. Against her orders, other survivors had followed her inland from the coast. They were here like her, to recover the bodies of loved ones. Give them a proper burial, say a few final words. They trickled up one by one, slowly, heads so full of questions. Many had gotten separated in the battle earlier today; it had all happened so fast. No one laid dead where they should have been, where they had left. Téadora had a couple hundred people now in the bloody grasses with her. She herself could not manage to go up and join them, lay her eyes on a sight she could not even in her wildest dreams imagine. She had a baby in her belly, and tears in her eyes. She could barely see anything. Téadora had been so stuck in her head, she didn't even notice what had happened to Varinius. She tossed her hand down behind her, trying to find his shoulder. When she couldn't find it, she turned to find the young man face down in the river, bobbing away from her with the current. He drowned himself in his sorrows. He'd only stayed alive long enough to tell Téadora that Spartacus was dead, and that Crassus had taken thousands of prisoners. His duty was done. All of his duties. Téadora's duties were not done. There were survivors that were going to look to her for guidance. If it were true that she was the last commander, then she needed to start acting like it. It felt like there was this gaping, growing hole in the center of her chest. With one hand over her heart, and one over her growing baby, she slowly began to ascend the hill and start searching through the bodies. There were twenty-thousand souls here however, all fallen on top of one another, face down, mutilated, swollen, slave and Roman alike. Crassus hadn't even had the decency to return for his own men. That explained so much though. Téadora could see her fellow soldiers, on hands and knees climbing through piles of the dead, rolling them over like sacks for identification. A loved one could also sense when a loved one was near. It was this unspoken attraction. You didn't need to see their face to know. It was like that with Téadora. She had been drawn to the top of the hill, where the flies were the thickest and the bodies piled sometimes six men high. It was this huge huddle of dead. But she knew. She knew this is where Spartacus had been, where a front line had been tested. Her eyes frantically searched the forearms of the tan skinned shreds hanging out of the pile. A handful of them had the seared B from the House of Batiatus, but only one had her matching dots. With all her strength she dug Spartacus out of the pile, and drug him into her lap so she could look at him. He slightly moaned from pain in her hold, and she surprised herself by how loudly she shrieked in a mixed combination of horror, amazement, and gratitude. He was alive! But barely. Some other survivors had been finding miraculous occurrences of dying loved ones as well, but they were much more calm about their discoveries. Téadora picked Spartacus' head up into her chest and began smothering his bloody, mud filled face with kisses.

"I'm going to help you, Spartacus. You are *not* dying in this river valley. I won't allow it. I'll get you back to the salt water. Salt water fixes everything, remember? You'll see. You'll see. You're not dying on me, Spartacus. You're not. You *can't*! Not today. You're going to be a father. Remember? Our baby needs its father. *I* need you. I need help! Spartacus is alive! I've found him! Honor your leader. Who will help me carry him? Please! I need help!"

At the sound that Spartacus was alive, there was no shortage of attention given to the Thracian leader. Survivors swarmed his body and lifted him on their shoulders to carry back to the coast. Téadora was a mess of thank you's. She could not be more grateful for the assistance, and took special care to hold Spartacus' head for the walk back to the coast. She smiled through the pain, and secured his mother's silver ring necklace back on his body. She didn't mind being the keeper of it for a short while, but Spartacus needed all the help he could get right now to recover, and the good will of his mother was not to be overlooked. Téadora pleaded with the gods in every language she knew to heal her man. Give him mercy. His good deeds had outweighed his bad. And if they hadn't, attach any of her good deeds to his record. Let her feel some of his pain. Let her alleviate some of his stressors. She would do anything for him in this moment, and every day forward. She would promise to be a good, kind, protective mother. She'd be an obedient, happy wife. She would not ask for anything ever again if she were allowed to live out her days with Spartacus like they had talked about. A gust of sea breeze hit her in the face like a sign from the gods. It would be so. She had a settling in her chest, the hole was slowly closing. The clouds had parted. It was a cool spring night on the shores of the Adriatic. Spartacus was laid out on the sands, with rocks propping up his head. A healer made their way to him, and began working on his various cuts, gashes, and varying degrees of broken bones and trauma. There was no plausible explanation for how the man was alive, but he was, and the healer promised to do everything in their power to keep it that way. Téadora in return would compensate the healer with their weight in coin, but the healer would not dare charge for helping Spartacus. There was the matter of supplies though. The four thousand remaining slaves had nothing to their name but the weapons in their hands and the clothes on their back. Blood soiled clothes at that. Empty stares. Téadora swallowed hard, and took a deep breath, urging volunteers to step forwards and help her.

"For years you have bled for Spartacus, and now I ask that you bleed for me. Our friends and family have died, or been taken prisoner. I don't know that I can be so bold as to look in your eyes right now and tell you I can make any of that better, but we left a camp behind. If anyone is strong enough to come with me, I am going to go back and salvage anything that we can, coin, food, armor, and human alike. I don't blame any of you if you want to stay on the water's edge. It has been a long, and trying day. Maybe one of the most difficult for a lot of us. But the night lives on. *We* live on, and we must make our friends and family proud. We are *free* men and women. That is no small victory. Perhaps, it is the greatest we have fought for. Let's not squander it by letting fear rule over us on tonight of all nights when our courage is needed the most."

Téadora took a deep breath and began walking back for the countryside. Not even for one second did she find herself walking alone. The walking wounded, some in better shape than others, came with her to the river valley. Some dropped off to survey the dead and say their final words with others who were still searching for their friends and families. Many remained with Téadora in the Silarius River, slogging upstream to get back to whatever remained of their camp. It wasn't much. In their victory march, the Romans had ravaged much of what the slaves had, but there were still tents to be saved, food to be collected. All weapons or armor had been taken. People could unbury their bags of coin they had stashed in the hillsides. Téadora loaded up as much coin as she could carry in the hopes of securing that ship to Samothraki. Those plans had not changed at all. But before she could leave the hills of Apulia for good, she had to go check on the prisoners. She could not live with herself if she didn't at least go and see what was to become of them. Four thousand survivors, of which only about four hundred had come out with Téadora tonight, were no match for the forty-thousand strong Roman army. There were massive celebratory bonfires, and lines of slaves all tied up in rope by their hands, feet, and necks. Everyone with Téadora, including the gladiatrix commander herself, cried heavy tears and asked the gods for swift deaths for those captured. But she, and everyone around her knew what was going to happen. Trees were being cut down in a hurry. Crosses were being made. Thousands of them. Crassus was giving a drunken, arrogant speech amongst his men. He made false claims and they cheered like he was a god. They would be going home now. The war was over. Téadora wanted to be relieved at that prospect of not being chased or hunted anymore, but it was the elder praetor's justification for the end of the war that sent chills down her spine. Being kicked around camp was the body of a man, a dead slave, so mutilated he was beyond the faintest of recognition. He was positively hacked to shreds. Crassus claimed this to be the body of Spartacus, the face of the war. With that body, there was no longer a face, and therefore, no longer a war. The men were excited to get back home for their rewards. For the slaves, Téadora hung her head in defeat, and led the survivors back downriver to the coast of the Adriatic Sea. Salt water didn't fix everything, but it did help.

In the days to come, the Romans would crucify all six thousand prisoners they had collected from the final battle in the valley of Campania. Whether the men and women had been dead, dying, or healthy, they were tied up all the same. Six thousand crosses were planted along either side of the Via Appia for miles and miles, which was a well-traveled thoroughfare from the south up to Rome. As the army marched home, more prisoners were strung up, and left to decay at the dismay of the locals who had often sympathized with the slaves during the course of the war. When news of this reached the coast, some of the survivors went out to see it with their own eyes, and most of them did not come back. Téadora assumed suicide, and she didn't blame them. Spartacus and the wounded were making slow recoveries. Many of them were bedridden with their injuries. Spartacus was among some of the worst being tended to by the healers. Téadora paid them handsomely for their services. She still reserved a solid two satchels worth of coin though for a ship. There were hopes when the fishing season opened up in the weeks ahead that someone might be willing to work a deal with her. She didn't have the best reputation though, and there was little she could to to fix that as her swollen belly grew. As luck would have it though, the city Téadora had chosen for her salvation, was also a city Damanicus had frequented on occasion to resupply his fleet of pirate ships. One night while Téadora was trying to walk off the day's worries by herself, she happened across the Cilician pirate king while he was struggling to swindle a shopkeeper into selling him jars of salt for half price. Téadora had been fond of this old woman running the seaside shop because she was giving the gladiatrix commander herbs to help with her morning sickness. Téadora promised the old woman she'd cover whatever the pirate refused to pay her, and then Damanicus smiled that crooked smile that she had once been so fond of and she couldn't help but blush. The young man with the strong jaw line offered to escort his former lover down to the lapping saltwater so she could rest her tired feet. It was getting difficult for her to sit without assistance now, but Damanicus was showing no shortage of support as he muscled her down to the sand, and invited himself to sit beside her.

"You're the last person I expected to see tonight, Damanicus."

"Well, news on the sea was that the slave war was over, so I thought it was safe to come into port here again. It's been a few years. You couldn't have picked a prettier night to watch the stars. Do you still do that?"

"I do, when the skies allow it."

"Will you teach your baby to watch the stars too?"

"I hope they will fall in love with the sea and sky like me, but I will love them whatever they choose."

"I'm happy for you and Spartacus."

"You are?"

"He will be a much better father than I could ever be. He can give you what I never could, a stable life. The baby is Spartacus', yes?"

"Yes. The baby is his."

"What's wrong, Téa?"

"I almost lost him in that battle a couple of weeks ago."

"I heard it got pretty nasty. I knew you'd pull through it though. No Roman would ever be so bold as to take *you* down."

"Our army was slaughtered. Some days I have questioned why I was allowed to live."

"That baby in your belly. That's why. You were meant to have a family, Téa, grow old, and be happy."

"I'd be happier if I was home. But no captains even want to give me the time of day. I had my heart set on giving birth on Samothraki."

"There's no reason that can't still happen."

"Dami, what am I going to do? *Swim* all the way home?"

"I'll take you."

"I could never ask that of you."

"It's the least I could do after everything I've put you through."

"And what of Spartacus? My people?"

"He once paid me for seventy-five thousand souls. As far as I'm concerned, that's what I still owe you."

"We number barely *two*-thousand now."

"Then I can get you home that much faster, if that's what you want?"

"How much will that cost me?"

"A couple of conversations by starlight is all that I ask. And that I am able to see your baby once it is born."

"No, Dami. I meant coin."

"I can't charge you."

"Then take it for your men, your fleet."

"I won't take anything from you but what I've already asked, conversation and visitation."

"You want to see my baby when it's born? Why?"

"I always knew you were going to be a great mother. I want to be able to see that, preferably more than once. My fleet has been looking for a good, safe port in the Aegean for years. If I could make a habit of stopping in on Samothraki, seeing you, Spartacus, the kids, it would give me some purpose in my life again."

"You always used to call me your anchor."

"You always *will* be my anchor. Do we have a deal?"

"We do. But on one condition."

"Anything."

"You must make it official and shake hands with Spartacus."

"I can do that."

"And that means you must tolerate my slow pace as I walk back and lead you to him."

"Walk as slow as you want. I'm in no hurry to leave your side."

"That's new."

"I know I've hurt you in the past. I've left you twice without any explanation. I've broken your heart. But this is me trying to make it up to you."

"And I will give you all the chances to do that, but I will also make you work for it."

"That's fair."

"Can you help me up?"

"Of course."

"What are the odds you found me here tonight? The gods must have been getting sick of my pleas."

"That…or…I might have been searching the coast for word of you."

"You were?"

Damanicus blushed and turned his head, offering his helpful hands and arm in place of his embarrassment. To Téadora, he would always be her Dami, and to the pirate king, she would always be his Téa, his anchor. Things might have been different now between them than they had in the past, but they were part of each other's lives again, and all the more happier for it. Spartacus was relieved to see the pirate king offering his services to help make his and Téadora's dreams come true. With only two-thousand people in their army of family, the Cilician pirate fleet was able to carry everyone into the Aegean in one trip, and without a moment to spare. Téadora gave birth to her and Spartacus' first child, a son, just a week after arriving on Samothraki. The slave army remnants and pirates were all there for the special occasion, and the pirates helped secure the army with materials to start building their own city, and homes over the next few months. Over the course of the next few years, Téadora and Spartacus would go on to have seven children. Their first son was named Téomachus after Spartacus' father, and their first daughter was named Marcia, after Spartacus' mother. Their second daughter was named Polycraetia, after Damanicus' sister. Then there were twin boys named Janus and Justus who were trouble from their first breath. Another son came along, and he was named Vestulus, after an officer who had been like a father to Spartacus when he had first been taken into the Romany army as a young man. And finally, a third daughter was born named Severa, after Téadora's childhood friend who she had reunited with and died in childbirth. Damanicus made many visits to Samothraki before finally retiring his fleet in his later years. Spartacus built a house for him on the same hillside where his own family lived, and together, they looked after Téadora and the children. Over the course of their quiet lives, they heard the news of many great and wonderful events around the Mediterranean. There was the rise and fall of Julius Caesar, the love affair with Cleopatra and Marc Antony. But the true gem of good news that made it's way out to the Aegean was during Téomachus' wedding festivities to his future wife, the sweetest Parthinian girl Téadora could have ever asked for. Crassus' luck and finally run out, and he was slaughtered in battle by the girl's own father and brother. Twenty years after the massacre in the valley of Campania, Crassus met his end in Carrhae, with a pair of sica blades in his chest.

Spartacus could finally lay his head down at night knowing the full meaning of the word, peace. A word many men who had crossed his path never thought possible. But Spartacus was at peace, and it was lovely. Seven healthy, ambitious children, a gorgeous wife who only got prettier and smarter as the years passed, and a best friend for life. As Téomachus danced with his bride at sunset, Spartacus sat down by the sea, and watched Téadora dance with Damanicus. Since the battle in Campania, Spartacus had a severe limp he was self-conscious of, and avoided being on his feet too long. While he enjoying his wife's laughter, his eyes were saying something else. Damanicus noticed, and held his hand out for Spartacus.

"Come dance with your wife, Spartacus."

"No, Damanicus. I've never been any good at it. Besides, you two are having fun. I don't want to spoil it."

"The woman wants to dance with her husband. Don't make me give her the bad news that he'd rather be a spectator."

"Come, my dear, Spartacus. Dance with me and hold me like we are young again."

"Every time I look at you, Téa, I *am* young again."

"Damanicus, help me get this stubborn old man to his feet, will you? Our son is marrying the love of his life, and the least you can do is give me one dance. Come, Spartacus, remind me of the young man I married. The warrior with a fire in his eyes."

"I'm afraid the fire has burned out over the years."

"No. I don't think so. Do you know what I see when I look upon you, dear husband? That smiling little boy, chasing me in the fields at sunset. You have given me love and laughter, Spartacus. Thank you. The gods themselves could not have given me a better life."

"Damanicus, help me to my feet. I owe my wife a dance."

Printed in Great Britain
by Amazon

1c755523-a723-4726-a06c-61deff22d682R01